T0203012

Lecture Notes in Computer Science   12054

More information about this series at http://www.springer.com/series/7408

Antonio Brogi · Wolf Zimmermann ·
Kyriakos Kritikos (Eds.)

Service-Oriented and Cloud Computing

8th IFIP WG 2.14 European Conference, ESOCC 2020
Heraklion, Crete, Greece, September 28–30, 2020
Proceedings

 Springer

Editors
Antonio Brogi ⓘ
Università di Pisa
Pisa, Italy

Wolf Zimmermann
Martin-Luther-Universität Halle-Wittenberg
Halle (Saale), Germany

Kyriakos Kritikos ⓘ
University of the Aegean
Karlovasi, Greece

ISSN 0302-9743   ISSN 1611-3349   (electronic)
Lecture Notes in Computer Science
ISBN 978-3-030-44768-7   ISBN 978-3-030-44769-4   (eBook)
https://doi.org/10.1007/978-3-030-44769-4   ˙

LNCS Sublibrary: SL2 – Programming and Software Engineering

This Springer imprint is published by the registered company Springer Nature Switzerland AG
The registered company address is: Gewerbestrasse 11, 6330 Cham, Switzerland

Preface

Service-oriented and cloud computing have made a huge impact both on the software industry and on the research community. Today, service and cloud technologies are applied to build large-scale software landscapes as well as to provide single software services to end users. Services today are independently developed and deployed as well as freely composed while they can be implemented in a variety of technologies, quite an important fact from a business perspective. Similarly, cloud computing aims at enabling flexibility by offering a centralized sharing of resources. The industry's need for agile and flexible software and IT systems has made cloud computing the dominating paradigm for provisioning computational resources in a scalable, on-demand fashion. Nevertheless, service developers, providers, and integrators still need to create methods, tools, and techniques to support cost-effective and secure development as well as the use of dependable devices, platforms, services, and service-oriented applications in the cloud.

The European Conference on Service-Oriented and Cloud Computing (ESOCC) is the premier conference on advances in the state of the art and practice of service-oriented computing and cloud computing in Europe. The main objectives of this conference are to facilitate the exchange between researchers and practitioners in the areas of service-oriented computing and cloud computing, as well as to explore the new trends in those areas and foster future collaborations in Europe and beyond. The 8th edition of ESOCC, ESOCC 2020, was held in the city of Heraklion in Crete, Greece, during September 28–30, 2020, under the auspices of FORTH-ICS.

ESOCC 2020 was a multi-event conference aimed to cover both an academic and industrial audience. The main event was associated with the main research track, which focused on the presentation of cutting-edge research in both the service-oriented and cloud computing areas. In conjunction, an industrial track was also held bringing together academia and industry by showcasing the application of service-oriented and cloud computing research, especially in the form of case studies, from industry. Overall, 20 submissions were received, out of which 6 outstanding full and 8 short papers were accepted.

Each submission was peer-reviewed by three main reviewers, either directly from the PC members or their colleagues. Due to the high quality of the manuscripts received, additional discussions were conducted, both among the PC members as well as between the two PC chairs, before the final selection was performed. The PC chairs would like to thank all the reviewers that participated in the reviewing process not only for enabling to increase the quality of the received manuscripts but also for sharing particular ideas on how the respective work, even if rejected in its current form in the ESOCC conference, could be substantially improved.

The attendees of ESOCC had the opportunity to follow two outstanding keynotes that were part of the conference program. The first keynote was conducted by Massimo Villari, Professor and Rector Delegate for ICT as well as Head of the Computer Science

School in the University of Messina, Italy. This keynote concerned recent research advances and trends towards realizing the vision of Osmotic Computing. The second keynote was conducted by Joseph Spillner, Head of the Service Prototyping Lab and Associate Professor at Zurich University of Applied Sciences in Switzerland. This second keynote concerned the presentation of methods for developing production-ready, Function-as-a-Service applications concentrating on scalable event-driven data processing that are well-suited for highly dynamic environments with varying loads.

The additional events held in ESOCC 2020 included the PhD symposium, enabling PhD students to present their work in front of real experts, as well as the EU projects track, supplying researchers with the opportunity to present the main research results that they have achieved in the context of currently operating EU projects. Further, ESOCC 2020 included the organization of satellite workshops. All these events were accompanied by respective proceedings which were published separately.

Finally, this 8th edition of ESOCC included a novel track dedicated to the conduction of tutorials. This enabled the workshop participants to get acquainted with the latest results of specific European projects as well as of specific European research groups in a practical manner which included demonstrations of research prototypes.

The PC chairs and the general chair would like to gratefully thank all the persons involved in making ESOCC 2020 a success. This includes both the PC members and their colleagues that assisted in the reviews as well as the organizers of the industry track, the PhD symposium, the EU projects track, and the workshops. A special applause should also go to the members of the Local Organizing Committee for their devotion, willingness, and hospitality. Finally, a special thanks goes to all the authors of all the manuscripts submitted to ESOCC 2020, the presenters of the accepted papers who made interesting and fascinating presentations of their work, as well as the active attendees of the conference who initiated interesting discussions and gave fruitful feedback to the presenters. All these persons not only enabled a very successful organization and execution of ESOCC 2020, but also formulate an active and vibrant community which continuously contributes to the research in service-oriented and cloud computing. This also encourages ESOCC to continue contributing with new research outcomes to further facilitate and enlarge its community as well as have a greater impact and share in both the service-oriented and cloud computing research.

September 2020

Antonio Brogi
Wolf Zimmermann
Kyriakos Kritikos

Organization

ESOCC 2020 was organized by FORTH-ICS, Greece.

Organizing Committee

General Chair

Kyriakos Kritikos   FORTH-ICS and University of the Aegean, Greece

Program Chairs

Antonio Brogi   University of Pisa, Italy
Wolf Zimmermann   Martin Luther University Halle-Wittenberg, Germany

Industry Track Chair

Marco Aiello   University of Stuttgart, Germany

Workshop Chairs

Christian Zirpins   University of Applied Sciences Karlsruhe, Germany
Iraklis Paraskakis   City College, Greece

EU Project Space Chairs

Pierluigi Plebani   Politecnico di Milano, Italy
Giuliano Casale   Imperial College, UK

PhD Symposium Chairs

Jacopo Soldani   University of Pisa, Italy
Massimo Villari   University of Messina, Italy

Steering Committee

Antonio Brogi   University of Pisa, Italy
Schahram Dustdar   TU Wien, Austria
Paul Grefen   Eindhoven University of Technology, The Netherlands
Winfried Lamersdorf   University of Hamburg, Germany
Frank Leymann   University of Stuttgart, Germany
Flavio de Paoli   University of Milano-Bicocca, Italy
Cesare Pautasso   University of Lugano, Switzerland
Ernesto Pimentel   University of Malaga, Spain
Pierluigi Plebani   Politecnico di Milano, Italy
Ulf Schreier   Hochschule Furtwangen University, Germany
Massimo Villari   University of Messina, Italy

Contents

Monitoring

Data Distribution and Analytics

Formal Methods

Testing Conformance in Multi-component Enterprise Application Management

Jacopo Soldani[1]([⊠]), Lars Luthmann[2], Malte Lochau[2], and Antonio Brogi[1]

[1] University of Pisa, Pisa, Italy
{soldani,brogi}@di.unipi.it
[2] TU Darmstadt, Darmstadt, Germany
{lars.luthmann,malte.lochau}@es.tu-darmstadt.de

Abstract. Modern enterprise applications integrate various heterogeneous components, which management has to be suitably coordinated. Being able to check whether the management allowed by the implementation of an application component conforms to a given specification hence becomes crucial. One may indeed wish to replace component specifications with conforming implementations, by ensuring that already planned management can be enacted, or that no additional (potentially undesired) management activities get enabled. In this perspective, we propose a parametric relation for testing the conformance of the management of application components, based on an existing formalism to model multi-component application management (i.e., management protocols). We also discuss how such relation can be exploited to ensure that replacing a specification with a conforming implementation continues to enable all already allowed management activities, and/or that no additional (potentially undesired) management activity gets enabled.

1 Introduction

Automating the management of enterprise applications is currently a major issue in IT [13]. Enterprise applications indeed integrate various components, and automating the management of an application requires to suitably coordinate the deployment, configuration and operation of its components [8]. This must be done by considering all dependencies and interactions occurring among application components, and the possibility of such components to fail or get stuck [15].

Replaceability is also to be supported [14], as application administrators may wish to replace the specification of desired components with suitable implementations. In this perspective, for suitably replacing a component specification, a candidate implementation must not only implement the specified business logic, but also conform to the specified management. The latter would indeed mean that the implementation of a component can be managed by executing the specified management operations in the specified order, that it properly interacts with the other components forming an application, and that it handles potential failures as specified. In other words, a proper notion of "management conformance"

ⓒ IFIP International Federation for Information Processing 2020
Published by Springer Nature Switzerland AG 2020
A. Brogi et al. (Eds.): ESOCC 2020, LNCS 12054, pp. 3–18, 2020.
https://doi.org/10.1007/978-3-030-44769-4_1

would hence allow application administrators to replace the specification of a component with implementations that can be managed as specified, by also getting guarantees on the way the implemented component interacts with the rest of the application (and on the overall application management automation).

To this end, we define the notion of management conformance based on *management protocols* [6], an existing approach for modelling multi-component application management. Intuitively, a management protocol specifies the management behaviour of a component by means of a finite state machine, which states model component states, and which transitions indicate which management operations can be performed in a state. States and transitions are enriched with conditions on the requirements of a component, and on the capabilities it offers to satisfy the requirements of other components (bound to such capabilities). Such conditions indicate which requirements must be satisfied while residing in a state or to perform a transition, and the capabilities offered during such state or transition to satisfy the requirements of other components. If some requirements assumed in a state stop being satisfied, a fault handler explicitly specifies how the component should react to such failure.

To define management conformance, we follow Tretmans' idea of input/output (I/O) conformance testing [21], by expressing the semantics of management protocols in terms of I/O labelled transition systems (IOLTS). We then exploit such semantics to define a parametric relation for testing management conformance, which can be instantiated into four different conformance testing relations. We focus on I/O conformance testing rather than on formal verification for two main reasons. I/O conformance testing is known to (i) be more suited for black-box scenarios [21]. It indeed allows us to test whether an existing third-party component conforms to a given specification, even if the such component is a "black-box", with the tester having no clue on how it has been implemented. Conformance testing is also known to (ii) provide a higher degree of implementation freedom, as it delegates to developers the choice of how to implement some under-/non-specified behaviour [19].

We then show how to instantiate the parametric relation for testing management conformance into four different relations. We also discuss how such relations can be used to check the replaceability of the specification of a component with a conforming implementation, as well as how they constitute different trade-offs among implementation freedom and guarantees obtained after replacing a specification with a conforming implementation. The choice of which conformance relation to employ hence depends on the context and requirements of the tester, who can reduce the amount of conforming implementations by considering relations fully preserving already allowed application management, or ensuring that no novel, potentially undesired management activity gets allowed.

To summarise, the contributions of this paper are threefold. We provide (a) an IOLTS semantics for the management protocols modelling the management behaviour of application components. We present (b) a parametric relation for testing management conformance (i.e., testing whether the management protocol of a component implementation conforms to that of a component specification), which permits instantiating four different conformance testing relations. We discuss (c) whether/how each relation ensures preserving the overall management of an application after replacing a component specification with a conforming implementation, or avoiding that undesired management activities gets enabled. The rest of the paper is organised as follows. Sections 2 and 3 provide some background and a motivating scenario, respectively. Section 4 illustrates how to test management conformance in multi-component applications. Sections 5 and 6 discuss related work and draw some concluding remarks, respectively.

2 Background: Management Protocols

Topology graphs allow to model multi-component applications [3]. Each node in a topology graph represents an application component, by describing its requirements, the operations to manage it, and the capabilities it features. Arcs then model inter-component dependencies, by associating the requirements of a node to the capabilities of other nodes that are used to satisfy such requirements.

Management protocols [6] describe how the management operations of a node N depend on (i) other operations of the same node N and on (ii) operations of other nodes providing the capabilities that satisfy the requirements of N. The first kind of dependencies is described by a transition relation τ specifying whether an operation o can be executed in a state s, and which state is reached by executing o in s. The second kind of dependencies is described by associating transitions and states with sets of requirements and capabilities. The requirements associated with a transition must be satisfied to allow its execution, while those associated with a state must continue to be satisfied in order for N to continue to work properly. The capabilities associated with a transition or state are those offered by N during such transition or while residing in such state.

Management protocols also specify how N reacts when a fault occurs, i.e. when N is in a state assuming some requirements to be satisfied, but some other node stops satisfying such requirements. This is described by a transition relation φ modelling the fault handling of N by specifying that its state changes from s to s' when some of the requirements it assumes in s stop being satisfied.

Definition 1 (Management protocol). *Let $N = \langle S_N, R_N, C_N, O_N, \mathcal{M}_N \rangle$ be a node, where S_N, R_N, C_N, and O_N are the finite sets of its states, requirements, capabilities, and management operations. $\mathcal{M}_N = \langle \overline{s}_N, \rho_N, \chi_N, \tau_N, \varphi_N \rangle$ is a finite state machine defining the management protocol of N, where:*

- *$\overline{s}_N \in S_N$ is the initial state,*
- *$\rho_N : S_N \rightarrow 2^{R_N}$ is a function indicating, for each state $s \in S_N$, which conditions on requirements must hold,*
- *$\chi_N : S_N \rightarrow 2^{C_N}$ is a function indicating which capabilities of N are concretely offered in a state $s \in S_N$,*
- *$\tau_N \subseteq S_N \times 2^{R_N} \times 2^{C_N} \times O_N \times S_N$ is a set of quintuples modelling the transition relation, i.e., $\langle s, P, X, o, s' \rangle \in \tau_N$ denotes that in state s, and if condition P holds, o is executable and leads to state s' (by maintaining the capability in X during the transition), and*

– $\varphi_N \subseteq S_N \times S_N$ *is a set of pairs modelling the* fault handling *for a node, i.e.,* $\langle s, s' \rangle \in \varphi_N$ *denotes that the node will change its state from s to s' if some of the requirements in* $\rho_N(s) - \rho_N(s')$ *stop being satisfied.*

We hereafter assume management protocols to be *complete* (i.e., handling all possible faults in all possible states) and *race-free* (i.e., handling faults so that the simultaneous removal of multiple requirements has the same effect on a node as any sequential removal of the same requirements). Construction rules for ensuring both properties on any management protocol can be found in [6].

3   Motivating Scenario

Consider the (toy) web-based application illustrated in Fig. 1. The application is composed by a gui to which clients connect, and which relies on a backend api to serve them. The api manages application data, by accessing the database where such data is stored. The connections from gui to api and from api to database are represented by arrows connecting a requirement of the source node to a capability of the target node, hence modelling which component is offering the capability used to satisfy a requirement of another component (i.e., the requirement db of api is satisfied by the homonym capability of database, while its capability endp is used to satisfy the homonym requirement of gui). The operations for managing the lifecycle of each component are instead listed next to it.

Suppose that the overall application management has been planned by assuming that the allowed management behaviour for api is that specified by the management protocol of api in Fig. 2(a). The latter indicates that the possible states of api are unavailable (initial), installed, started and failed. Operation transitions allow the component to transit from a state to another by executing the corresponding operation, with configure self-looping on state installed and requiring db to be satisfied for being executable. No requirements are needed to reside in states unavailable and failed, while requirement db is needed to reside in states installed and started (hence requiring database to provide its capability db to satisfy such requirement). If requirement db stops being satisfied while api is installed or started, api gets failed. No requirement is instead needed by api to perform any other transition or reside in any other state. Finally, state started is the only state where api is actually providing its capability endp, hence also being able to satisfy the requirement endp of gui.

Suppose now that we have a candidate implementation of api, provided by a third-party and whose internals are not known. Suppose also that we observed

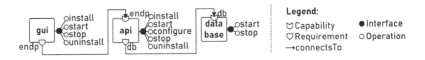

Fig. 1. Example of multi-component application.

that such implementation can be managed according to the management protocol in Fig. 2(b). Can we use the candidate implementation of api in place of its
specification? If yes, which guarantees would we get on the overall application
management when enacting the replacement? For instance, we may wish to be
sure that the overall management behaviour of the application is preserved, so
that already developed management plans will continue to work properly.

4   Testing Conformance in Application Management

I/O conformance is usually defined between two IOLTS defining the operational
semantics of the formalism under consideration [21]. Thus, before defining management conformance, we first need to introduce an IOLTS semantics for management protocols.

4.1   IOLTS Semantics of Management Protocols

Given a node $N = \langle S_N, R_N, C_N, O_N, \mathcal{M}_N \rangle$, we consider two kinds of *input
actions* for each state $s \in S_N$, i.e., *operation-invocation* actions and *requirement-
set* actions. An operation-invocation action $o^\uparrow$ denotes the input due to the
invocation of an operation $o \in O_N$ in a state, while a *requirement-set* action R
(with $R \in R_N$) denotes a subset of the requirements of N that are satisfied by
capabilities provided by other components in the application.

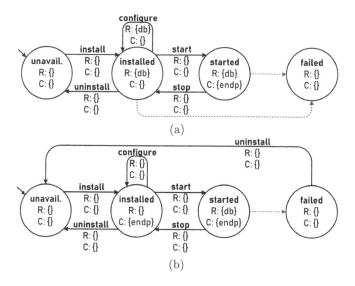

Fig. 2. Examples of management protocols. States are denoted by circles, operation
transitions by solid arrows, and fault-handling transitions by dashed arrows. Conditions
on requirements and capabilities are specified by sets R and C, respectively.

We instead consider three different kinds of output actions for a node N, for observing outputs possibly occurring after input actions. An *operation termination* action $o^{\downarrow}$ notifies the completion of a previously invoked operation $o \in O_N$. A *capability-set* action allows to denote the set of capabilities that are provided by N to the rest of the application. In addition, a special output symbol $\perp \notin (R_N \cup C_N \cup O_N)$ is used to denote *fault-handling* actions, i.e., to explicitly observe the activation of fault handlers.

Definition 2 (Input/output actions). *Let $N = \langle S_N, R_N, C_N, O_N, \mathcal{M}_N \rangle$. The I/O actions labelling alphabet is a set $Act_N = In_N \cup Out_N$ where*

$$In_N = \{o^{\uparrow} \mid o \in O_N\} \cup 2^{R_N} \quad and \quad Out_N = \{o^{\downarrow} \mid o \in O_N\} \cup 2^{C_N} \cup \{\perp\}.$$

We now define the IOLTS semantics of the management protocol $\mathcal{M}_N = \langle \overline{s}_N, \rho_N, \chi_N, \tau_N, \varphi_N \rangle$ of a node N. The configurations X_N of the IOLTS denoting the semantics of $\mathcal{M}_N$ are given by the set of states S_N of N, to which we add a set of fresh configurations denoting the execution of operation and fault-handling transitions, i.e., $X_N = (S_N \cup \tau_N) \cup \varphi_N$. The initial configuration of the IOLTS corresponds to the initial state of $\mathcal{M}_N$, i.e., $\overline{s}_N$.

The transition relation over the configurations of the IOLTS semantics of $\mathcal{M}_N$ are instead obtained as follows.

- For each state $s \in S_N$, two self-looping IOLTS transitions on s indicate the sets of assumed requirements and capabilities provided by N in s.
- For each management protocol transition $t = \langle s, R, C, o, s' \rangle \in \tau_N$, four IOLTS transitions are added. An input transition corresponding to the invocation of o outgoes from s and targets t, while an output transition notifying the completion of o outgoes from t and targets s'. Two transitions self-looping on t instead indicate the sets R and C of requirements and capabilities associated with t, i.e., the input requirement-set and output capability-set.
- For each fault handler $f = \langle s, s' \rangle \in \varphi_N$, and for each subset of requirements assumed in s and handled by $\langle s, s' \rangle$, two IOLTS transitions are added. An input transition labelled with the set R of remaining requirements (i.e., the requirements that were assumed in s and that continue to be satisfied by the rest of the application) goes from s to f, modelling the reaction of N to the handled fault (i.e., the requirements in $\rho_N(s) - R$). An output transition labelled with $\perp$ instead goes from f to s', allowing to explicitly observe the issuing of a fault handler.

Definition 3 (IOLTS semantics). *Let $N = \langle S_N, R_N, C_N, O_N, \mathcal{M}_N \rangle$ be a node, with $\mathcal{M}_N = \langle \overline{s}_N, \rho_N, \chi_N, \tau_N, \varphi_N \rangle$. The IOLTS semantics of the management protocol $\mathcal{M}_N$ of N is defined as a triple $\mathcal{I}_N = \langle \overline{s}_N, X_N, \rightarrow_N \rangle$ where*

$$X_N = S_N \cup \tau_N \cup \varphi_N \quad and \quad \rightarrow_N \subseteq (X_N \times Act_N \times X_N),$$

with $\rightarrow_N$ being the least relation such that

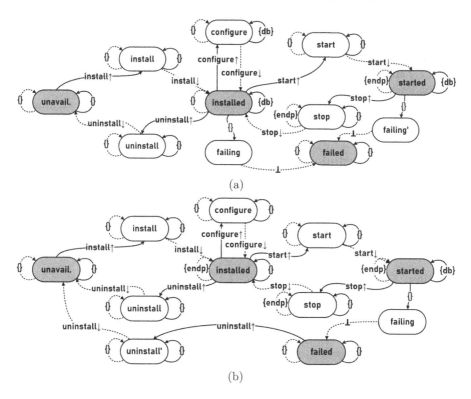

Fig. 3. IOLTS semantics of the management protocols in Fig. 2. Transitions labelled with input actions are solid, while those labelled with output actions are dashed. Configurations corresponding to states of management protocols are highlighted in grey.

- $\forall s \in S_N . \{\langle s, \rho_N(s), s\rangle, \langle s, \chi_N(s), s\rangle\} \subseteq \rightarrow_N,$
- $\forall t = \langle s, R, C, o, s'\rangle \in \tau_N . \{\langle s, o^\uparrow, t\rangle, \langle t, R, t\rangle, \langle t, C, t\rangle, \langle t, o^\downarrow, s'\rangle\} \subseteq \rightarrow_N,$
- $\forall f = \langle s, s'\rangle \in \varphi_N .$
  $\forall R \subset \rho_N(s) : (\rho_N(s') \subseteq R \wedge (\nexists\langle s, s''\rangle \in \varphi_N . \rho_N(s') \subset \rho_N(s'') \subseteq R)) .$
  $\{\langle s, R, f\rangle, \langle f, \bot, s'\rangle\} \subseteq \rightarrow_N.$

Example. Figure 3 illustrates the IOLTS semantics of the management protocols for api in our motivating scenario (Fig. 2). In both IOLTS, configurations are given by the union of the sets of states and transitions of the original management protocol. One can readily observe how intermediate configurations allow to split operation transitions into operation-invocation and operation completion.

Self-loops then model the conditions on requirements and capabilities associated with states and transitions. For instance, the configuration (corresponding to state) started has two self-loops. The dashed self-loop models the fact that the node is offering the capability endp while residing in state started, since it can produce {endp} as output. The solid self-loop instead indicates that the node keeps residing in state started if the requirement db continues to be satisfied, since the configuration does not change when {db} is given as input.

The figure also shows how fault-handling transitions are split into two transitions. Consider again started, whose corresponding state assumes db to be satisfied. If no requirement is given as input, this means that db stops being satisfied and the configuration of the IOLTS changes from started to failing, from which (the configuration corresponding to) state failed can be reached by producing the output ⊥. The two transitions in the IOLTS model the corresponding fault-handling transition in the original management protocol.

4.2   Input-Enabledness

A crucial assumption in I/O conformance testing is *input-enabledness* of implementations under test, i.e., a candidate implementation under test will never block any input action [21]. During our case, this means that a management protocol is input enabled if its IOLTS semantics accepts any possible input in any configuration corresponding to a state in the original management protocol.

Notation. *Given the IOLTS semantics $\mathcal{I}_N = \langle \overline{s}_N, X_N, \to_N \rangle$ of a management protocol $\mathcal{M}_N$ and a configuration $x \in X_N$, $x \xrightarrow{\sigma}_N x'$ and $x \xrightarrow{\sigma}_N$ (with $\sigma \in Act_N^*$) denote traces σ corresponding to valid paths in $\mathcal{I}_N$.*

Definition 4 (Input-enabledness). *Let $\mathcal{I}_N = \langle \overline{s}_N, X_N, \to_N \rangle$ be the IOLTS semantics of the management protocol of a node N. $\mathcal{I}_N$ is input-enabled iff*

$$\forall x \in S_N \,.\, \forall i \in In_N : x \xrightarrow{i} .$$

The input-enabledness of a given management protocol can be ensured automatically. Intuitively, its IOLTS semantics can be automatically completed by adding an input transition targeting a distinct sink configuration $s_\perp$ (with $s_\perp \notin X_N$) for each unspecified input of each state $s \in S_N$. Namely, an input transition labelled with the set R of requirements is added if there is no input transition outgoing from s and labelled with R. An input transition labelled with the invocation of operation o is instead added if o cannot be invoked in s.

The sink state $s_\perp$ is also made input-enabled, by adding a self-looping input transition for each possible input. Furthermore, a self-looping output transition on $s_\perp$ is added, which is labelled with the special symbol ⊥. This allows to explicitly observe that an unspecified input has been provided to the IOLTS, as whenever this happens the IOLTS can provide ⊥ as output. Any unspecified input action hence results in an (implicit) fault handling under input completion.
Example (cont.). Consider again the (a) management protocol specification and (b) candidate implementation in our motivating example (Fig. 2). By looking at their corresponding IOLTS semantics, shown in Fig. 3, one can readily observe that both management protocols are not input-enabled, as each configuration corresponding to a state of the protocol lacks some outgoing input transitions. More precisely, there are some operation-invocation actions that are available in each of such configurations, e.g., in the IOLTS semantics of both protocols there is only one out of five operation-invocation actions defined for started.

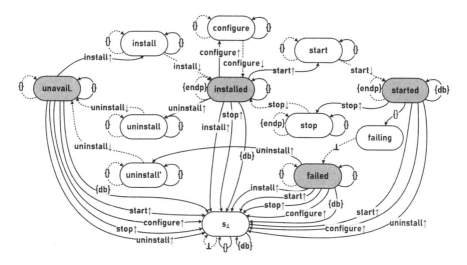

Fig. 4. Input-enabled version of the IOLTS in Fig. 3(b), obtained by input completion.

I/O conformance testing requires implementations to be input-enabled [21]. To be able to test whether the candidate implementation of api conforms to its specification, we hence need to make the IOLTS in Fig. 3(b) input-enabled. The latter can be obtained by applying it to the above listed construction rules, which results in the IOLTS shown in Fig. 4.

4.3 Conformance Testing Based on Management Protocols

We now introduce a formal framework for testing management conformance between application components. Suppose N to constitute the (fully known) *specification* of the intended management behaviour of an application component and N' to constitute a candidate (black-box) *implementation* for N, both defined over the same sets of requirements, capabilities and operations. Intuitively, we wish to formally define an I/O conformance relation on management protocols (mpioco), such that N' mpioco N denotes that the management behaviour implemented by N' *conforms* to that specified by N, i.e., given the same inputs, N' can produce the outputs specified by N. Given how we relate input and outputs to requirements, operations and capabilities (Definition 2), this intuitively means that given the same requirements and operations, N' can offer the capabilities expected in N, hence meaning that N' can be used to replace N in a multi-component application.

For defining mpioco, we first need to introduce the notions of *quiescence* and *suspension traces*. We introduce a special output symbol $\delta \notin (R_N \cup C_N \cup O_N)$ denoting *quiescence*, i.e., the observable absence of any output. In the IOLTS semantics of a management protocol, *quiescence* occurs whenever a configuration corresponds to a state not providing any capability. Suspension traces are then defined by extending existing traces and allowing to explicitly observe quiescence.

Definition 5 (Quiescence and suspension traces). *Let* $N = \langle S_N, R_N, C_N,$ $O_N, \mathcal{M}_N \rangle$ *be a node and let* $\mathcal{I}_N = \langle \overline{s}_N, X_N, \rightarrow_N \rangle$ *be the IOLTS semantics of* $\mathcal{M}_N$. *Let also* $x \in X_N$ *be a configuration in* $\mathcal{I}_N$.

- x *is* quiescent, *denoted by* $\delta(x)$ *iff* $\forall C \subseteq C_N : C \neq \emptyset . x \not\xrightarrow{C}_N$, *and*
- $\mathsf{straces}(x) = \{\sigma \mid x \xrightarrow{\sigma}_N\}$, *where* $\forall x' \in X_N . x' \xrightarrow{\delta}_N x'$ *if* $\delta(x')$.

We also need to introduce the notions of *enabled outputs* and *reachability*, to identify the set of output symbols enabled by a set of configurations, and the configurations that can be reached by performing a trace σ in a configuration x.

Definition 6 (Enabled outputs). *Let* $N = \langle S_N, R_N, C_N, O_N, \mathcal{M}_N \rangle$ *be a node and let* $\mathcal{I}_N = \langle \overline{s}_N, X_N, \rightarrow_N \rangle$ *be the IOLTS semantics of* $\mathcal{M}_N$. *The set of outputs enabled in a configuration* $x \in X_N$ *is the least set* $\mathsf{out}(x)$ *such that*

$$C \subseteq \mathsf{out}(x) \text{ if } x \xrightarrow{C} \quad \text{and} \quad \{\bot\} \subseteq \mathsf{out}(x) \text{ if } x \xrightarrow{\bot} \quad \text{and} \quad \{\delta\} \subseteq \mathsf{out}(x) \text{ if } \delta(s).$$

We also write $\mathsf{out}(X)$ *to denote the outputs enabled in at least one of the configurations in the set* $X \subseteq X_N$, *i.e.,* $\mathsf{out}(X) = \bigcup_{x \in X} \mathsf{out}(x)$.

We define two different versions of reachability, distinguished by parameter γ. If γ is "=", transitions involving a set of requirements or capabilities are considered only if the trace is delivering exactly that set of requirements or capabilities. In the relaxed version with γ set to "$\geq$", a transition labelled with a set R' of requirements is considered if the trace is delivering at least the requirements in R', while one labelled with a set C' of capabilities is considered if the trace is delivering at most the capabilities in C'. Operation-invocation and operation-completion transitions are instead always considered, independently of γ.

Definition 7 (γ-reachability). *Let* $N = \langle S_N, R_N, C_N, O_N, \mathcal{M}_N \rangle$ *be a node and let* $\mathcal{I}_N = \langle \overline{s}_N, X_N, \rightarrow_N \rangle$ *be the IOLTS semantics of* $\mathcal{M}_N$. *Let also* $x \in X_N$ *be a configuration in* $\mathcal{I}_N$ *and* $\sigma \in \mathsf{straces}(x)$ *be a suspension trace for* x. *The set of* γ-reachable *configurations from* x *with* σ *is* $\mathsf{reach}_\gamma(x, \sigma) \subseteq X_N$, *i.e., the least set satisfying the following recursive rules:*

$-x \in \mathsf{reach}_\gamma(x, \epsilon),$

$-x \in \mathsf{reach}_=(x', \sigma) \text{ if } x' \xrightarrow{R'}_N x'' \wedge R' \subseteq R_N \wedge \sigma = R' \cdot \sigma'' \wedge x \in \mathsf{reach}_=(x'', \sigma''),$

$-x \in \mathsf{reach}_\geq(x', \sigma) \text{ if } x' \xrightarrow{R'}_N x'' \wedge R' \subseteq R \subseteq R_N \wedge \sigma = R \cdot \sigma'' \wedge x \in \mathsf{reach}_\geq(x'', \sigma''),$

$-x \in \mathsf{reach}_=(x', \sigma) \text{ if } x' \xrightarrow{C'}_N x'' \wedge C' \subseteq C_N \wedge \sigma = C' \cdot \sigma'' \wedge x \in \mathsf{reach}_=(x'', \sigma''),$

$-x \in \mathsf{reach}_\geq(x', \sigma) \text{ if } x' \xrightarrow{C'}_N x'' \wedge C \subseteq C' \subseteq C_N \wedge \sigma = C \cdot \sigma'' \wedge x \in \mathsf{reach}_\geq(x'', \sigma''),$

$-x \in \mathsf{reach}_\gamma(x', \sigma) \text{ if } x' \xrightarrow{o^\uparrow} x'' \wedge o \in O_N \wedge \sigma = o^\uparrow \cdot \sigma'' \wedge x \in \mathsf{reach}_\gamma(x'', \sigma''), \text{ and}$

$-x \in \mathsf{reach}_\gamma(x', \sigma) \text{ if } x' \xrightarrow{o^\downarrow} x'' \wedge o \in O_N \wedge \sigma = o^\downarrow \cdot \sigma'' \wedge x \in \mathsf{reach}_\gamma(x'', \sigma''),$

where $\cdot$ *denotes concatenation (i.e.,* $\alpha \cdot \omega$ *denotes an I/O action* α *followed by a sequence* ω *of I/O actions).*

We now formally define how to test the management conformance between application components, by means of a parametric relation for testing management conformance, which allows to obtain four different testing operators. The latter are distinguished based on (a) the employed notion of γ-reachability and on (b) the way non-deterministic output-behaviour is handled. Concerning (b), we introduce some shorthand notations for comparing sets of sets, i.e., we write $Z' \sqsupset Z''$ to indicate that Z'' contains all sets in Z', and $Z' \sqsupseteq Z''$ to indicate that Z'' contains a superset of each set in Z'.

Notation. *Let Z' and Z'' be two sets. We write $Z' \sqsupset Z''$ iff $\forall z' \in Z' : (\exists z'' \in Z'' : z'' = z')$, and $Z' \sqsupseteq Z''$ iff $\forall z' \in Z' : (\exists z'' \in Z'' : z'' \subseteq z')$.*

Intuitively, the implemented management of a node conforms to its specification if, given a set of inputs, it can produce the expected outputs.

Definition 8 (mpioco). *Let $N = \langle S_N, R_N, C_N, O_N, \mathcal{M}_N \rangle$ be a node, with $\mathcal{M}_N = \langle \overline{s}_N, \rho_N, \chi_N, \tau_N, \varphi_N \rangle$. Let $N' = \langle S'_N, R_N, C_N, O_N, \mathcal{M}'_N \rangle$ be another node, with $\mathcal{M}_N = \langle \overline{s}'_N, \rho'_N, \chi'_N, \tau'_N, \varphi'_N \rangle$ being input-enabled. Let also $\beta \in \{\sqsupset, \sqsupseteq\}$ and $\gamma \in \{=, \geq\}$.*

$$N' \text{ mpioco}_{\beta,\gamma} N \Leftrightarrow \forall \sigma \in \text{straces}(\overline{s}_N) . \text{out}(\text{reach}_\gamma(\overline{s}'_N, \sigma)) \beta \text{ out}(\text{reach}_\gamma(\overline{s}_N, \sigma)).$$

Note that if γ is $=$ and β is $\sqsupset$, an implementation conforms to a specification only if it produces the set of desired capabilities given exactly the same sets of requirements. Setting γ to $\geq$ or β to $\sqsupseteq$ results in more flexibile relations of management conformance. With γ set to $\geq$, conformance occurs also if the implementation needs less requirements and provides more capabilities. With β set to $\sqsupseteq$, conformance occurs also if the implementation can produce at least one of the expected sets of capabilities, hence allowing specifications to exhibit non-deterministic output behaviour.

Example (cont.). Consider again our motivating scenario, where we have a specification of api and a possible implementation for such component, which we hereafter denote with api_S and api_I, for simplicity. The IOLTS semantics of the management protocol of api_S is in Fig. 3(a), while the input-complete IOLTS semantics of the management protocol of api_I is in Fig. 4.

By applying the different conformance testing relations to both IOLTS, one can check that $\text{api}_I \text{ mpioco}_{\sqsupset,\geq} \text{api}_S$ and $\text{api}_I \text{ mpioco}_{\sqsupseteq,\geq} \text{api}_S$ (while the same does not hold for the relations with γ set to $=$). This means that the candidate implementation api_I can be used to replace the desired specification api_S. However, which guarantees on the overall application management are given when enacting the replacement? Is every possible trace of management preserved? Is there any (potentially undesired) additional trace that gets enabled?

4.4   Which Conformance Tests to Run?

The different notions of mpioco not only allow to check management conformance, but they can also ensure different properties while replacing a component

Table 1. Additional guarantees on overall application management, after replacing a specification with a conforming implementation, with mpioco varying on β and γ.

	γ **set to** $=$	γ **set to** $\geq$
β **set to** $\sqsupset$	*existing traces preserved* *no additional traces*	*existing traces preserved*
β **set to** $\sqsupseteq$	*no additional traces*	–

specification with a conforming implementation. More precisely, mpioco relations vary based on the parameters γ and β, and stricter mpioco relations are obtained when employing stricter constraints on γ and β, i.e., setting γ to $=$ and β to $\sqsupset$. Both restrictions induce additional guarantees on the overall management behaviour of a multi-component application (Table 1).

Whenever the implementation of a node conforms to a specification with γ set to $=$, this means that the implementation needs the same sets of requirements in states and transitions, and that it provides the same sets of capabilities. As a result, after replacing the specification with the conforming implementation in an applicaton, *no additional trace* in the overall management behaviour is introduced. This intuitively holds since the execution of operations and fault handlers is constrained by conditions on requirements and capabilities, which do not change after enacting the replacement.

On the other hand, the implementation of a node can conform to a specification with β set to $\sqsupset$ only if such specification is deterministic in its output behaviour. The latter happens only if the specification does not contain non-deterministic branches, and (given Definition 8) it can be proved that this means that any conforming implementation implements all its viable paths. This in turn means that setting β set to $\sqsupset$ results in *preserving all possible traces* in the overall management behaviour of an application.

Which of the restrictions to employ strictly depends on the guarantees that an application administrator wishes to have. If an application administrator wishes to replace the specification of a component by preserving the overall management behaviour of the application it appears in, she must test the management conformance of a candidate implementation with β set to $\sqsupset$. The latter was precisely the case in our motivating scenario, and since the candidate implementation of api shown to be conforming to the desired specification with β and γ set to $\sqsupset$ and $\geq$, we can use such implementation to replace the given specification.

Alternatively, if an application administrator wishes to replace the specification of a component by ensuring that no additional management trace is introduced, she has to test for management conformance with γ set to $=$. This is not to be underestimated, as enabling additional management activities while considering interdepedent components may result in some undesired situation. For instance, suppose that a component specification requires a VPN in some state to encrypt its communications. By employing the relaxed version of γ, an implementation not requiring any VPN would conform the specification, even if it this would mean that after enacting the replacement the component would not be exploiting any VPN to encrypt its communications.

5   Related Work

Various approaches allow to check whether an existing implementation can be used to replace the specification of a desired application component, e.g., [4], [5], [9], [11], and [12] just to mention some. Such approaches typically consider an implementation as suitable to replace a specification if the implementation can provide (at least) the desired outputs if provided with (at most) the same inputs, by also providing techniques for adapting matching implementations to exhibit the specified I/O behaviour. Their goal is indeed to enact the replacement of a component specification with a suitable implementation, by ensuring that the overall application behaviour is preserved, which in our case can be obtained by exploiting mpioco with β restricted to $\sqsupseteq$. Our approach is instead intended to support application administrators in a wider set of scenarios, varying on the guarantees she wishes to get on the overall management of an application.

Similar arguments apply to the approach proposed in [17]. The latter propose an approach for checking that the interactions with a service in a multi-service application (including the handling of potential exceptions) conforms the behaviour specified by the service itself, hence focusing on preserving the overall application behaviour. Our approach applies to a wider set of scenarios, depending on desired guarantees on the overall application management behaviour.

To offer such a wider support, we exploit the potentials of Tretmans' I/O conformance testing theory [21]. There exists various heterogeneous extensions and variations of the I/O conformance testing theory, and the closest to ours are those dealing with (i) the implementation freedom given by specifications with non-deterministic output behaviour, with (ii) fault handling, and with (iii) guarantees on the overall application behaviour after replacing a component specification with a conforming implementation.

Approaches worth mentioning for what concerns implementation freedom are [2,10,18]. [2] extends I/O conformance testing for dealing with software product lines, by allowing them to exhibit a fine-grained behavioral variability controlled by feature selection. [10,18] give implementation freedom by introducing modality in I/O conformance testing, i.e., allowing to distinguish between mandatory and optional output behaviour. Various other existing approaches define modal conformance as alternating simulation relations [1], where conformance is lifted from simple trace inclusion to an alternating simulation preorder [16,22]. However, none of the above approaches allows to capture the implementation freedom characterising conformance testing on management protocols, e.g., allowing an implementation to conform to a given specification even if the former needs less requirements or provides more capabilities.

To the best of our knowledge, ours is also the first approach for testing conformance for software systems with explicit fault-handling. Only [19,20] consider explicit failure states, but for different purposes. They indeed consider failure states as forbidden states, to suspend test runs in case of forbidden inputs. However, [19,20], as well as no other approach for conformance testing, currently support the explicit specification and testing of fault-handling mechanisms such as those provided by management protocols.

In summary, to the best of our knowledge, ours is the first approach for testing conformance of the *management* allowed by the implementation of a component with respect to that of its specification. Our approach distinguishes from existing solutions for checking behaviour-aware replaceability in terms of supported scenarios, enabled by the proposed relation of conformance testing. The latter is itself the first relation providing the freedom to implement a specification by requiring less and offering more, as well as dealing with explicit fault-handling and with different operators for combining the behaviour of application components.

6   Conclusions

We have presented an approach for testing management conformance in multi-component applications. More precisely, we proposed a parametric relation for testing whether the management allowed by an existing component conforms to a desired specification, modelled with management protocols [6]. Our parametric relation can be instantiated into four different conformance testing relations, spanning from that giving higher implementation freedom, to more restricting relations ensuring that replacing a specification with a conforming implementation continues to enable all already allowed management activities, and/or that no additional (potentially undesired) management activity gets enabled.

We also discussed how the different conformance testing relations can be used to check the replaceability of the specification of a component with a conforming implementation, and how the choice of which relation to exploit strictly depends on the desiderata of an application administrator. She may decide to reduce implementation freedom (hence restricting the set of implementations conforming to a given specification), if she wishes to ensure that the overall application management is fully preserved after replacing a specification with a conforming implementation, or that no undesired management activity gets enabled.

We now plan to provide a first prototype for testing management conformance in multi-component applications and to use such a prototype to validate our approach in practice. We also plan to extend the supported conformance tests, by relying on more expressive versions of management protocols (e.g., truly concurrent management protocols [7]), and by extending the degree of implementation freedom (e.g., by introducing modality, as [10,18] do for different purposes). We also plan to investigate whether and how to adapt our conformance testing approach to other approaches for modelling the management of multi-component applications, e.g., the Aeolus component model [13].

Acknowledgments. This work is partly funded by the projects *AMaCA* (POR-FSE, Regione Toscana) and *DECLware* (PRA_2018_66, University of Pisa). This work was funded by the Hessian LOEWE initiative within the Software-Factory 4.0 project.

References

1. Alur, R., Henzinger, T.A., Kupferman, O., Vardi, M.Y.: Alternating refinement relations. In: Sangiorgi, D., de Simone, R. (eds.) CONCUR 1998. LNCS, vol. 1466, pp. 163–178. Springer, Heidelberg (1998). https://doi.org/10.1007/BFb0055622
2. Beohar, H., Mousavi, M.R.: Input-output conformance testing for software product lines. J. Log. Algebr. Methods Program. **85**(6), 1131–1153 (2016)
3. Binz, T., Fehling, C., Leymann, F., Nowak, A., Schumm, D.: Formalizing the cloud through enterprise topology graphs. In: 2012 IEEE Fifth International Conference on Cloud Computing, pp. 742–749. IEEE (2012)
4. Bonchi, F., Brogi, A., Canciani, A., Soldani, J.: Simulation-based matching of cloud applications. Sci. Comput. Program. **162**, 110–131 (2018)
5. Bonchi, F., Brogi, A., Corfini, S., Gadducci, F.: A net-based approach to web services publication and replaceability. Fundam. Inform. **94**(3–4), 305–330 (2009)
6. Brogi, A., Canciani, A., Soldani, J.: Fault-aware management protocols for multi-component applications. J. Syst. Softw. **139**, 189–210 (2018)
7. Brogi, A., Canciani, A., Soldani, J.: True concurrent management of multi-component applications. In: Kritikos, K., Plebani, P., de Paoli, F. (eds.) ESOCC 2018. LNCS, vol. 11116, pp. 17–32. Springer, Cham (2018). https://doi.org/10.1007/978-3-319-99819-0_2
8. Brogi, A., Rinaldi, L., Soldani, J.: TosKer: a synergy between TOSCA and Docker for orchestrating multicomponent applications. Soft. Pract. Exp. **48**(11), 2061–2079. https://doi.org/10.1002/spe.2625
9. Brogi, A., Soldani, J.: Finding available services in TOSCA-compliant clouds. Sci. Comput. Program. **115–116**, 177–198 (2016)
10. Bujtor, F., Sorokin, L., Vogler, W.: Testing preorders for dMTS: deadlock-and the new deadlock-/divergencetesting. ACM Trans. Embed. Comput. Syst. **16**(2), 41:1–41:28 (2016)
11. Castagna, G., Gesbert, N., Padovani, L.: A theory of contracts for web services. ACM Trans. Program. Lang. Syst. **31**(5), 19:1–19:61 (2009)
12. Cavallaro, L., Di Nitto, E., Pradella, M.: An automatic approach to enable replacement of conversational services. In: Baresi, L., Chi, C.-H., Suzuki, J. (eds.) ICSOC/ServiceWave -2009. LNCS, vol. 5900, pp. 159–174. Springer, Heidelberg (2009). https://doi.org/10.1007/978-3-642-10383-4_11
13. Di Cosmo, R., Mauro, J., Zacchiroli, S., Zavattaro, G.: Aeolus: a component model for the cloud. Inf. Comput. **239**, 100–121 (2014)
14. Dragoni, N., et al.: Microservices: yesterday, today, and tomorrow. Present and Ulterior Software Engineering, pp. 195–216. Springer, Cham (2017). https://doi.org/10.1007/978-3-319-67425-4_12
15. Durán, F., Salaün, G.: Robust and reliable reconfiguration of cloud applications. J. Syst. Softw. **122**, 524–537 (2016)
16. Gregorio-Rodríguez, C., Llana, L., Martínez-Torres, R.: Input-output conformance simulation (iocos) for model based testing. In: Beyer, D., Boreale, M. (eds.) FMOODS/FORTE -2013. LNCS, vol. 7892, pp. 114–129. Springer, Heidelberg (2013). https://doi.org/10.1007/978-3-642-38592-6_9
17. Heike, C., Zimmermann, W., Both, A.: On expanding protocol conformance checking to exception handling. Serv. Oriented Comput. Appl. **8**(4), 299–322 (2013). https://doi.org/10.1007/s11761-013-0146-2
18. Luthmann, L., Mennicke, S., Lochau, M.: Towards an I/O conformance testing theory for software product lines based on modal interface automata. In: Formal Methods and Analysis in SPL Engineering. EPTCS, vol. 182, pp. 1–13 (2015)

19. Luthmann, L., Mennicke, S., Lochau, M.: Compositionality, decompositionality and refinement in input/output conformance testing. In: Kouchnarenko, O., Khosravi, R. (eds.) FACS 2016. LNCS, vol. 10231, pp. 54–72. Springer, Cham (2017). https://doi.org/10.1007/978-3-319-57666-4_5
20. Luthmann, L., Mennicke, S., Lochau, M.: Unifying modal interface theories and compositional input/output conformance testing. Sci. Comput. Program. **172**, 27–47 (2019)
21. Tretmans, J.: Test generation with inputs, outputs and repetitive quiescence. Soft. Concepts Tools **17**(3), 103–120 (1996)
22. Veanes, M., Bjørner, N.: Input-output model programs. In: Leucker, M., Morgan, C. (eds.) ICTAC 2009. LNCS, vol. 5684, pp. 322–335. Springer, Heidelberg (2009). https://doi.org/10.1007/978-3-642-03466-4_21

Formalizing Event-Driven Behavior
of Serverless Applications

Matthew Obetz, Anirban Das, Timothy Castiglia, Stacy Patterson,
and Ana Milanova[✉]

Rensselaer Polytechnic Institute, Troy, NY 12180, USA
{obetzm,dasa3,castit,pattes3,milana2}@rpi.edu

Abstract. We present new operational semantics for serverless computing that model the event-driven relationships between serverless functions, as well as their interaction with platform services such as databases and object stores. These semantics precisely encapsulate how control transfers between functions, both directly and through reads and writes to platform services. We use these semantics to define the notion of the service call graph for serverless applications that captures program flows through functions and services. Finally, we construct service call graphs for 12 serverless JavaScript applications, using a prototype of our call graph construction algorithm, and we evaluate their accuracy.

Keywords: Serverless computing · Formal semantics · Call graph

1 Introduction

Serverless computing has grown significantly in recent years and so has the need for abstractions and program analysis tools that target serverless applications [8]. Existing abstractions emphasize unique features of the environment where serverless functions execute [4,6]. However, these abstractions do not consider effects of transmitting data to other services and functions. Data transmitted in this fashion triggers new executions of serverless functions that spawn in response to a change in state on their associated service. Without *operational semantics* that capture this behavior, program analysis cannot construct a precise call graph and cannot reason about dataflow between parts of a serverless application. The lack of formal semantics also hinders more advanced reasoning about data privacy, application correctness, and resource usage.

To address this gap, we propose new operational semantics for event-driven serverless computation. These semantics describe how writes and reads to platform services create inter-function control transfer in serverless applications. Our semantics formalize the most common platform services including object stores, databases, notification services, queues, and stateless services. The semantics gives rise to the *service call graph*, which extends the classical call graph to include new nodes and edges. The new nodes represent the platform services

© IFIP International Federation for Information Processing 2020
Published by Springer Nature Switzerland AG 2020
A. Brogi et al. (Eds.): ESOCC 2020, LNCS 12054, pp. 19–29, 2020.
https://doi.org/10.1007/978-3-030-44769-4_2

written to or read by application code; the new edges represent the writes and reads to services from serverless functions.

We make the following contributions:

- We formulate new operational semantics for the execution of serverless programs. These semantics model (1) interactions of serverless functions with platform services, including event triggers that cause additional functions to execute, and (2) function composition.
- We extend the traditional notion of a call graph with new types of nodes and edges that represent event-driven behavior on serverless platforms. These new nodes and edges capture the inter-function control and state transfer represented in our operational semantics.
- We design and implement an algorithm for constructing service call graphs and evaluate its accuracy on 12 serverless programs collected from GitHub.

Related Work. Our semantics for the lifecycle of a single serverless function are closely related to those used in a recent formalization of serverless computing [6]. That work focused on modeling low-level behavior of serverless systems. Such models are useful for capturing behavior such as program non-determinism that can arise from reading state from previous executions of serverless functions. Our semantics start from this model to describe initiating requests, language-agnostic computation steps, and generated responses. However, the semantics defined in [6] do not capture inter-function communication and program flows that span multiple serverless functions. Specifically, these semantics limit data persistence to a locking transactional key-value store. Our semantics introduce several new state domains that model common services. More importantly, the previous semantics also lack a conceptualization of serverless events, which initiate execution of a serverless function when state is manipulated on a data storage service. We model these interactions with a new collection of event semantics that capture state transfer between serverless components.

The service call graph shares some features of message flow graphs for distributed event-based systems that communicate through publish-subscribe middleware [5], however, retrieval of data from databases and object stores cannot be succinctly captured in publish-subscribe semantics. Our work considers not only notification-based communication, but also messages that pass through other channels available to serverless applications.

In preliminary work [10], we introduced the notion of the service call graph. In this paper, we formalize the definition in terms of our new operational semantics. Further, we design and implement a call graph construction algorithm and present experimental results on 12 real-world serverless applications.

Outline. Section 2 summarizes the operational semantics, and Sect. 3 presents our serverless call graph construction. We evaluate the call graph construction accuracy in Sect. 4 and conclude in Sect. 5. Our technical report [9] presents an expanded discussion on the serverless model and our semantics and algorithms.

2   Semantics for Serverless Computation

We introduce operational semantics for the execution of serverless applications. The goals of these serverless semantics are to: (1) precisely model the semantics of communication between serverless functions and platform services, and (2) capture program flows that are introduced as a result of this communication.

$f \in F$	defined functions
$\sigma \in \Sigma$	internal state
$init \in F \times V \to \Sigma$	initial state
$v := \dots$	value
$x := \dots$	request ID
$y := \dots$	instance ID
$\mathbb{C} := \mathbb{F}(f, \sigma, y)$	executing serverless function
$\mid \mathbb{R}(f, x, v)$	received request
$\mid \mathbb{S}(x, v)$	generated response
$step_f \in F \times \Sigma \to \Sigma$	computational step

$$\text{RECEIVE} \;\; \frac{x \text{ is fresh}}{\mathbb{C} \Rightarrow \mathbb{CR}(f, x, v)}$$

$$\text{START} \;\; \frac{}{\mathbb{CR}(f, x, v) \Rightarrow \mathbb{CR}(f, x, v)\mathbb{F}(f, init(f, v), y)}$$

$$\text{COMPUTE} \;\; \frac{step_f(\sigma) = \sigma'}{\mathbb{CF}(f, \sigma, y) \Rightarrow \mathbb{CF}(f, \sigma', y)}$$

$$\text{RESPOND} \;\; \frac{step_f = respond(v')}{\mathbb{CR}(f, x, v)\mathbb{F}(f, \sigma, y) \Rightarrow \mathbb{CS}(x, v')\mathbb{F}(f, \sigma, y)}$$

$$\text{DIE} \;\; \frac{}{\mathbb{CF}(f, \sigma, y) \Rightarrow \mathbb{C}}$$

Fig. 1. In-process semantics models the sequence of steps in an individual serverless functions. A full serverless application $\mathbb{C}$ is modeled as a set of requests $\mathbb{R}$, executing functions $\mathbb{F}$, and generated responses $\mathbb{S}$. Functions and requests are appended to $\mathbb{C}$ as they become active, and are removed from $\mathbb{C}$ as they terminate or are responded to.

2.1   In-process Semantics

In-process semantics are defined in Fig. 1. These semantics capture the sequence of steps in an individual serverless function. When an *external* gateway service initiates a request for the execution of the serverless program, the platform applies the RECEIVE rule which adds a new request $\mathbb{R}$. The request contains a serverless function f and a data value v that is passed to the function. Most commonly, RECEIVE represents a request made to a public web endpoint for the serverless application. When an unhandled request exists, the platform applies the START rule which initializes f with an initial state $init(f, v)$ and starts the execution of f. We note that $init(f, v)$ captures both initial state at cold and warm start. COMPUTE models the execution steps in function f. Similarly to [6], COMPUTE is a language agnostic representation of transitions on state σ. COMPUTE absorbs interactions with platform services, e.g., *upload* to object stores (see Sect. 2.2). A serverless function may issue a response, in which case the platform applies the RESPOND rule. This rule removes the unhandled request $\mathbb{R}(f, x, v)$ from the system and replaces it with a response $\mathbb{S}(x, v')$, where v' is the value provided by the responding serverless function. Responses represent data which is sent back to the external service that initiated the request; they are terminal states and are not used for further computation within the platform.

Finally, functions may terminate through the application of the DIE rule. The system reaches a stable state when all requests have been responded to and no serverless functions are still executing.

2.2   Event Semantics

We extend the in-process semantics with an event semantics to capture interaction of functions with platform services, as well as direct invocation. We develop semantics for each service: object stores, databases, notifications, queues, and stateless services. These semantics detail how serverless functions interface with that specific service during execution. In this section, we detail the semantics of object stores. We include the semantics for the remaining services in the technical report [9]; these semantics follow the structure of the object store semantics, however, each details behavior specific to the service they model.

The semantic rules can be broadly grouped into rules that *write* the state of a service (UPLOAD and REMOVE for object stores; INSERT, UPDATE, and DELETE, for databases; and ENQUEUE for queues), and rules that *read* data from a service into the state of an executing serverless function (READ for object stores, SELECT for databases, and DEQUEUE for queues).

```
functions:
    processor:
        handler: index.process
        events:
        - s3:
            bucket: photos
            event: s3:ObjectCreated:*
```

Fig. 2. An example event configuration. The serverless function `processor` is triggered when an object is added to the `photos` bucket. In the semantics, this event is represented as the fact $e(c, processor)$ where $c = (photos, upload)$.

Our semantics introduce a domain of events E that captures function invocations due to service state transitions. An event $e(c, f) \in E$ consists of two parts: a triggering condition c and an associated serverless function f. Triggering conditions are generally defined by a unique service identifier sid and an operation op (e.g., *upload* to an object store); we write $c = (sid, op)$. Program configurations unambiguously reference their associated services and the associated serverless functions. We reduce configurations to set of events $e(c, f)$ during static analysis. We present an example configuration in Fig. 2. An event is *triggered* when a serverless function performs a step that fires the event condition. For instance, an upload to an object store b will activate all events tied to upload to b. To capture the effect of these triggering events, our semantics introduce the function *trigger*. This function accepts a triggerring condition $c = (sid, op)$, and returns the set of functions f for which there is $e(c, f)$, i.e., the set of functions that will execute when a function runs operation op on service sid. We note that some types of triggering conditions defined in our semantics are officially supported by serverless platforms but rarely occur in practice, such as the trigger associated with a REMOVE from an object store.

Our semantics distinguish between functions triggered by external requests and functions triggered by events on services. The platform applies RECEIVE followed by START on functions triggered by external requests. It immediately applies START on functions triggered by "internal" events on services. Our semantics allow that any function that is part of the serverless application may issue a response to the external request. RECEIVE and RESPOND define the "boundary" of the serverless application, although functions may continue to execute and modify services after a RESPOND.

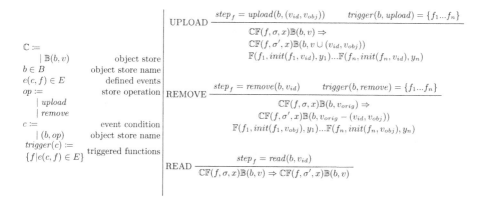

$$
\begin{aligned}
\mathbb{C} := & \\
& | \ \mathbb{B}(b, v) \quad && \text{object store} \\
b \in B \quad && \text{object store name} \\
e(c, f) \in E \quad && \text{defined events} \\
op := \quad && \text{store operation} \\
& | \ upload \\
& | \ remove \\
c := \quad && \text{event condition} \\
& | \ (b, op) \quad && \text{object store name} \\
trigger(c) := \quad && \text{triggered functions} \\
& \{f \, | \, e(c, f) \in E\}
\end{aligned}
$$

$$
\text{UPLOAD} \ \frac{step_f = upload(b, (v_{id}, v_{obj})) \qquad trigger(b, upload) = \{f_1...f_n\}}{\begin{array}{c} \mathbb{CF}(f, \sigma, x)\mathbb{B}(b, v) \Rightarrow \\ \mathbb{CF}(f, \sigma', x)\mathbb{B}(b, v \cup (v_{id}, v_{obj})) \\ \mathbb{F}(f_1, init(f_1, v_{id}), y_1)...\mathbb{F}(f_n, init(f_n, v_{id}), y_n) \end{array}}
$$

$$
\text{REMOVE} \ \frac{step_f = remove(b, v_{id}) \qquad trigger(b, remove) = \{f_1...f_n\}}{\begin{array}{c} \mathbb{CF}(f, \sigma, x)\mathbb{B}(b, v_{orig}) \Rightarrow \\ \mathbb{CF}(f, \sigma', x)\mathbb{B}(b, v_{orig} - (v_{id}, v_{obj})) \\ \mathbb{F}(f_1, init(f_1, v_{obj}), y_1)...\mathbb{F}(f_n, init(f_n, v_{obj}), y_n) \end{array}}
$$

$$
\text{READ} \ \frac{step_f = read(b, v_{id})}{\mathbb{CF}(f, \sigma, x)\mathbb{B}(b, v) \Rightarrow \mathbb{CF}(f, \sigma', x)\mathbb{B}(b, v)}
$$

Fig. 3. Object store event semantics.

We define semantics for object stores in Fig. 3. Each object store has a unique identifier $b \in B$, the set of object stores defined for the application. Object stores provide a filesystem-like interface for writing and reading data. In the semantics, this interaction is encoded by allowing serverless functions to write or overwrite some value v in a named bucket by applying the UPLOAD rule. When a file is uploaded, all events triggered by state transition on the receiving bucket initialize their respective function(s). Serverless functions can also delete data contained in a bucket through application of the REMOVE rule. When a function retrieves a data value from a bucket, the READ rule accesses the associated data and assigns it to a variable inside the function's local state.

Our event semantics are synchronous in the sense that a request to a service and the execution of the request by the service happen in "one step". This facilitates static reasoning. In practice, a request is decoupled from the execution; we conjecture that the synchronous semantics are sufficient as programs implicitly synchronize events on services: a read in f_2 *is triggered* by a write in f_1. Further, for reads and writes within the same function, standard libraries typically provide only synchronous methods for interacting with platform services. We will formalize sufficiency conditions on programs in future work.

2.3   Platform Behavior Encoded in Semantics

Our semantics are sufficiently expressive to capture features of serverless platforms that impact system state in unintuitive ways. We illustrate below.

```
export.shortenUrl = function(event, context, callback) {
    let url = event.body;
    let slug = crypto.randomBytes(8).toString(...).replace(...);
    callback(null, {shortUrl: context.domainName + slug});
    dynamodb.put({
        TableName: "ShortUrls",
        Item: {slug: slug, long_url: url}
    });
}
```

Fig. 4. Example of execution continuing after response. RESPOND is applied when the `callback` passed in to the serverless function is invoked, but a database is written to after this response. Code adapted from the `url-shortener` project [11].

Non-finality of RESPOND. Unlike **return** statements in normal functions, responses from a serverless function do not return from the function. Consider the example in Fig. 4. This serverless function accepts a URL string and generates a random short slug for that URL. It immediately responds with the generated shortened URL, then afterward, writes the association between the slug and the original URL to a database. Our semantics models the execution of this serverless function by the following transitions ($\mathbb{D}$ represents the database service. INSERT has semantics similar to UPLOAD in Fig. 3):

$$\mathbb{CD}(\mathit{ShortUrls}, v)$$
$$\implies \mathbb{CD}(\mathit{ShortUrls}, v)\mathbb{R}(f, x, v_1) \qquad\qquad \text{by rule RECEIVE } (f, x, v_1)$$
$$\implies \mathbb{CD}(\mathit{ShortUrls}, v)\mathbb{R}(f, x, v_1)\mathbb{F}(f, \sigma, y) \qquad \text{by START}(y)$$
$$\implies \mathbb{CD}(\mathit{ShortUrls}, v)\mathbb{R}(f, x, v_1)$$
$$\qquad \mathbb{F}(f, \sigma' = \sigma[url \leftarrow ev.body, slug \leftarrow rand()], y) \qquad \text{by COMPUTE}(f)$$
$$\implies \mathbb{CD}(\mathit{ShortUrls}, v)\mathbb{S}(x, v')\mathbb{F}(f, \sigma', y) \qquad \text{by RESPOND}(x, v' = \sigma'[slug])$$
$$\implies \mathbb{CD}(\mathit{ShortUrls}, v' \cup v)\mathbb{S}(x, v')\mathbb{F}(f, \sigma', y) \qquad \text{by INSERT}(\mathit{ShortUrls}, v')$$
$$\implies \mathbb{CD}(\mathit{ShortUrls}, v' \cup v)\mathbb{S}(x, v') \qquad \text{by DIE}(y)$$

The application of the INSERT rule affects the final state of the system $\mathbb{C}$ by introducing the value v' to the database $\mathbb{D}$. This insertion occurs even though the serverless function has already generated a response in an earlier step.

Failures and Retried Executions. A serverless function may fail during execution for two reasons: (1) the function code enters an error state as the result of an uncaught exception, or (2) the container runtime kills the function, either because execution has timed out, or because the language interpreter fails with an error. When a function fails, the platform can retry the function by starting a new execution with a clone of the data from the original request [1].

Our semantics capture the effects of failures and retried executions that may impact system state. In particular, serverless functions that are not idempotent may emit messages to platform services that are repeated in retried executions, affecting final system state. In our semantics, these retries are modeled as an application of the DIE rule, followed by a subsequent application of START to handle a still-unsatisfied request. Consider a serverless function that uses the UPDATE rule to increment a view count. It is retried due to a spontaneous failure in the data center where the function is executing. This series of events are modeled under our semantics as:

$\mathbb{CD}(ViewCount, v)$
$\implies \mathbb{CD}(ViewCount, v)\mathbb{R}(f, x, v)$ by RECEIVE(f, x, v)
$\implies \mathbb{CD}(ViewCount, v)\mathbb{R}(f, x, v)\mathbb{F}(f, \sigma, y)$ by START(y)
$\implies \mathbb{CD}(ViewCount, v + 1)\mathbb{R}(f, x, v)\mathbb{F}(f, \sigma, y)$ by UPDATE$(ViewCount, (v) \to v + 1)$
$\implies \mathbb{CD}(ViewCount, v + 1)\mathbb{R}(f, x, v)$ by DIE(y)
$\implies \mathbb{CD}(ViewCount, v + 1)\mathbb{R}(f, x, v)\mathbb{F}(f, \sigma, y')$ by START(y')
$\implies \mathbb{CD}(ViewCount, v + 2)\mathbb{R}(f, x, v)\mathbb{F}(f, \sigma, y')$ by UPDATE$(ViewCount, (v) \to v + 1)$
$\implies \mathbb{CD}(ViewCount, v + 2)\mathbb{S}(x, v)\mathbb{F}(f, \sigma, y')$ by RESPOND$(x, \{\})$
$\implies \mathbb{CD}(ViewCount, v + 2)\mathbb{S}(x, \{\})$ by DIE(y')

Following these state transitions, *ViewCount* has been incremented twice, despite only a single request being made to the serverless function. Such faults are representative of data inconsistencies that exist in real serverless applications that violate the idempotency recommended by serverless providers [1].

2.4   Platform Supported Function Composition

Function composition frameworks, such as AWS Step Functions, allow developers to statically define pathways for messages through a serverless application. When one of these pathways is defined, the return value of a serverless function implicitly becomes a message passed to the serverless function or service following it in the composition. Our semantics are expressive enough to capture such behavior using the same set of state transitions as other serverless events.

Consider a Step Function composition that defines a chain of two serverless functions, f_1 and f_2. ([9] shows the real-world Step Function declaration that we model in this example.) Our semantics models the execution as follows:

$$\mathbb{C}$$
$$\implies \mathbb{CR}(f_{step}, x, v) \qquad\qquad\qquad \text{by RECEIVE}(f_{step}, x, v)$$
$$\implies \mathbb{CR}(f_{step}, x, v)\mathbb{F}(f_1, \sigma, y) \qquad\qquad \text{by START}(y)$$
$$\implies \mathbb{CR}(f_{step}, x, v)\mathbb{F}(f_1, \sigma', y) \qquad\qquad \text{by COMPUTE}(f_1)$$
$$\implies \mathbb{CR}(f_{step}, x, v)\mathbb{F}(f_1, \sigma', y)\mathbb{F}(f_2, \sigma'', y) \qquad \text{by INVOKE}(f_2, v')$$
$$\implies \mathbb{CR}(f_{step}, x, v)\mathbb{F}(f_2, \sigma'', y) \qquad\qquad \text{by DIE}(f_1, \sigma', y)$$
$$\implies \mathbb{CR}(f_{step}, x, v)\mathbb{F}(f_2, \sigma''', y) \qquad\qquad \text{by COMPUTE}(f_2)$$
$$\implies \mathbb{CS}(x, v'')\mathbb{F}(f_2, \sigma''', y) \qquad\qquad \text{by RESPOND}(x, v'')$$
$$\implies \mathbb{CS}(x, v'') \qquad\qquad\qquad\qquad \text{by DIE}(f_2, \sigma''', y)$$

This execution illustrates an important difference between standalone serverless functions and those defined as part of a composition chain. The platform starts the Step Function chain by issuing a request $\mathbb{R}(f_{step}, x, v)$ by RECEIVE. Only the final serverless function in the chain RESPONDs to the request. The "return" of all other functions in the chain is encoded into an event rule that INVOKEs the next function in the chain. Since compositions are static, the target of each INVOKE in the composition is known. To preserve the connection to the originating Step Function request that started $\mathbb{F}(f_1, \sigma, y)$, f_2 inherits the identifier y from f_1 when it is invoked (the semantics assume that y reflects the request identifier x). Thus, the lifecycle of the first function in the composition chain is RECEIVE, START, COMPUTE, DIE; the lifecycle of the final one is START, COMPUTE, RESPOND, DIE.

3   Service Call Graphs

Our semantics enable construction of a *service call graph* that explicitly models interaction between services and serverless functions. The service call graph extends the classical call graph by adding nodes that represent platform services and edges that represent reads from services, writes to services, and transfer of control to functions triggered by state transition on services. Our graphs treat an entire intra-function call graph as a single node in order to clearly capture the interaction between serverless functions and platform services.

Construction of the service call graph proceeds in two phases: *configuration analysis* and *code analysis*. Configuration analysis processes configuration files and identifies the serverless functions and services for the given application. Each serverless function $f \in F$, and each service $b \in B$ (object store), $d \in D$ (database), $q \in Q$ (queue), and $t \in T$ (notification topic) becomes a node in the service call graph. In addition, configuration analysis also identifies the set of events $e(c, f) \in E$ and triggering conditions $c = (sid, op)$ (recall Sect. 2 for the explanation of e and c); each event $e(c, f) \in E$ where $c = (sid, op)$ gives rise to an edge from sid to f.

Code analysis processes each serverless functions $f \in F$. It constructs the standard interprocedural control flow graph (ICFG) of f (here, "interprocedural" refers to the local helper functions in f). The analysis tracks the set of service identifiers sid that flow to call sites in the ICFG corresponding to rules of the event semantics (such as UPLOAD, ENQUEUE, INSERT, or NOTIFY). At each such call site, the analysis adds an edge from the current serverless function f to each service sid that may reach the call site corresponding to the event rule.

4   Call Graph Implementation and Evaluation

We implement service call graph construction as an extension of the Type Analysis for JavaScript (TAJS) framework [7]. We employ a branch of TAJS that supports reasoning about asynchronous behavior [12]. Our analysis includes code that summarize the effects of third party libraries, including the AWS SDK. We constructed summaries of library functions to overcome limitations in TAJS that prevented us from performing standard whole-program analysis. We searched GitHub for repositories that included serverless configuration files that defined more than one serverless function, sorted by repository popularity. We analyze the top 12 applications that fit these criteria. To evaluate the accuracy of our generated call graphs, we compare the output of our analysis against call graphs drawn by manual inspection of the programs.

Table 1. Service call graph results.

Application	Lines of code	# Functions	Sound?	Missed edges
Hello-retail	2288	14	Y	0
Citizen-dispatch	865	3	N	6
Galleria	641	5	Y	0
Rating-service	412	2	Y	0
LEX	323	2	Y	0
Lending-app	258	4	Y	0
Url-shortener	172	3	Y	0
Zen-beer	155	4	Y	0
Greeting-app	99	2	Y	0
Lane-breach	98	2	N	1
Wombat	88	2	Y	0
Serverless-chaining	28	2	Y	0

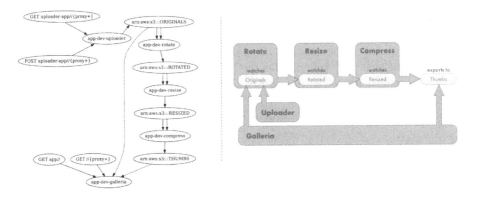

Fig. 5. Comparison of service call graph generated by our analysis for the galleria serverless application [3], and pipeline diagram provided in the repository's user documentation. In the call graph at left, the GET and POST API gateway events trigger the **app-dev-uploader** serverless function. This function then writes to the ORIGINALS S3 bucket, which in turn triggers the **app-dev-rotate** serverless function. This function reads from its triggering bucket then writes to a ROTATED bucket. The process repeats for two more image processing functions before the final image is uploaded to THUMBS.

Table 1 presents the analysis results. For 10 of the 12 applications, our analysis produced a service call graph *identical to the ground truth*. One such comparison is shown in Fig. 5. For two applications, our analysis missed edges. In the case of **lane-breach**, the missed edge corresponded to a web request made directly to another function through the external web API. We note that it is not possible, in general, to determine whether a web address belongs to the application under analysis or a third-party web site. Fortunately, this behavior represents a discouraged pattern [2]; the program could be made more efficient using a direct invocation, which would be captured through our INVOKE rule.

In the case of **citizen-dispatch**, the analysis missed edges from serverless functions to a set of database tables that corresponded to database queries made by third-party library calls. This program violated our assumption that third-party libraries do not interact with services. Though constant service identifiers flow to the library calls, it is difficult to statically infer which tables will be accessed by a particular call due to the nature of the query inference engine. Future versions of our tool could safely over-approximate this behavior by assuming that any library call has the potential to query all tables. If we could perform standard whole-program analysis, interactions with the database through the library would have been soundly detected. (Whole-program analysis is trivially supported in tools for languages such as Java, but it is not supported by TAJS due to the difficulty of analyzing JavaScript.)

5 Conclusion

We introduced new operational semantics for serverless computing and demonstrated how these semantics give rise to the service call graph. Finally, we presented a prototype of our service call graph construction algorithm and showed its efficacy on real-world serverless programs. In future work, we will construct analyses for improving performance and security of serverless applications.

References

1. Amazon Web Services: AWS Lambda Documentation (2019). https://docs.aws. amazon.com/lambda/index.html
2. Baldini, I., et al.: Serverless computing: current trends and open problems. In: Chaudhary, S., Somani, G., Buyya, R. (eds.) Research Advances in Cloud Computing, pp. 1–20. Springer, Singapore (2017). https://doi.org/10.1007/978-981-10-5026-8_1
3. Chiu, E.: Serverless galleria (2019). https://github.com/evanchiu/serverless-galleria
4. Gabbrielli, M., Giallorenzo, S., Lanese, I., Montesi, F., Peressotti, M., Zingaro, S.P.: No more, no less. In: Riis Nielson, H., Tuosto, E. (eds.) COORDINATION 2019. LNCS, vol. 11533, pp. 148–157. Springer, Cham (2019). https://doi.org/10.1007/978-3-030-22397-7_9
5. Garcia, J., Popescu, D., Safi, G., Halfond, W.G.J., Medvidovic, N.: Identifying message flow in distributed event-based systems. In: Proceedings of the 9th Joint Meeting on Foundations of Software Engineering, pp. 367–377 (2013)
6. Jangda, A., Pinckney, D., Brun, Y., Guha, A.: Formal foundations of serverless computing. PACMPL 3(OOPSLA), pp. 149:1–149:26 (2019)
7. Jensen, S.H., Møller, A., Thiemann, P.: Type analysis for Javascript. In: Palsberg, J., Su, Z. (eds.) SAS 2009. LNCS, vol. 5673, pp. 238–255. Springer, Heidelberg (2009). https://doi.org/10.1007/978-3-642-03237-0_17
8. Jonas, E., et al.: Cloud programming simplified: a berkeley view on serverless computing. Technical report, University of California at Berkeley (2019)
9. Obetz, M., Patterson, S., Milanova, A.: Formalizing event-driven behavior of serverless applications. CoRR abs/1912.03584 (2019). http://arxiv.org/abs/1912.03584
10. Obetz, M., Patterson, S., Milanova, A.: Static call graph construction in AWS lambda serverless applications. In: HotCloud (2019)
11. Onan, M.: URL-shortener (2019). https://github.com/mdonan90/url-shortener/blob/master/create/index.js
12. Sotiropoulos, T., Livshits, B.: Static analysis for asynchronous JavaScript programs. CoRR abs/1901.03575 (2019). http://arxiv.org/abs/1901.03575

Probabilistic Verification of Outsourced Computation Based on Novel Reversible PUFs

Hala Hamadeh[1]([✉]), Abdallah Almomani[2], and Akhilesh Tyagi[1]

[1] Iowa State University, Ames, IA 50010, USA
hamadeh@iastate.edu
[2] Jordan University of Science and Technology, Irbid 22110, Jordan

Abstract. With the growing number of commercial cloud-computing services, there is a corresponding need to verify that such computations were performed correctly. In other words, after a weak client outsources computations to an untrusted cloud, it must be able to ensure the correctness of the results with less work than re-performing the computations. This is referred to as verifiable computation. In this paper we present a new probabilistic verifiable computation method based on a novel Reversible Physically Unclonable Function (PUF) and a binomial Bayesian Inference model. Our scheme links the outsourced software with the cloud-node hardware to provide a proof of the computational integrity and the resultant correctness of the results with high probability. The proposed Reversible SW-PUF is a two-way function capable of computing partial inputs given its outputs. Given the random output signature of a specific instruction in a specific basic block of the program, only the computing platform that originally computed the instruction can accurately regenerate the inputs of the instruction correct within a certain number of bits. To explore the feasibility of the proposed design, the Reversible SW-PUF was implemented in HSPICE using 45 nm technology. The probabilistic verifiable computation scheme was implemented in C++, and the Bayesian Inference model was utilized to estimate the probability of correctness of the results returned from the cloud service. Our proof-of-concept implementation of Reversible SW-PUF exhibits good uniqueness compared to other types of PUFs and exhibits perfect reliability and acceptable randomness. Finally, we demonstrate our verifiable computation approach on a matrix computation. We show that it enables faster verification than existing verification techniques.

1 Introduction

Verifiable computations (VC) have attracted enormous interest and attention with the recent growth in cloud computing. The concept of verifiable computation allows a lower-resource client to outsource the computation of a program to an untrusted cloud. With a proof provided by the cloud, the client can verify that

© IFIP International Federation for Information Processing 2020
Published by Springer Nature Switzerland AG 2020
A. Brogi et al. (Eds.): ESOCC 2020, LNCS 12054, pp. 30–37, 2020.
https://doi.org/10.1007/978-3-030-44769-4_3

the results produced are consistent with the program specification and that the computations were performed correctly. To be viable, the effort of performing the verification must be negligible compared to the actual computation. Three main solutions were proposed to support verifiable computation: VC based on Trusted Computing [2]. The main drawback of this approach was the assumption that the physical protections cannot be defeated. A second method, VC with a Non-Interactive Argument, is described in [8]. This approach is not practical because it relies on complex Probabilistically Checkable Proofs (PCPs) or fully-homomorphic encryption (FHE). Finally, VC with Interactive Proofs [9] has been propose. While this approach is often efficient, it applies to only a narrow class of computations.

In recent years, interest in physically-unclonable functions (PUFs) has evolved. PUFs have been deployed in different applications because of their ability to generate "digital fingerprints" of unique identities for a physical system. SW-PUF [6] is a specific type of PUF that binds software execution to the exact hardware platform and produces unique signatures at various points in the software's execution. The SW-PUF signature is a promising candidate for providing a proof that a specific computation was performed on a specific platform. By expanding the capabilities of a SW-PUF to include invertibility and commutativity, we achieve elements of verifiable computation. Invertibility is achieved by capturing a physical attribute such as time when an output bit settles using reversible functions. Reversibility is obtained with transmission gates.

2   The Reversible SW-PUF

The design of the Reversible SW-PUF is an extension of our previous work on the SW-PUF [6]. As in the original SW-PUF, the ALU signatures of an instruction on the reversible SW-PUF are generated from an early sampling of the ALU results. However, in the reverse mode, the roles of inputs and outputs are reversed, and the early sampling is done on the original input end. Reversible SW-PUF has two modes: forward and reverse. The forward mode is similar to the SW-PUF where it generates a unique signature by capturing the delay variations of carry propagation in ripple-carry adders (which is a basic component in an ALU). The delay variation is caused by instruction input values and the silicon fabrication foundry variations. The reverse mode computes the partial inputs from the signature and the instruction output. Early sampling captures a subset of original input bits correctly in a platform specific manner, which itself is a platform specific secret. Only the computing platform that originally computed the instruction can regenerate the inputs of the instruction accurate within a certain number of bits. In this design, Reversible SW-PUF is implemented in reversible logic. Fredkin gate [4] is used as the Boolean basis for conservative logic because it is universal.

Since Fredkin gates are based on transmutation gates, and TGs are slow compare to a regular gate, we propose to use two ALUs (fast-ALU, rev-ALU). The actual computation values consumed by the following program instructions occur at the fast-ALU. The rev-ALU is used only for verification.

3   Verifiable Computation Scheme

In this section an efficient Verifiable Computation Scheme based on Reversible SW-PUF is proposed. The proposed scheme fits with a probabilistic consistency guarantee. In this scheme, we are interested in estimating the probability of a cloud service to return a correct result for the outsourced function. The main idea is to bind the verification scheme to the cloud service hardware by entangling the computation with the SW-PUF. When the cloud computes the function, an instruction sequence for each instruction generates relevant attributes which are the two data inputs for the lth instruction - X_0^l, X_1^l, the instruction output Y^l, and the PUF output P_l. Effectively, the cloud node generates a signature (response) for each instruction (challenge) in the execution path. This entire sequence of challenge-response pairs will be returned to the client as a proof of computational consistency.

For the verification process, the client can verify the behavior of a program of variable granularities. Most straightforward granularity is to verify an individual instruction behavior. Pick a random challenge-response (C_k, R_k) pair of an instruction I_k to verify. The client needs to send the response part (the instruction output Y^k, and the PUF output P_k) to the cloud node. The cloud instantiates the reversible SW-PUF to re-compute the challenge from the response (the data inputs of the instruction $(X_0'^k, X_1'^k)$. Only the cloud node that computed the original signature will be able to compute the inverse PUF, so that $(X_0'^k, X_1'^k)$ is consistent with the (X_0^k, X_1^k) in the original computation's proof of consistency within a large number of bits. We assume that over all the clients and programs, the amount of data is too large to be archived by the cloud node preventing a look-up based response to the verification step.

Repeating this verification process for all the n instructions is not feasible because a large number of instructions could be executed during a program run. As we discuss later, an alternative approach to pick a subset of instructions is used to increase the confidence interval for the verification while maintaining an efficient verification.

Static program slices raise this granularity naturally. It is a technique for reducing a program to a minimal form that still retains the original program computation for a given variable at a chosen point. Merging the program slicing technique with our verification scheme leads to a more efficient Verifiable Computation. A program slice's input/output consistency can be established with the Reversible SW-PUF method. For a program slice, all of the instructions in its execution flow can be verified leading to a deterministic verification. The program slices can be extracted to maximize certain static properties.

Figure 1 describes an example of a client that wants to run the program on a cloud server using the proposed protocol:

For choosing the slice set in our scheme, two elements are critical: the size of the slice, and the number of slices. Since small slices result in more efficient verification, we propose to use a selection method based on the super-node [10] algorithm to reduce the verification effort. However, certain types of program control flow graphs may not be amenable to small slices, and in such a case,

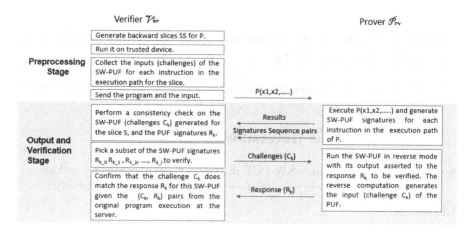

Fig. 1. The proposed protocol

different methods could be applied. As in any interactive proof system, increasing the number of slices will increase confidence in the computed results. To provide a desired probabilistic proof about the server's results, we propose to use a Bayesian Inference [3] model to determine the appropriate number of static slices required.

Slices Selection:
Given a program P that contains a set of instructions S, our goal is to find a subset of S called M such that M exhibits the same behavior as S with respect to one of the program outputs. Once we find M, while we want to generate static slices SS that go through M, the selection of M must be based in some randomized algorithm to prevent an adversary from producing the same M to cheat. For choosing M, we used the algorithm in [10], for selecting all the super-nodes in P as our set of desired nodes. A super-node is formed from a strict dominator-post-dominator pair. A node X is defined as a dominator to a node Y if every path from the start node to Y goes through X. Similarly, a node X is defined as a post-dominator to a node Y if all paths to the exit node of the graph starting at Y go through X. The super-node method will reduce the proposed verification scheme overhead. Verifying at least one instruction from each super-node block will be sufficient to verify the entire slice.

Probabilistic Verification Algorithms:
In this section, we propose use of a Bayesian inference on a binomial proportion method to verify the outsourced computation statistically. Bayesian inference is a statistical technique to update our subjective beliefs as new evidence or data becomes available. Our objective here is to characterize the probability density function for the outsourced computation correctness given that a set of slices were run correctly. In particular, we are interested in estimating confidence in verifying the correctness of the calculation results returned by an untrusted cloud server. Bayesian computation of probability distributions starts with a

prior belief about a model parameter, then updates this distribution based on observed data to produce new posterior beliefs. The mathematical definition of the Bayesian method is as follows:

$$p(H|D) = \frac{p(D|H) \times p(H)}{p(D)} \tag{1}$$

4   Evaluation of the Reversible SW-PUF

We evaluate 32-bit Reversible SW-PUF in HSPICE using predictive technology model. We studied three metrics: uniqueness, randomness, and reliability.

Uniqueness:
Uniqueness measures the capability to distinguish between different devices. Hamming distances (HD) between PUF responses are used to measure uniqueness. An ideal HD between any two PUF responses is 50% (16-bit). To evaluate the uniqueness of the Reversible SW-PUF on the same ALU under different data inputs (Intra-chip), we measured the average HD distribution between a pair of output data on the same device PUF instance with different set of input data. The uniqueness of the forward signature for the Reversible SW-PUF has been measured the same way as the regular SW-PUF [6]. Figure 2(A) shows the HD in Forward mode. For the reverse computation, both ALU inputs were measured on ten different PUF instances with identical output (response, which constitutes the input for a reversible PUF in reverse mode). The HD between each pair of different ALUs was calculated. Figure 2(B) shows the HD in Reverse mode.

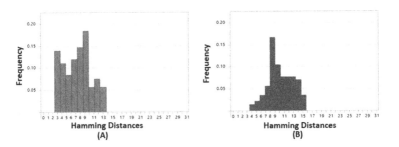

Fig. 2. Hamming distance distribution of reversible SW-PUF: (A) Forward mode; (B) Reverse mode

Randomness: Randomness evaluates a PUF signature by analyzing the distribution of 0's and 1's. The standard statistical test suite of the National Institute of Standard and Technology (NIST) was used to evaluate the responses of the reversible SW-PUF. We have applied the NIST tests to 512-bit stream that was produced from the 16 PUF instances. Only two categories (rank and linear complexity), out of fifteen statistical tests, failed.

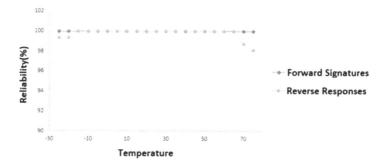

Fig. 3. The reliability of reversible SW-PUF against temperature variations.

Reliability: Reliability measures robustness of a PUF in the presence of environmental variations. Temperature variations are the main factor that affect the stability of a PUF response. Figure 3 shows the reliability results for the responses of the Reversible SW-PUF for both the forward and backward computations. The reversible PUF is very stable under the temperature variation from $-10\,^{\circ}\mathrm{C}$ to $65\,^{\circ}\mathrm{C}$.

Case Study: Verification of Matrix Multiplication

We evaluate the proposed method thorough a matrix multiplication experiment, a widely-used example in Verifiable Computation Systems. We considered the following scenario: a client C needs to multiply two large scale matrices $A(n \times n)$ and $B(n \times n)$ using a cloud service S. However, since the client C does not completely trust the cloud S to return the correct results for multiplication, the client C could verify the results in many ways. A naive algorithm could replicate the multiplication using another cloud service and compare the results, but this method is expensive, e.g., multiplying $n \times n$ matrices execute $O(n^3)$ time using the standard method. A faster check could use Freivalds' algorithm [5], a probabilistic randomized algorithm that verifies matrix multiplication in $O(kn^2)$ with a probability of failure less than 2^{-k}. Our approach improves Freivalds' algorithm by reducing the running time of the verification process by a factor of $O(n)$. Finally, we compare the execution time of our approach with the Verifiable Computation method proposed in [11].

Experimental Setup: We implemented a C++ tool to generate the random slices and perform the verification, and a LLVM compiler framework to compile the matrix multiplication program into LLVM Immediate Representation (IR). We used the Symbiotic 3 tool [1] to obtain the backward static slice for the program. Symbiotic 3 linked with C++ code to generate the random slices in which the slicing criterion was one element of the output matrix. The number of slices was chosen based on the Bayesian Inference model. For simplicity, we assumed that client C challenges must completely match the server signatures, and any failure will result in rejection of the verification. Finally, a Pin tool was used to generate the desired instruction traces, while HSPICE was used to represent the Reversible SW-PUF to generate the signatures.

Performance Evaluation: We performed the experiments for evaluating our scheme and present the computation time cost for each of its elements. The resultant time cost was obtained by averaging the outcomes of testing 10 different randomly generated inputs of the matrix multiplication code for matrix sizes ranging from 1000 to 7000. Table 1 shows a computational cost comparison between the server S (i.e. Matrix Multiplication, Reverse computations) and the client C (i.e. Slices Generation "the number of slices was picked to produce a probability of more than 0.97", Signatures Verification) sides.

We evaluate the advantage of our scheme by comparing our experiment with the PVCBMM scheme proposed in [11]. Both of the experiments are performed on the same computer properties. However, we used the Strassen's algorithm [7] to reduce the time required to multiply matrices. We studied seven dimensions size ranging from 1000 to 7000. As shown in Table 2, the experimental results reveal that our scheme is more efficient than the PVCBMM scheme.

Table 1. Computation cost of proposed scheme for different problem size.

Dimension	Verification at client side		Computations at server side	
	Slices generation	Signatures verification	Matrix multiplication	Reverse computations
$n = 1000$	10.025 ms	0.570 ms	0.201 s	0.008 s
$n = 2000$	11.504 ms	0.684 ms	2.129 s	0.078 s
$n = 3000$	12.753 ms	0.746 ms	6.372 s	0.183 s
$n = 4000$	15.025 ms	0.866 ms	12.479 s	0.366 s
$n = 5000$	16.875 ms	0.925 ms	20.692 s	0.675 s
$n = 6000$	17.752 ms	0.990 ms	29.668 s	1.065 s
$n = 7000$	20.057 ms	1.136 ms	44.050 s	1.523 s

Table 2. Computation and verification cost between two schemes.

Dimension	The proposed scheme		PVCBMM scheme [11]	
	Computations cost	Verification cost	Computations cost	Verification cost
$n = 1000$	0.201 s	0.018 s	1.75 s	6.94 s
$n = 2000$	2.12 s	0.090 s	4.36 s	14.86 s
$n = 3000$	6.37 s	0.19 s	8.35 s	32.26 s
$n = 4000$	12.47 s	0.38 s	24.62 s	61.37 s
$n = 5000$	20.69 s	0.69 s	36.31 s	85.03 s
$n = 6000$	29.66 s	1.08 s	65.16 s	178.54 s
$n = 7000$	44.05 s	1.54 s	105.28 s	193.86 s

5   Conclusions

We present reversible SW-PUF, a novel PUF design for computing partial inputs given a set of outputs. We implemented the reversible SW-PUF in HSPICE and established its desirable properties (uniqueness, randomness, and reliability). We then provided an efficient interactive verifiable computation scheme based on the proposed PUF and based on the Bayesian method. Our approach links outsourced computation with server cloud node hardware to provide proof of correctness of the results with high probability.

References

1. Chalupa, M., Jonáš, M., Slaby, J., Strejček, J., Vitovská, M.: Symbiotic 3: new slicer and error-witness generation. In: Chechik, M., Raskin, J.-F. (eds.) TACAS 2016. LNCS, vol. 9636, pp. 946–949. Springer, Heidelberg (2016). https://doi.org/10.1007/978-3-662-49674-9_67
2. Chen, L., Landfermann, R., Löhr, H., Rohe, M., Sadeghi, A.-R., Stüble, C.: A protocol for property-based attestation. In: Proceedings of the First ACM Workshop on Scalable Trusted Computing (STC 2006), pp. 7–16. ACM, New York (2006)
3. Dempster, A.P.: A generalization of Bayesian inference. J. Roy. Stat. Soc. Ser. B (Methodol.) **30**(2), 205–232 (1968)
4. Fredkin, E., Toffoli, T.: Conservative logic. Int. J. Theor. Phys. **21**(3), 219–253 (1982)
5. Freivalds, R.: Fast probabilistic algorithms. In: Bečvář, J. (ed.) MFCS 1979. LNCS, vol. 74, pp. 57–69. Springer, Heidelberg (1979). https://doi.org/10.1007/3-540-09526-8_5
6. Hamadeh, H., Tyagi, A.: Physical unclonable functions (PUFs) entangled trusted computing base. In: 2019 IEEE International Symposium on Smart Electronic Systems (iSES)(Formerly iNiS). IEEE (2019)
7. Huss-Lederman, S., Jacobson, E.M., Johnson, J.R., Tsao, A., Turnbull, T.: Implementation of strassen's algorithm for matrix multiplication. In: Supercomputing 1996: Proceedings of the 1996 ACM/IEEE Conference on Supercomputing, p. 32. IEEE (1996)
8. Parno, B., Howell, J., Gentry, C., Raykova, M.: Pinocchio: nearly practical verifiable computation. Commun. ACM **59**(2), 103–112 (2016)
9. Vu, V., Setty, S.T.V., Blumberg, A.J., Walfish, M.: A hybrid architecture for interactive verifiable computation. In: IEEE Symposium on Security and Privacy, pp. 223–237. IEEE Computer Society (2013)
10. Zhang, M., Gu, Z., Li, H., Zheng, N.: WCET-aware control flow checking with super-nodes for resource-constrained embedded systems. IEEE Access **6**, 42394–42406 (2018)
11. Zhang, X., Jiang, T., Li, K.-C., Castiglione, A., Chen, X.: New publicly verifiable computation for batch matrix multiplication. Inf. Sci. **479**, 664–678 (2019)

Cloud Service and Platform Selection

Multiplayer Game Backends: A Comparison of Commodity Cloud-Based Approaches

Nicos Kasenides$^{(\boxtimes)}$(iD) and Nearchos Paspallis(iD)

University of Central Lancashire—Cyprus Campus,
12-14 University Avenue, 7080 Pyla, Cyprus
{nkasenides,npaspallis}@uclan.ac.uk

Abstract. The development of resource-intensive complex distributed systems such as the backend side of Massively Multiplayer Online Games (MMOGs) has shifted towards cloud-based approaches in recent years. Despite this shift, researchers and developers have mostly utilized proprietary clouds to provide services for such applications—thus leaving the area of commodity clouds largely unexplored. The use of proprietary clouds is almost always applied at the Infrastructure-as-a-Service layer, thereby enforcing restrictions on the development of MMOGs. In a previous work we focused on the characteristics of MMOGs, outlining certain factors that prohibit their deployment on commodity clouds. In this paper, we evaluate the suitability of common public cloud platforms in developing and deploying the backend side of MMOGs. In our approach, we implement a simple MMOG over three popular public cloud platforms. Then, we evaluate their performance by measuring the latency of the game over each platform as well as the maximum size of game worlds supported by each approach. Our measurements show that approaches based on the Infrastructure-as-a-Service layer perform better than those based on the Platform-as-a-Service layer—which was expected. However, our results indicate that MMOGs based on the Platform-as-a-Service layer can also perform relatively well and within the bounds of real-time latency. Coupled with accelerated development and lower maintenance costs, Platform-as-a-Service technology paves the way for further development of MMOG specific Backend-as-a-Service platforms.

Keywords: Software engineering · Distributed systems · Cloud computing · MMOG · Backend · Commodity clouds

1 Introduction

The use of commodity cloud platforms to power enterprise applications has become the default choice in recent years. Cloud computing offers numerous advantages, most notably scalability, elasticity, and cost efficiency [6]. Despite their scale, enterprise applications exhibit moderate synchronization requirements that rarely cause any significant issues with their scalability. On the

© IFIP International Federation for Information Processing 2020
Published by Springer Nature Switzerland AG 2020
A. Brogi et al. (Eds.): ESOCC 2020, LNCS 12054, pp. 41–55, 2020.
https://doi.org/10.1007/978-3-030-44769-4_4

other hand, resource-intensive applications such as *Multiplayer Online Games* (MOGs) and especially *Massively Multiplayer Online Games* (MMOGs) typically limit their scale using game-imposed constraints—such as game "rooms" with specific capacities—to cope with the very high resource demands. Such games have traditionally pushed the limits of cloud computing: they have certain peculiarities and present a different set of challenges that must be tackled before they can be enabled to run on commodity clouds [16,18,24,37]. In the past, the resource-intensive nature of such applications has led game providers to opt for on-premise rather than for public cloud solutions to host their game's backend [13,38,45]. However, trends emerging from a recent study we conducted [28] show that the use of cloud technology has become the most popular option for deploying MMOGs, and also that it is moving towards higher abstraction layers such as *Platform-as-a-Service* (PaaS).

In this paper, we assess how commercial-grade, public cloud solutions can be used to realize the backends of MOGs and MMOGs. While *Backend-as-a-Service* (BaaS) technology has already been used for secondary functionalities—such as analytics, score-keeping, etc.—we investigate how PaaS-based backends can be used for core tasks that cover the state management and core operations typically placed at the backend. We believe there is an opportunity to utilize these higher layers of cloud computing to provide inherent scalability, offer higher abstraction during development and decrease maintenance costs for game producers.

Our approach realizes a simple MOG which is implemented and tested on top of commodity cloud services at the *Infrastructure-as-a-Service* (IaaS) and PaaS layers. By implementing the game in multiple layers, we aim to identify some of the constraints, peculiarities, and challenges presented when moving from on-premise solutions to private clouds and then to public clouds. Our main objective is to allow a comparison between these approaches, based on their performance. Performance—frequently measured in terms of latency—significantly affects the *Quality of Experience* (QoE) perceived by players and can have a remarkable impact on a game provider's success in the market. We evaluate each approach by running tests that give insight into their performance and enable comparison between them. First, we compare their data stores in terms of the maximum size of game worlds supported. Secondly, we conduct simulations to measure the latency in each service and thus the performance of each approach. Our results show that approaches based on the IaaS layer perform better than those based on the PaaS layer in terms of latency—as we initially expected. However, the PaaS-based approach still performed reasonably well and within the bounds of real-time MMOG latency. Consequently, we believe that the PaaS layer can offer a viable alternative for the development of MMOGs on commodity cloud platforms which pushes the development boundaries of cloud-enabled MMOGs past the IaaS layer. Our results motivate us to explore the possibility of utilizing alternative emerging technologies to enable MMOGs at progressively higher levels of abstraction: PaaS, BaaS and *Function-as-a-Service* (FaaS). The utilization of these higher-level solutions may offer additional advantages to those offered by current cloud solutions based on IaaS. For instance, PaaS, BaaS and FaaS solutions can offer significantly higher levels of abstraction—therefore facilitating faster, more efficient and more sustainable development of MMOG backends.

The rest of this paper is organized as follows: We first discuss related work in Sect. 2. Then we describe our experimental approach and enumerate which platforms we evaluate in Sect. 3. Our pilot implementation of a Minesweeper-themed MOG and its related architecture are discussed in Sect. 4. Then, our evaluation and results are critically presented in in Sect. 5. Finally, we list the conclusions and discuss future work in Sect. 6.

2   Related Work

As good performance is one of the most important features of MOGs and MMOGs [16,38], a large number of related studies have focused on evaluating their platforms using various techniques, such as those we have discussed in a previous work [28]. In their evaluations, various authors also focus on measuring different types of metrics such as:

- Latency – [10,16,17,23,27,32,39,42].
- Bandwidth – [27].
- Network distance between peers/servers – [16,43].
- The number of players – [31].
- Messages per second – [31].
- Moves per second – [27].
- The number of connections – [42].

According to [16], *"ensuring an acceptable Quality of Experience (QoE) for all players is a fundamental requirement [for cloud-based games]"*. By proposing a mathematical model for measuring the QoE in MMOGs, the authors identify the *global response delay* as the most notable metric. Global response delay—also known as latency—is highly dependent on several other parameters such as the CPU and memory capacity. Furthermore, they argue that other factors, such as network distance between the players and the servers can significantly affect latency. These authors evaluate: (i) the performance of a cloud-based MMOG in terms of latency using simulations, and (ii) the degradation of the QoE as a function of the number of allocated Virtual Machines (VMs) and the number of players, using an empirical approach. Similarly, the authors of [22] state that to maintain the quality of experience, game state updates *"must be delivered within specific time bounds"*, depending on the type of MMOG. The study points to the players' *flocking* behavior in certain *hotspots* as a significant challenge because of the high bandwidth load it places on servers. DynFilter [22], a game-oriented message processing middleware based on the publisher-subscriber pattern, filters out state-update messages from entities located far away to reduce bandwidth demand. Experiments on Amazon's EC2 platform have proven that it can maintain bandwidth use within quotas while maintaining the QoE. Another approach is CloudFog [30], a system utilizing fog computing in conjunction with cloud computing to distribute intensive tasks—such as graphics rendering—to powerful super-nodes which are located closer to the end-user. As a result of its offloading strategy and closer proximity to the players, CloudFog manages to reduce latency, bandwidth consumption and to improve user coverage.

3   Experimental Approach

As argued earlier, developers and researchers alike have used a plethora of approaches to implement, deploy and evaluate the performance of backends for MMOGs. To compare various on-premise and native cloud approaches, we have implemented a version of Minesweeper [9], modified to run as a multiplayer game. While Minesweeper is a relatively simple game in terms of complexity and graphics, it still demonstrates the requirement for a backend which can be used to maintain consistence, persistence, and push updates to the clients—all while maintaining an *acceptable* performance. This section describes the general architecture of our implementation and enumerates the approaches we have used. Last, it discusses how we developed the necessary software to evaluate them.

Minesweeper is a game in which the player has to clear a rectangular board that contains hidden mines, without detonating them. It was initially created in the 1960s as a single-player game and gained wide popularity when it was included in Microsoft Windows [14]. As a result, it has seen many offshoots including ones that feature multiplayer competitive gameplay [35].

3.1   Game State

The game state of Minesweeper can be represented as a two-dimensional grid/ array—also known as a *tilemap* [15]—which is a common type of game state. Examples of other popular games based on 2D grids are Pac Man, the Civilization series, and the more recent Clash of Clans. Our research focuses on this type of games because their worlds are *persistent* in the long run, meaning that their state is sustained in memory and does not cease to exist after certain conditions are met. In contrast, other types of games such as Call of Duty (first person shooter) are not persistent, which means their state is lost when certain conditions are met and the game is over.

Rather than using match-based gameplay, persistent worlds allow players to control entities that co-exist in a common world which is constantly updated—thus meeting the requirements of our target systems. Theoretically, a Minesweeper game could feature a very large game board with a large number of players accessing it simultaneously and either competing or co-operating with each other to solve the puzzle. Based on previously implemented games, we created several classes which represent the main elements of the game, such as: *BoardState*, *CellState*, *GameState*, etc.

3.2   Actions and Rules

We chose to implement Minesweeper because of the relative simplicity of its components, such as its *actions* and *rules*. In terms of actions, the player can either *reveal, flag* or *unflag* a selected cell on the board. We have also identified and implemented the following rules: (a) A player can make a single move on a single cell per turn, (b) when an empty cell is revealed, the game displays the number of mines in adjacent cells, (c) if the revealed cell has no adjacent mines, all adjacent cells without a mine are also revealed recursively, (d) when a cell containing a hidden mine is revealed, a penalty is applied, and (e) the game ends when there are no hidden mines left.

3.3 Evaluation Strategy

Our evaluation strategy is to develop nearly identical multiplayer Minesweeper games, targeting a set of popular public cloud platforms and use them to compare their performance in terms of latency—the most notable performance metric according to the related work. We specifically target the following platforms which are widely considered to be the most popular/widely used:

- Amazon Web Services: EC2 and DynamoDB (IaaS).
- Microsoft Azure: VM and CosmosDB (IaaS).
- Google Cloud Platform: App Engine and Cloud Datastore (PaaS).

We have chosen these platforms because they allow a meaningful comparison between the services of three major, commodity cloud providers. For this experiment, we kept the same code base for every project but we modified the rules to allow for longer simulations. For instance, we have introduced a score element and award players with points when they reveal an empty cell, and deduct points when they erroneously reveal a cell with a hidden mine. Consequently, instead of ending the game when all mines are flagged (win) or when the player reveals a mine (loss), we consider a game as finished when all cells have been revealed. Our simulations can therefore run for longer periods and allow for a bigger range of tests to take place.

4 Implementation

All projects were developed using Java 8 and are based on the client-server architecture, which is the preferred choice for most MMOG systems [23,27,29]. We identify several architectural components necessary to build an MMOG system: a client application, a server/backend application, a data store, and a state update mechanism.

Our client applications have been kept completely identical throughout the three approaches. The objectives of the client are: (a) to allow visualization of the game state, (b) initiate simulations with multiple players, and (c) gather data regarding performance and save it in a local files.

The purpose of the backend is to provide access to services of the game so that the clients can perform in-game actions. The functionality of the backend is exposed through a set of commands that can be accessed through an *Application Programming Interface* (API). When a client issues a request, the backend resolves it, executes the logic that enforces the game's rules, and performs the necessary actions by updating the state stored in the data store.

The data store component is used to persistently store the game worlds/states as well as information about the players and their game sessions. Lastly, the state-update mechanism component is responsible for updating the client's view of the game state, once an update to the game state has occurred, or periodically when latency allows for it. Figure 1 summarizes the general architecture used in our implementations.

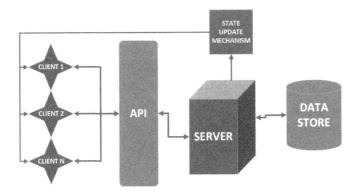

Fig. 1. General architecture for all approaches.

To allow communication between the clients and the servers, we provide a command interface that allows clients to issue commands to servers as requests, and servers to respond with the corresponding data after retrieving the state from their data store. We use the following minimal interface which contains five core functions. /createGame creates a new Minesweeper game, /join allows a player to join a game, /list lists all the available games, /getState allows players who have joined a game to get its state, and /play allows players in a game to perform an action on a selected cell.

All of our implementations utilize the *Area of Interest* (AoI) [7,20,23,40] concept to reduce the bandwidth required to communicate the game's state. We use a class called *BoardState* to store the state of each game's board, which is an abstract class that can store game cells. We use *FullBoardState* and *Partial-BoardState*, which are both derived from BoardState, to distinguish states which contain the *full* game state from those containing a specific, *partial* part of the game state. While the server utilizes the former for storage and computation, each client can only see a part of that full state—they receive a partial state based on their location in the game. The location of each client's partial state can be moved by issuing a move command to the /play service and specifying the new desired location within the game board. To support game state updates for the clients we use Ably, a real-time WebSocket infrastructure [1] that enables a publish-subscribe mechanism supporting the concept of AoI.

Client-Side. Our client application uses Java Swing forms to visualize the Minesweeper board for testing purposes. To carry out simulations, we have created a simple Minesweeper solver—with no GUI—that tries to solve the game by opening cells sequentially – i.e. moving rightwards and then downwards as the game progresses. Naturally this is a sub-optimal approach to play Minesweeper, but our study focuses on the performance of the backend in terms of serving player requests rather than the efficiency of solving the game.

We run our simulations by initializing the client programs with information such as the width and height of the game board, the number of players in the game, the size of their partial states and the delay between the execution of moves by each player. Our simulations instantiate a new thread for each player in the game, with each player going through a series of steps that simulate real player actions in a multiplayer game. Firstly, our bot players request a list of all available games from the server by calling the /list service. Upon acquiring this list, they always select the first available game and try to join it by calling /join and specifying their name. The names of players are automatically set when created (e.g. $Player_1$, $Player_2$,... $Player_N$). After successfully joining the game, a player requests the initial partial game state using/getState. Upon receiving the initial game state, the players run the solver and submit their moves—*reveal* or *flag/unflag*—using the /play call. When all cells in their visible area have been revealed, the players try to shift their position rightwards and then downwards by calling /play and issuing a *move* command.

To allow multiplayer gameplay, we define an additional entity called *Session*, which couples a certain player to a specific game that the player has joined. Using sessions, we track the locations and actions of players, award or deduct points for their actions, and choose which players to send game state updates to, based on their proximity to those updates.

Our client records the time the request is sent and the response is received for each of these calls, using timestamps. The time taken for the round trip of the request-response (latency) is found in terms of milliseconds, by subtracting the two timestamps. The recorded values are stored in memory and saved in a comma-separated value (CSV) file, as shown in Table 1.

Amazon Web Services Backend. Our Amazon Web Services (AWS) project is hosted by an Amazon EC2 t2.micro instance, running on Linux Ubuntu 18 and features 1 vCPU, 1GB of RAM and *"low to moderate"* network performance [3]. Our server does not store any game data but instead utilizes an instance of DynamoDB with a provisioned capacity within the free tier [4]. DynamoDB is Amazon's NoSQL data store which stores data in tables that contain items consisting of key-value pairs. Amazon claims that DynamoDB has *"single-digit millisecond performance at any scale"* [4]. We have implemented our project using Java Servlets running on Apache Tomcat 9 [21], with each Servlet implementing an endpoint of the API. Client-server communication occurs through the HTTP protocol, with each client issuing requests to the server and the server carrying out the request and responding with the necessary information. To retrieve data

Table 1. The format used for the simulation results file.

players	endpoint	latency(ms)
2	GAME_LIST	1414
2	JOIN	310
2	STATE_GET	141
2	PLAY	335
...	...	...

from DynamoDB we use DynamoDBMapper [5], a library which maps client-side classes to DynamoDB tables using code annotations. As with all platform setups, we use Ably [1] for state updates. Ably allows state update messages to be sent from the server through a channel in real time. Clients subscribe to a channel once they have an active game session and listen for state updates from the server. For these experiments, we used the free package of Ably [2].

Microsoft Azure Backend. Our Microsoft Azure backend project is powered by a B1S-type virtual machine running on Linux Ubuntu 14 and featuring 1 vCPU and 1 GB of RAM [33]. As in the AWS project, we achieve client-server communication using HTTP and Java Servlets powered by Apache Tomcat 9. The two projects are almost identical (i.e. we use the same endpoints, algorithms, etc.). The only difference is the code which utilizes the data store since we opt to use an Azure product in this approach. To store data, we use Azure's CosmosDB [34], a NoSQL data store that saves data in documents as key-value pairs. In terms of performance, Microsoft also claims that projects utilizing CosmosDB can *"take advantage of fast, single-digit-millisecond data access"* [34]. Just as in our AWS project, we realize server-to-client state updates using Ably's free package, and identical code in our state update function.

Google App Engine Backend. Our third and last approach is based on a server-less PaaS infrastructure. We use *Google App Engine* (GAE) [25], a fully-managed platform that allows application development without the need to deal with server configuration—i.e. realizing *serverless* computing [11]. App Engine allows applications to scale *seamlessly* and without developer supervision, which is a major advantage over the other approaches. The serverless architecture of this approach lets App Engine manage the server resources—we only had to create an App Engine instance and select our environment (Java 8). App Engine Java projects utilize Jetty 9 [19], an HTTP server that is similar to Apache Tomcat, which also enables clients to communicate with the server using Java Servlets. Our web-based API is kept identical to the other two native cloud approaches, with the only difference being the code utilizing the data store. In this approach, we use Google's NoSQL solution, the Cloud Datastore [26]. Google claims that its Cloud Datastore *"scales seamlessly [...] with your data* *allowing applications to maintain high performance as they receive more traffic"* [26]. The Cloud Datastore saves data in documents called *Entities* that contain key-value associations. To easily interact with the Cloud Datastore we utilize a Java library called Objectify [41], which allows us to annotate classes as entities and easily perform CRUD operations. Just like with the other approaches, we have implemented game state updates using Ably. Figure 2 shows the selection of architectural components for all three approaches.

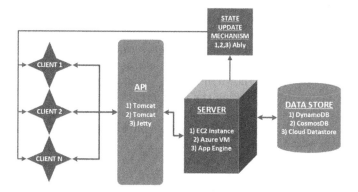

Fig. 2. Architectures used for all three platforms: (1) Amazon Web Services, (2) Microsoft Azure, (3) Google Cloud Platform.

5   Evaluation

Our evaluation is driven by the performance aspect of MMOGs. We evaluate each approach independently, while maintaining identical secondary components such as game-solving algorithms and game logic. We focus on performance because we believe it is the most important performance metric, as also indicated in several related works [10, 16, 17, 23, 27, 32, 39, 42].

In our data collection experiments we aimed to keep secondary factors in control as follows:

– We aimed to keep the network conditions as similar as possible by running the experiments within the same wired network. We also (a) monitored the network, verifying that it was not being utilized by other programs at the time and (b) ran the experiments at similar times and days of the week to avoid different network conditions.
– We kept the client device conditions as similar as possible by running all simulations on the same computer while it was initially idle.
– We used comparable data center locations (Eastern United States) for all experiments.
– We used NoSQL data stores for all cloud approaches to allow a comparison between them. We use this type of persistence because it can be easily scaled and appears to better match the needs of MMOG backends [8, 12, 44].

- We created virtual machines with similar specifications to keep the backend processing power as comparable as possible.
- We conducted our experiments based on a set of identical commands and made sure that the parameters and logic of those calls stayed the same throughout all simulations.

To establish a base latency for each approach, we created a Servlet that performs no operations and returns an empty result. The purpose of the *BaseServlet* is to allow us to establish a minimum latency for each approach. Given that our code is kept the same for game logic, this helps compare the latency between calls that utilize the backend extensively and those that do not—thus determining the latency caused by our backend implementations. Secondly, we measured the latency of each endpoint in our API by running our simulations and obtaining the data from a local file, as shown in Table 1. In each case, we ran simulations 10 times for each endpoint, including the base latency endpoint and took averages from these results. We ran the base latency test first, which yielded an average of 97.2 ms for Google's App Engine, 144.2 ms for Microsoft Azure and 167.3 ms for the Amazon Web Services approach.

Before testing each of the actual backend services, we performed several tests to establish the maximum size of the game board state possible in each approach. In our approach, the size of game state is limited by the size of the *unit* element used in the corresponding data store. While there exist ways to circumvent these limitations to create bigger game sizes, we kept our implementations free of these modifications for three reasons: First, state modeling is beyond the scope of this paper. Second, a workaround implemented on a specific platform may not necessarily work on all platforms – thus making it harder to compare our results. Third, we aimed to keep our implementations as simple and consistent as possible.

We conducted these tests by creating square-sized boards where the width is the same as the height. Initially, we attempted to create games of size 100×100 – if that game size could be created we incremented the size by 50% and tried again. When the game could not be created anymore because of platform-enforced limitations, we reduced the size by 25% and tried again until we found the exact size of game boards supported by each approach. Our experiments showed that Microsoft's CosmosDB supports a game state up to 229×229 cells, Google's Cloud Datastore takes the middle ground, with up to 158×158 game boards and Amazon's DynamoDB supports a maximum size of up to 98×98 board states for Minesweeper. These hard limitations are subject to change from game to game and are dependent on each platform.

Upon establishing the maximum state size for each approach, we used the minimum of those values as input to evaluate the performance of the /createGame service. We performed HTTP GET requests by specifying the administrator password, the maximum number of players allowed, the game size and the difficulty of the game. We kept the parameters of all these calls constant throughout all experiments by using a game size of 98—the minimum out of the three approaches—setting the difficulty to *Easy* and the maximum number of players to 10. Our results from ten calls indicate an average latency of 332.7 ms for AWS, 346.3 ms for Azure and 496.6 ms for App Engine.

Our next test focused on the /list service, which returns a list of all available games. It is important to indicate that the list service only retrieves information about a game (such as its ID, width and height) but not its actual state. To conduct this test, we created two games in each of the three data stores and called the list service. Our results from ten rounds of simulations show that Azure took 555 ms to respond, AWS took 568.5 ms, while App Engine took 1153.2 ms.

To test the /join, /getState and /play services, we ran ten simulations with the following configuration: a game size of 10 × 10 with two players, difficulty set to easy and a partial state of 5 × 5 for each player. AWS performed best in joining the game, with a latency of 201.8 ms, compared to Azure's 234.8 ms and App Engine's 554.6 ms. AWS also performed marginally better when retrieving the initial state of the game at 176.3 ms, while App Engine took 176.7 ms and Azure 245.4 ms. When calling the play service, Azure performed marginally better with 175.8 ms while AWS took just a bit longer at 176.9 ms. App Engine took an average of 201.2 ms to respond to play requests. Table 2 summarizes our latency test results.

Table 2. A summary of average latencies for all approaches for various API calls. All time measurements are in milliseconds.

Approach	Base latency	Create game	List	Join	Get state	Play
Amazon EC2	167.3	332.7	568.5	201.8	176.3	176.9
Microsoft Azure	144.2	346.3	555	234.8	245.4	175.8
Google App Engine	97.2	496.6	1153.2	554.6	176.8	201.2

Data gathered during the evaluation shows that IaaS-based approaches generally performed better than their PaaS counterpart, which was expected because of the larger overhead of computational layers being present in the PaaS approach. From the latency results of our game service calls, we observe that AWS IaaS approach performed better in three of those services (create game, join and get state), while Azure performed better in two (list and play).

In contrast, App Engine performed significantly better—about 33% faster—compared to the other two approaches in the base latency test, something that may reveal a higher latency caused by Google's Cloud Datastore which was utilized in the Minesweeper services but not in the base latency test.

In the create game service, the AWS approach performed slightly better (4%) compared to the Azure approach. The opposite applies for the list service, where Azure performs marginally better (3%) compared to AWS. The difference between the two is more significant when joining the game, with AWS scoring a 15% improvement compared to Azure. In these services, App Engine scores relatively poorly compared to the two IaaS approaches.

In the get state service, App Engine performs better and almost ties AWS's better-performing service – the two have a negligible difference (1%) with Azure falling behind by a relatively large margin (-28%).

The most significant test is conducted on the play service which we regard as the most important of all services because it is the one which is most frequently called by the players during a game. This means it can impact the performance of the MMOG most significantly. In this test, AWS and Azure performed within 1% difference of each other, with Azure performing better by about 1ms. App Engine also scores a relatively low latency (201.2 ms) but ends up performing about 13% worse than Azure.

By combining this relatively good performance with (1) inherent elasticity, (2) code abstraction and (3) the elimination of infrastructural management from developers, the PaaS layer appears to offer a viable alternative development approach for cloud-enabled games—one that many game developers could benefit from in the future.

6   Conclusions and Future Work

In this paper, we selected a set of public cloud platforms to assess the suitability of public clouds for developing MMOG backends. To do this, we implemented a modified version of Minesweeper in each of three selected approaches. Our implementation extended a traditionally single-player game to run as an MMOG on the infrastructure of three major cloud providers: Amazon Web Services, Microsoft Azure and Google App Engine. Our findings suggest that MMOGs can be engineered to run on high-level commodity cloud platforms, something that game providers have generally avoided so far. We compare the performance of our game's services in terms of latency, using simulations. Our results show that the two IaaS approaches (AWS and Azure) have performed better than the PaaS approach (App Engine), which is what we initially expected. Based on related work, the expected latency of real-time MMOGs is near or below 250ms [23,36,46]. From our results, we conclude that the PaaS layer offers acceptable performance which indicates that it could provide a suitable environment for realizing MMOG backends—at least for game types that do not require very low latency. While not as good as in IaaS, the performance of our PaaS approach puts it within the limits even of real-time MMOGs. With its extra benefits—easier, faster and more economical development—we argue that PaaS is becoming a competitive option for realizing MMOG backends.

For the future, we aim to improve our understanding of developing and deploying MMOGs on public clouds by studying related models, methods and tools. Our priority is to complement our work by exploring another important aspect of MMOGs—scalability—through the evaluation of models that allow varying sizes of game worlds. Due to technical limitations, our approach was limited to ten players, which is not representative of MMOGs but rather of MOGs. Furthermore, Minesweeper is a turn-based game and is therefore different from more popular types of online games. It does not fall into popular categories such as First Person Shooter (FPS), Real-Time Strategy (RTS) and so on, which is not the focus of this research. Lastly, our approach utilizes various data stores. Some of these may be optimized towards read operations, while others may be optimized towards write operations—perhaps skewing the latencies scored by some approaches. Despite that, we argue that our work is a good starting point and showcases the possibilities that lie ahead, especially when more work is done with respect to scalability. Such an advancement will allow MMOGs running on public clouds to handle workloads with far larger numbers of players and game world sizes than what we have used in the present study.

References

1. Ably: Ably realtime (2019). https://www.ably.io/. Accessed 10 Dec 2019
2. Ably: Pricing — ably realtime (2019). https://www.ably.io/pricing. Accessed 10 Dec 2019
3. Amazon Web Services: Amazon ec2 instance types (2019). https://aws.amazon.com/ec2/instance-types/. Accessed 10 Dec 2019
4. Amazon Web Services: Dynamodb - overview (2019). https://aws.amazon.com/dy-namodb/pricing/provisioned. Accessed 10 Dec 2019
5. Amazon Web Services: Dynamodbmapper - amazon dynamodb (2019). https://docs.aws.amazon.com/amazondynamodb/latest/developerguide/Dynamo-DBMapper.html. Accessed 10 Dec 2019
6. Armbrust, M., et al.: A view of cloud computing. Commun. ACM **53**(4), 50–58 (2010)
7. Assiotis, M., Tzanov, V.: A distributed architecture for massive multiplayer online role-playing games. In: Proceedings of 5th ACM SIGCOMM Workshop on Network and System Support for Games (NetGames' 06), Article no. 4 (2005)
8. Baker, J., et al.: Megastore: providing scalable, highly available storage for interactive services. In: Proceedings of the Conference on Innovative Data system Research (CIDR), pp. 223–234 (2011)
9. Becker, K.: Teaching with games: the minesweeper and asteroids experience. J. Comput. Sci. Coll. **17**(2), 23–33 (2001)
10. Burger, V., et al.: Load dynamics of a multiplayer online battle arena and simulative assessment of edge server placements. In: Proceedings of the 7th International Conference on Multimedia Systems, p. 17. ACM (2016)
11. Castro, P., Ishakian, V., Muthusamy, V., Slominski, A.: The rise of serverless computing. Commun. ACM **62**(12), 44–54 (2019). https://doi.org/10.1145/3368454
12. Chang, F., et al.: Bigtable: a distributed storage system for structured data. ACM Trans. Comput. Syst. (TOCS) **26**(2), 4 (2008)
13. Chu, H.S.: Building a simple yet powerful MMO game architecture. Verkkoarkkitehtuuri, Part (2008)
14. Cobbett, R.: The most successful game ever: a history of minesweeper, May 2009. https://www.techradar.com/news/gaming/the-most-successful-game-ever-a-history-of-minesweeper-596504. Accessed 12 Dec 2019
15. Coleman, R., Roebke, S., Grayson, L.: Gedi: a game engine for teaching videogame design and programming. J. Comput. Sci. Coll. **21**(2), 72–82 (2005)
16. Dhib, E., Boussetta, K., Zangar, N., Tabbane, N.: Modeling cloud gaming experience for massively multiplayer online games. In: 2016 13th IEEE Annual Consumer Communications & Networking Conference (CCNC), pp. 381–386. IEEE (2016)

17. Dhib, E., Zangar, N., Tabbane, N., Boussetta, K.: Resources allocation trade-off between cost and delay over a distributed cloud infrastructure. In: 2016 7th International Conference on Sciences of Electronics, Technologies of Information and Telecommunications (SETIT), pp. 486–490. IEEE (2016)
18. Ducheneaut, N., Yee, N., Nickell, E., Moore, R.J.: Building an MMO with mass appeal: a look at gameplay in world of warcraft. Games Cult. 1(4), 281–317 (2006). https://doi.org/10.1177/1555412006292613
19. Eclipse: Jetty - servlet engine and http server (2019). https://www.eclipse.org/jetty/. Accessed 10 Dec 2019
20. El Rhalibi, A., Al-Jumeily, D.: Dynamic area of interest management for massively multiplayer online games using OPNET. In: 2017 10th International Conference on Developments in eSystems Engineering (DeSE), pp. 50–55. IEEE (2017)
21. Foundation, A.: Apache tomcat (2019). http://tomcat.apache.org/. Accessed 10 Dec 2019
22. Gascon-Samson, J., Kienzle, J., Kemme, B.: DynFilter: limiting bandwidth of online games using adaptive pub/sub message filtering. In: Proceedings of the 2015 International Workshop on Network and Systems Support for Games, p. 2. IEEE Press (2015)
23. GauthierDickey, C., Zappala, D., Lo, V.: Distributed architectures for massively multiplayer online games. In: ACM NetGames Workshop. Citeseer (2004)
24. Ghobaei-Arani, M., Khorsand, R., Ramezanpour, M.: An autonomous resource provisioning framework for massively multiplayer online games in cloud environment. J. Netw. Comput. Appl. (2019). https://doi.org/10.1016/j.jnca.2019.06.002
25. Google Cloud: App engine - google cloud (2019). https://cloud.google.com/appengine/. Accessed 10 Dec 2019
26. Google Cloud: Datastore - nosql schemaless database (2019). https://cloud.google.com/datastore/. Accessed 10 Dec 2019
27. Jardine, J., Zappala, D.: A hybrid architecture for massively multiplayer online games. In: Proceedings of the 7th ACM SIGCOMM Workshop on Network and System Support for Games, pp. 60–65. ACM (2008)
28. Kasenides, N., Paspallis, N.: A systematic mapping study of MMOG backend architectures. Information 10, 264 (2019). https://doi.org/10.3390/info10090264. Switzerland
29. Kavalionak, H., Carlini, E., Ricci, L., Montresor, A., Coppola, M.: Integrating peer-to-peer and cloud computing for massively multiuser online games. Peer-to-Peer Netw. Appl. 8(2), 301–319 (2015)
30. Lin, Y., Shen, H.: Cloud fog: towards high quality of experience in cloud gaming. In: 2015 44th International Conference on Parallel Processing, pp. 500–509. IEEE (2015)
31. Lu, F., Parkin, S., Morgan, G.: Load balancing for massively multiplayer online games. In: Proceedings of 5th ACM SIGCOMM workshop on Network and system support for games, p. 1. ACM (2006)
32. Meiländer, D., Gorlatch, S.: Modeling the scalability of real-time online interactive applications on clouds. Future Gener. Comput. Syst. 86, 1019–1031 (2018)
33. Microsoft Azure: Introducing B-series, our burstable VM size (2019). https://azure.microsoft.com/en-au/blog/introducing-b-series-our-new-burstable-vm-size/. Accessed 10 Dec 2019
34. Microsoft Azure: Introduction to Azure Cosmos DB (2019). https://docs.microsoft.com/en-us/azure/cosmos-db/introduction. Accessed 10 Dec 2019
35. Minesweeper.io: Minesweeper.io (2019). https://minesweeper.io/. Accessed 10 Dec 2019

36. Nae, V., Iosup, A., Prodan, R.: Dynamic resource provisioning in massively multiplayer online games. IEEE Trans. Parallel Distrib. Syst. **22**(3), 380–395 (2011)
37. Nae, V., Prodan, R., Fahringer, T., Iosup, A.: The impact of virtualization on the performance of massively multiplayer online games. In: Proceedings of the 8th Annual Workshop on Network and Systems Support for Games, p. 9. IEEE Press (2009)
38. Nae, V., Prodan, R., Iosup, A.: Massively multiplayer online game hosting on cloud resources. In: Cloud Computing: Principles and Paradigms, pp. 491–509 (2011)
39. Najaran, M.T., Krasic, C.: Scaling online games with adaptive interest management in the cloud. In: 2010 9th Annual Workshop on Network and Systems Support for Games (NetGames), pp. 1–6. IEEE (2010)
40. Negrão, A.P., Veiga, L., Ferreira, P.: Task based load balancing for cloud aware massively multiplayer online games. In: 2016 IEEE 15th International Symposium on Network Computing and Applications (NCA), pp. 48–51. IEEE (2016)
41. Objectify: Objectify (2019). https://github.com/objectify/objectify. Accessed 10 Dec 2019
42. Plumb, J., Kasera, S., Stutsman, R.: Hybrid network clusters using common gameplay for massively multiplayer online games, pp. 1–10, August 2018. https://doi.org/10.1145/3235765.3235785
43. Plumb, J.N., Stutsman, R.: Exploiting Google's edge network for massively multiplayer online games. In: 2018 IEEE 2nd International Conference on Fog and Edge Computing (ICFEC), pp. 1–8. IEEE (2018)
44. Shabani, I., Kovaçi, A., Dika, A.: Possibilities offered by Google App Engine for developing distributed applications using datastore. In: 2014 Sixth International Conference on Computational Intelligence, Communication Systems and Networks (CICSYN), pp. 113–118. IEEE (2014)
45. Shaikh, A., Sahu, S., Rosu, M.C., Shea, M., Saha, D.: On demand platform for online games. IBM Syst. J. **45**(1), 7–19 (2006)
46. Shea, R., Liu, J., Ngai, E.C.H., Cui, Y.: Cloud gaming: architecture and performance. IEEE Netw. **27**(4), 16–21 (2013)

Are Cloud Platforms Ready for Multi-cloud?

Kyriakos Kritikos[1(✉)], Paweł Skrzypek[2], and Feroz Zahid[3]

[1] ICS-FORTH, Crete, Greece
kritikos@ics.forth.gr
[2] AI Investments, Skierniewice, Poland
pskrzypek@aiinvestments.pl
[3] Simula Research Laboratory, Fornebu, Norway
feroz@simula.no

Abstract. Multi-cloud computing is getting a momentum as it offers various advantages, including vendor lock-in avoidance, better client proximity and application performance improvement. As such, various multi-cloud platforms have been developed, each with its own strengths and limitations. This paper aims at comparing all these platforms to unveil the best one as well as ease the selection of the right platform based on the user requirements and preferences. Further, it identifies the current gaps in the platforms to be covered so as to enable the full potential of multi-cloud computing. Finally, it draws directions for further research.

1 Introduction

Cloud computing promises the on-demand delivery of infrastructural and other kinds of services to assist in the applications development, deployment and adaptive provisioning. Further, it promises the reduction of costs, flexibility in resource management plus the ability to supply a potentially infinite amount of resources. As such, it has been widely adopted, leading to a multitude of applications being migrated to the Cloud. However, the initial Cloud computing platforms and providers offered services that encouraged vendor lock-in while these services performance was not always as expected or promised.

To this end, multi-cloud computing popped up [1], promising to address the above issues. This computing kind enables applications to be deployed in multiple clouds, one at a time. This allows not only to avoid vendor lock-in but also to achieve customer proximity via application spreading across different physical locations. Further, it enables application providers to select more reliable cloud providers in terms of the service level being delivered by their services. In addition, it allows to better satisfy application requirements and preferences, leading to applications with improved performance. A certain form of multi-cloud computing, cross-cloud computing, [1,2] has been also introduced, promising to deploy applications each time in not one but multiple cloud providers. This has the inevitable advantage of achieving true optimality, as application developers can select the best cloud services to realise their applications' functionality.

Based on the above analysis, multi-cloud computing is now getting a momentum such that a multitude of multi-cloud management platforms (MCMPs) have been developed. Such MCMPs are either extensions of existing platforms (see Google Anthos[1]) or new ones that rushed to cover the respective market gap. These MCMPs have their own strengths and weaknesses. For instance, one MCMP can support a diversity of clouds while another deployment automation. Thus, users find it difficult to select the MCMP best suiting their needs.

As such, this paper attempts to review all these MCMPs by adopting an hierarchical criteria set, organised according to three main aspects: (a) how well the orchestration of multiple clouds is supported; (b) what is the support level for multi-cloud applications; (c) what is the MCMP intelligence extent for increasing the automation in application provisioning. All these aspects complement each other and together lead exploiting the full potential of multi-cloud computing.

The MCMP review based on the aforementioned set fulfills multiple purposes: (a) it enables to nominate one MCMP as the best; (b) it facilitate MCMP selection based on user requirements and preferences; (c) it unveils those functional gaps in MCMPs which need to be covered to fully support multi-cloud computing. Another contribution is the supply of interesting challenges, which, when addressed, can further boost the MCMP adoption.

The rest of the paper is structured as follows. The next section explains the MCMP selection process. Section 3 introduces the hierarchical set of criteria which can be regarded as multi-cloud computing goals. Section 4 presents and analyses the evaluation results. Finally, the last Sect. 5 concludes the paper and supplies some research challenges for further boosting the MCMP adoption.

2   Platform Selection Process

We aimed at assessing only proprietary MCMPs, as these are complete products which can be actually exploited by users in the cloud market. To this end, our simplified MCMP selection process involved the following two main steps:

MCMP Search. To conduct the MCMP search, we have relied on: (i) using sophisticated web search engines (e.g., Google) by applying the following query string: "Multi-cloud AND Platform"; (ii) the snowball crawling method [3] where forwarding links are visited from the main web site currently inspected – useful in case the web site was suggesting or evaluating multiple from these platforms/tools; (iii) our own knowledge about some well-known MCMPs. While conducting (i) and (ii), we also came across two articles from Forrester [4] and Gartner [5] which enabled us to both identify MCMPs and validate those already discovered.

Filtering. Apart from the fact that the MCMPs should be either proprietary or offered in dual licensing mode, we have applied additional selection criteria

---

[1] https://cloud.google.com/anthos/

which included: (i) the MCMP should be still in operation; (ii) it should have existing clients; (iii) it should support multi-cloud and not just hybrid application deployment; (iv) finally, it should also support application reconfiguration.

In result, 17 MCMPs were discovered (see Appendix 1 in https://tinyurl. com/rby7m37). In fact, the MCMP market is overruled by US companies and only 2 MCMPs reside in Europe and just one in Canada. Further, with the exception of Google, no other major cloud provider is offering a MCMP. A subset of these MCMPs (see Table 1), the top-7, will be reviewed in Sect. 4 based on the criteria identified in the next section due to paper length restriction reasons.

Table 1. Overview of assessed MCMPs

Platform	Location-Cloud	Description
Cisco Cloud Center Suite[a]	US	Multi-cloud management platform with special focus on cost optimisation and CI/CD
Rackware Hybrid Cloud Platform[b]	US	A multi-function solution for workload migration to the cloud, disaster recovery, and multi-cloud resource management
Morpheus Data[c]	US	A multi-cloud management platform for hybrid IT and DevOps automation with special focus on cost and performance optimisation
CloudBolt[d]	US	A multi-cloud and hypervisor management platform featuring continuous infrastructure testing and blueprints for repeatable and standardised application deployment
Google Anthos	US	Hybrid application management platform for on-premise and public clouds with support for service mesh, containers, micro-services and functions as well as strong focus on security and workload migration
Cloudify[e]	US	End-to-end modular orchestration platform that abstracts applications and networks from underlying infrastructures. Provides also support for edge computing
Melodic[f]	Poland	Cross-cloud, data-intensive application management platform with strong focus on utility- and model-driven application reconfiguration

[a]https://www.cisco.com/c/en/us/products/cloud-systems-management/cloudcenter/index.html
[b]https://www.rackwareinc.com/platform-1
[c]https://www.morpheusdata.com/
[d]https://www.cloudbolt.io
[e]cloudify.co/
[f]melodic.cloud/

3 Requirements

To evaluate the selected MCMPs, a sophisticated evaluation framework in form of an assessment criteria hierarchy was devised. The main focus is on three main dimensions: (a) *cloud orchestration support* – the degree of cloud service orchestration support and automation even across multiple abstraction levels; (b) *cloud application support* – the degree and level of management for cloud applications; (c) *platform intelligence* – what knowledge is derived from intelligent mechanisms to optimise the multi-cloud application provisioning. In the following, we present all dimensions and their hierarchy of criteria in separate sub-sections.

3.1 C1 – Cloud Orchestration Support

This criteria category evaluates the capability of an MCMP to orchestrate cloud services, even coming from different providers and/or different abstraction levels. It also covers aspects like the possibility to orchestrate private clouds in hybrid deployment scenarios and the support to cloud-related standards.

C1.1 – Cloud Support. This sub-category assesses the orchestration support that a certain MCMP has on different clouds.

C1.1.1 – Cloud Diversity. This criterion assesses the diversity of public clouds that can be supported. As such, the evaluation of this criterion on a MCMP can take the following values: (a) *low*: only two public clouds are supported; (b) *medium*: three to six clouds are supported; (c) *good*: six to nine clouds are supported; (d) *high*: ten or more clouds are supported by the MCMP.

C1.1.2 – Private Cloud. This criterion assess the capability of an MCMP to support application deployment in private clouds to cover hybrid application provisioning scenarios. This capability can be assessed as follows: (a) *no*: it is not exhibited by an MCMP; (b) *yes*: it is indeed featured.

C1.1.3 – Cross-Cloud. As indicated in Sect. 1, cross-cloud computing enables to achieve true optimisation of application deployment. As such, an MCMP can be evaluated on this as follows: (a) *no*: the MCMP does not support cross-cloud computing; (b) *yes*: otherwise.

C1.2 – Resource Diversity. Due to various factors, including better workload and security isolation, other deployment alternatives have been presented apart from Virtual Machines (VMs) like containers and specialised resources kinds (e.g., GPUs) which enable boosting the performance of compute-intensive applications. As such, the more resource kinds are handled, the more kinds of workloads can be supported. Thus, an MCMP can be evaluated as follows here: (a) *low*: only the traditional resource of a VM is supported; (b) *medium*: also containers are supported; (c) *good*: three to four resource kinds are supported; (d) *high*: more than four resource kinds are supported.

C1.3 – BYON. Users might have existing resources hosted in specialised infrastructures or private clouds. Thus, if an MCMP is able to exploit and manage such resources, it can increase the alternative deployment options for applications plus cater for hybrid application provisioning scenarios. As such, it can be evaluated on this criterion as follows: (a) *no*: this BYON capability is not featured by the MCMP; (b) *yes*: the MCMP can support deployment on user-specific resources.

C1.4 – Service Support. This criteria sub-category assesses the kinds of services supported by an MCMP and the support versatility per each handled service kind with the rationale that the diversity of services in different abstraction levels leads to covering more advanced multi-cloud application provisioning scenarios.

C1.4.1 – Service Kinds Versatility. This criterion assesses the different abstraction levels (i.e., IaaS, PaaS, SaaS & BPaaS) covered by an MCMP in terms of respective cloud services. The rationale is that higher abstraction levels coverage enables to reduce administration burden and cost while facilitates completing the functionality of multi-cloud applications. As such, an MCMP can be evaluated as follows: (a) *low*: one service kind is only supported; (b) *medium*: two to three service kinds are supported; (c) *high*: all service kinds are supported.

C1.4.2 – Service Versatility. This criterion attempts to assess the versatility of support for the same service kind to enable moving or selecting multiple services of the same kind in the context of multi-cloud application provisioning. C1.1 covered this for infrastructural but not higher-level of services. As such, an MCMP can be evaluated as follows: (a) *low*: only one service is supported for a higher-level service kind; (b) *medium*: two to five services are supported; (c) *high*: more than five services are supported.

C1.5 – Automation. This criterion assesses the level of automation in cloud service orchestration. Ideally, it is expected that based on a model of the user application, an MCMP could derive and execute a concrete orchestration plan to relieve users from manually specifying it and the burden to delve into cloud-specific details. As such, an MCMP can be evaluated as follows: (a) *low*: the orchestration is manually conducted by the user; (b) *medium*: some orchestration parts can be automated by the MCMP; (c) *good*: the MCMP can orchestrate a plan given by the user; (d) *high*: it can automatically derive and execute a plan based on the user input (e.g., an application model).

C1.6 – Standards. The conformance to standards comes with various benefits, also related to multi-cloud computing, like the ability to operate software plus exchange information and knowledge across different technologies, platforms and infrastructures. Already multiple cloud standards exist spanning, e.g., how cloud applications can be specified (e.g., TOSCA [6]) and the format of VM images (e.g., OVF), although their adoption level by the providers is not as expected. As such, we can evaluate a MCMP on this as follows: (a) *no*: no cloud standard is supported; (b) *low*: one standard is supported; (c) *medium*: two to three standards are supported; (d) *high*: more than three standards are supported.

3.2 C2 – Cloud Application Support

An outmost MCMP goal is to support the multi-cloud applications' management, spanning their whole lifecycle. This support needs to be built under solid bases, like model-driven engineering, which abstract from low-level technicalities and increase the automation level. Applications could also process and produce data, which can be large in volume in many cases. As such, these data should be also managed accordingly by the MCMPs. Finally, an MCMP must allow for high-levels of management flexibility plus cater for the continuous application evolution. All these aspects are covered by the following categories of criteria.

C2.1 – Modelling Support. An MCMP should provide the right support level for multi-cloud application modelling, spanning the supply of a modelling framework, the capturing of multiple component configuration kinds, the rich resource specification plus the re-use of existing model parts for new application models.

C2.1.1 – Modelling Language. An MCMP should use a modelling language for the specification of multi-cloud applications which is rich enough to cover all relevant application management aspects (e.g., deployment, monitoring) while providing the right abstraction level. As such, an MCMP can be evaluated as follows: (a) *no*: no modelling language is offered; (b) *low*: it is offered but covers only one aspect; (c) *medium*: the MCMP's modelling language covers two to three management aspects; (d) *high*: it covers all necessary aspects;

C2.1.2 – Configuration Diversity. To support true multi-cloud computing, application components in one form need to be coupled with different cloud-specific configuration specifications. Further, the same functionality/component can take different forms (e.g., functions or big data processing tasks), each coming with its own configuration alternatives. Thus, an MCMP must support as many of these configuration kinds as possible to increase its applicability level. So, it can be evaluated on this criterion as follows: (a) *low*: the MCMP supports only one configuration kind; (b) *medium*: the MCMP supports two or three configuration kinds; (c) *high*: more than three configuration kinds are supported.

C2.1.3 – Resource/Service Modelling. Cloud service offerings must be modelled to support matching service requirements and capabilities and the selection of the best possible services. This modelling is also imperative to realise BYON scenarios. However, it needs to cover all service kinds across multiple clouds. As such, an MCMP can be evaluated as follows: (a) *no*: the MCMP does not support service modelling; (b) *low*: it features a language via which only one service kind can be modelled; (c) *medium*: the language covers two service kinds; (d) *high*: the language covers the modelling of any service kind.

C2.1.4 – Policy Modelling & Enforcement. User organisations can have non-functional requirements and policies that should hold for any of their applications or for specific ones. For instance, due to privacy low conformance reasons, any data manipulated by any application must reside in its origin country. Further, an application's response time could be restrained to be lower than an upper bound. Besides, different requirement kinds might need to be specified, like location, scaling, and quality requirements. Thus, an MCMP can be evaluated as follows: (a) *no*: it does not support requirement modelling; (b) *low*: only one requirement kind is supported; (c) *medium*: two to three requirement kinds can be modelled; (d) *good*: more than three kinds can be specified; (e) *high*: same as (d) but requirements are enforced at both the global and application level.

C2.1.5 – Editing Capabilities. Cloud modelling languages mostly adopt representation formats like YAML or JSON coming with their own generic editors. However, language-specific editors must be used instead so as: (a) to cover the modelling preferences and habits of the main target users (devops); (b) to have specialised language features (e.g., error highlighting, auto-completion) that enhance user experience and speedup the modelling process. Thus, an MCMP can be evaluated as follows: (a) *no*: no modelling language is supplied; (b) *low*: no editor is offered but generic editors exist for the language representation formats; (b) *medium*: a language editor exists with no special features; (c) *high*: a sophisticated editor is offered with the aforementioned added-value features.

C2.1.6 – Model Re-use. Model re-use is essential to not only allow the rapid creation of language models but also to reduce the learning curve. It can also lead to a community-lead effort where both complete multi-cloud application models plus model fragments covering common elements like metrics become available. As such, we evaluate a MCMP as follows: (a) *no*: no model-reuse is allowed; (b) *low*: complete models can be re-used by just copying their parts; (c) *medium*: whole models and some complex model elements can be re-used/cross-referenced; (d) *high*: any kind of model element can be re-used/cross-referenced.

C2.2 – Lifecycle Management. Suitable support to any application management activity (e.g., design and deployment) reduces the management burden and enables devops to focus more on the core application functionality and its improvement. As such, we can assess an MCMP as follows: (a) *low*: only one activity (usually deployment) is covered; (b) *medium*: two to three activities are covered; (c) *good*: four to five activities are covered; (d) *high*: all activities are supported.

C2.3 – Data Management. (Big) Data are becoming a critical asset for organisations which strive to derive added-value knowledge from them to improve existing products and services. Due to their importance, they need to be properly managed to increase the automation level in data manipulation and reduce operational costs (e.g., by moving computation near data to save communication cost). With this criteria sub-group, we assess the pure data management activities offered by an MCMP.

C2.3.1 – Data Creation. Data sources can already exist outside the application management scope. However, in other cases, data sources and their encapsulated data must be created before a specific application can be deployed and executed. To this end, an MCMP can be evaluated as follows: (a) *no*: no data (source) creation facility is offered; (b) *yes*: otherwise.

C2.3.2 – Secure Data Migration. Data are not always bound to a certain place and might require to be moved for various reasons; e.g., the level of availability of the node currently storing them has been greatly reduced. However, data migration is not a simplified activity while it needs to be properly secured for privacy and protection reasons. As such, an MCMP can be assessed as follows: (a) *no*: data migration is not supported; (b) *medium*: only insecure data migration is supported; (c) *high*: secure data migration is fully supported.

C2.3.3 – Secure Data Destruction. While output data can be moved to a new place or intermediate data can be deleted, a new user of the same host or the cloud provider could still read them. As such, for security and privacy reasons, an MCMP must securely destruct data when they are no more needed and can be, thus, evaluated as follows: (a) *no*: data are simply destructed; (b) *yes*: data are securely destructed by utilising state-of-the-art mechanisms.

C2.3.4 – Data Source Versatility. Data can be encapsulated in different data source kinds, including relational or NoSQL DBs, and triples stores. Thus, data management should be conducted across all such kinds. As such, an MCMP can be evaluated as follows: (a) *no*: no data source is supported; (b) *low*: only one data source kind is supported; (c) *medium*: two to three data source kinds are supported; (d) *high*: the MCMP supports more than three data source kinds.

C2.4 – Workflow Support. With this sub-group of activities, we assess the support level towards management and application workflows.

C2.4.1 – Management Flexibility. In many cases, MCMPs encode the management of application lifecycle activities in code form. This is inflexible as each time the handling of such activities must be modified, the code must be re-engineered. However, if lifecycle activities are encoded in a workflow form, the highest possible flexibility is achieved as workflows can be easily and effortlessly modified by using well-known workflow editors without changing any kind of code. Thus, we can evaluate an MCMP with: (a) *no*: management workflows are not directly supported; (b) *yes*: such workflows can be both edited and executed.

C2.4.2 – Workflow Automation. Applications do not take just the form of component agglomerations. They could also be BPaaSes realised in form of workflows that must be properly provisioned and managed. Thus, we can assess an MCMP as follows: (a) *no*: it does not support application workflows; (b) *yes*: it offers specialised workflow facilities and services.

C2.5 – Containerization. By adopting the well-known and used micro-service paradigm, modern cloud applications are built and deployed as containers which can be easily managed in separation. With the following two criteria, we assess the support level towards building and managing a diversity of container forms.

C2.5.1 – Container Versatility. Docker is the most widely used container form. However, new container forms were recently developed (e.g., singularity [7]), which are more secure and lightweight, specializing for particular workload kinds (i.e., high performance ones). Thus, an MCMP must support handle all these container forms during application deployment to increase its applicability. So, it can be evaluated as follows: (a) *no*: containers are not supported; (b) *low*: only one container form is supported; (c) *medium*: two container forms are supported; (d) *high*: the MCMP handles more than two container forms.

C2.5.2 – Container Image Management. An MCMP must offer suitable facilities to manage container images; this is handy in the context of manipulating and building containerised application components. Thus, we can evaluate it as follows: (a) *no*: container images are not managed; (b) *yes*: the MCMP offers tools or facilities to manage container images.

C2.6 – CI/CD Support. Applications can evolve over time due to market competition, requirements change and the advent of new technologies. Thus, an MCMP must support this evolution by adopting different continuous integration and deployment (CI/CD) paradigms. For instance, it could allow old and new application versions to be concurrently provisioned. As such, an MCMP can be assessed as follows: (a) *no*: CI/CD is not supported; (b) *low*: it is not directly supported but users can push new application versions for deployment; (c) *medium*: it directly supported; (d) *high*: it can also be properly configured.

3.3 C3 – Platform Intelligence

An MCMP must derive extra knowledge to optimise the client's application in terms of its initial deployment and its continuous reconfiguration. The ability to derive new knowledge plus exploit it relates to monitoring & runtime capabilities covering the user application's functionality and data. As such, respective criteria categories were devised to assess MCMPs with respect to such capabilities.

C3.1 – Optimisation. This criterion assesses how well a multi-cloud application is continuously optimised by an MCMP.
  C3.1.1 – Utility Functions. Optimisation is usually accompanied by utility functions to derive a candidate solution's utility. This enables checking the solution space to discover the solution with the highest utility, i.e., the optimal one. The formulation of such utility functions must be rich and precise via the use of complete mathematical specifications. As such, an MCMP can be evaluated as follows: *no*: it does not consider any optimisation objective; *low*: the objective is rather fixed; *medium*: the objective is indirectly produced via the user specification of partial objectives (e.g., metrics) and their relative importance (in form of weights); *high*: a complete mathematical formula can be expressed.
  C3.1.2 – Objective Versatility. Even if an optimisation objective is mathematically defined, we argue that apart from mathematical operators and functions, its content should include as variables: (a) *metrics*: these connect with the monitoring feedback to properly compute a solution's utility; (b) *attributes*: they denote some quantities related to the solution space or the current application configuration. For instance, one attribute could express the maximum cost among all candidate offerings of an application component. Thus, an MCMP can be evaluated as follows: *no*: metrics and attributes cannot be used in objective specification; *low*: only fixed metrics can be used; *medium*: also fixed attributes can be used; *high*: any kind of metric or attribute can be involved.
  C3.1.3 – Continuous Reasoning. An MCMP must continuously reason to derive new application deployment plans that more optimally address the

current situation. This is an essential ability in the dynamic cloud environments under which applications operate (as various functional and non-functional faults can occur) while allows grabbing new opportunities for optimisation when they appear (e.g., better offerings for application components). As such, an MCMP can be evaluated with: *no*: reasoning is performed once for initial application deployment; *medium*: it is also performed at runtime for very limited occasions (e.g., SLO violations); *high*: deployment reasoning is continuously performed.

C3.2 – Monitoring. This criterion assesses an MCMP's monitoring features, including the monitoring and aggregation of any kind of metric plus the proper configuration of such measurement.

C3.2.1 – System Metrics. By allowing the automatic computation of some metrics, the client's development effort in terms of application monitoring is reduced. This signifies the need to support system metrics across different abstraction levels. Thus, an MCMP is evaluated with: *no*: no system metric is offered; *low*: only infrastructural metrics are covered; *medium*: metrics at two abstraction levels are offered; *high*: system metrics cover all possible levels.

C3.2.2 – Custom Metrics. An MCMP cannot realise any metric kind, especially domain-specific ones, so clients must be able to inject their own metrics in the MCMP. Such an injection must be properly performed by defining sensor components within the application model and subsequently installing them in the application's deployment infrastructure. Thus, an MCMP can be evaluated on this criterion with: *no*: no custom metrics can be exploited; *low*: only external sensors (to the application deployment infrastructure) can be utilised; *medium*: also internal sensor components can be indirectly incorporated but the devops must properly install them in the deployment infrastructure and integrate them with the MCMP's monitoring sub-system; *high*: internal sensor components are properly installed and integrated with the MCMP's monitoring sub-system.

C3.2.3 – Metric Aggregation. Application requirements rely on high-level measurements as aggregations of raw-level ones. Such an aggregation must be computed via mathematical formulas that apply basic or statistical functions over metrics and attributes. This enables to compute any kind of composite metric, mapping to the outmost monitoring flexibility. Thus, an MCMP can be evaluated with: *no*: measurement aggregation is not supported; *low*: only fixed statistical functions can be applied on raw measurements; *medium*: mathematical expressions using fixed statistical functions can be expressed; *high*: any kind of mathematical expression including any kind of function can be utilised.

C3.2.4 – Metric Configuration. Metric measurement should be properly configured based on: the measurement schedule, i.e., how often to conduct it; the measurement window, i.e., how many measurement values are used to compute the aggregated measurement. While such information could be specified by users, this may lead to situations where mistakes can be performed or the monitoring sub-system becomes overloaded. Thus, an MCMP must optimally derive this information by finding the best trade-off between monitoring accuracy and performance. So, it can be evaluated with: *no*: it does not allow specifying such information and cannot derive it; *low*: it has a fixed mapping of metrics to schedules and windows based on their type (raw or composite); *medium*: it allows the user to specify this information; *high*: it automatically derives this information by respecting user preferences (e.g., bounds on both information pieces).

C3.3 – Runtime Adaptation. An MCMP must globally adapt the user application according to the current situation and across multiple abstraction levels.

C3.3.1 – Scaling Support. Local application reconfiguration can be conducted in less critical situations through application (component) scaling. Different scaling kinds (horizontal and vertical) must be supported to cover different local reconfiguration scenarios. As such, an MCMP can be evaluated on this criterion as follows: *no*: scaling is not supported at all by the MCMP; *medium*: only horizontal scaling is supported; *high*: also vertical scaling is supported.

C3.3.2 – Global Reconfiguration. In more critical situations, single application component scaling does not suffice; a more radical application reconfiguration must be performed, even across multiple clouds, which can be guided through utility functions for discovering the best possible application deployment solution. As such, an MCMP can be evaluated as follows: *no*: it does not support global reconfiguration; *yes*: it does support it.

C3.3.3 – Higher-Level Adaptation. Problematic situations relate to issues which occur in one abstraction level and can be propagated up to higher levels. To this end, a workflow of level-specific adaptation actions must be executed in a coordinated manner to avoid conflicting action effects. As such, we can evaluate an MCMP on this as follows: *no*: it does not offer higher-level adaptation actions; *low*: adaptation actions at two levels are offered; *medium*: adaptation actions in all possible levels are supplied; *high*: workflows of level-specific adaptation actions can be specified to address problematic situations.

C3.4 – Event Management. Problematic situations need to be detected before they can lead to triggering any kind of adaptation action. Thus, any kind of event needs to be captured, to cover all possible situation kinds, irrespectively of whether it is within the MCMP's control sphere or not.

C3.4.1 – Event Versatility. As different kinds of events might occur in an application system spanning both functional and non-functional aspects, an MCMP must capture them all. As such, an MCMP can be assessed on this as follows: *no*: it cannot capture any event kind; *medium*: it is able to capture either functional or non-functional events; *high*: it can capture both event kinds.

C3.4.2 – Complex Events. In many cases, a problematic situation cannot be characterised by a single but multiple events, related to each other in different ways. This requires capturing hierarchical compositions of events on which time and logic-based operators can be applied. Thus, an MCMP can be evaluated with: *no*: composite events cannot be captured; *low*: only time or logical operators can be used in the event composition; *medium*: a limited set of both operator kinds can be used; *high*: a rich operator set of both kinds can be used.

C3.4.3 – External Event Integration. A diversity of applications might receive from as well as propagate events to their environment. In the context of cloud & edge computing, the environment could comprise sensors or external services like message queues. Thus, all such (external) entities must be properly integrated with an MCMP in a provider-independent way to support multi-cloud application deployment. So, an MCMP can be evaluated with: *no*: integration with external services is not possible; *medium*: there is a provider-specific integration; *high*: external event integration is realised across multiple providers.

C3.5 – Data Management. Data may not be just consumed by an application but may have to be migrated for various reasons (e.g., they must move towards external sources). As such, data must be properly maintained and accounted for in application deployment optimisation.

C3.5.1 – MetaData Maintenance. To control and manage data, there is a need to support their continuous characterisation in terms of metadata. Such metadata could cover static information about the data like what is their origin plus dynamic information like their current size. As such, an MCMP can be evaluated as follows: *no*: metadata are not kept at all; *medium*: only static metadata are maintained; *high*: both static and dynamic metadata are preserved.

C3.5.2 – Data Monitoring. Dynamic metadata observation and data quality measurement require suitable data monitoring mechanisms, independent of the data source and format to increase an MCMP's applicability in handling different data-intensive application kinds. Thus, an MCMP can be evaluated with: *no*: data monitoring is not supported at all; *medium*: data monitoring is supported but only for certain data sources and/or formats; *high*: the MCMP features a data-source and format-independent data monitoring mechanism.

C3.5.3 – Data-aware Optimisation. Data placement could have a tremendous effect on both application cost and performance as well as the component placement. Thus, there is a need to support data-aware optimisation of application deployment. This can be realisable by: (a) considering resource, platform and other kinds of constraints for the nodes on which data should be placed; (b) incorporating data-related metrics in the optimization objective(s). As such, an MCMP can be evaluated with: *no*: it does not support data-aware optimisation; *medium*: it only accounts for constraints on data nodes; *high*: it also incorporates data-related metrics in the optimisation objectives.

C3.6 – Dynamic Resource Offering Discovery. Due to the dynamicity in cloud environments plus the periodic upgrading of cloud offerings, cloud services might go down or cease to exist. Thus, if these services' offerings are not properly observed, an MCMP might propose deployment solutions that do not work or are not optimal. Further, cloud providers do not advertise all possible information for such services, especially their non-functional capabilities. As such, there is a need for mechanisms (e.g., benchmarking, monitoring) that enhance the service performance profiles with the missing knowledge. Thus, an MCMP can be evaluated with: *no*: it does not support dynamic resource offering discovery; *medium*: it does support this but cannot derive extra performance-oriented knowledge; *high*: both dynamic resource offering discovery and enhancement are supported.

4   Evaluation

Before we supply and analyse the evaluation results, we first explain how they were produced, especially in terms of aggregating the raw assessment values per each individual criterion. To this end, the following approach has been adopted:

- Per each individual criterion, the qualitative values are mapped to quantitative ones. As such, the following mappings were introduced:
  - $no \rightarrow 0.0$
  - $low \rightarrow 1.0$
  - $medium \rightarrow 3.0$
  - $high \rightarrow 5.0$
- we aggregate the evaluation results via a weighted sum in the two higher hierarchy levels. First, aggregation is conducted on the composite criteria level, where each individual criterion gets the same weight (same relative importance with the others). Then, aggregation is performed on the global dimensions level, where each component criterion gets again the same weight.
- Finally, for the global level the aggregated quantitative values are mapped to qualitative ones as follows:
  - $[0.0, 1.0) \rightarrow very\ low$
  - $[1.0, 2.0) \rightarrow low$
  - $[2.0, 3.0) \rightarrow medium$
  - $[3.0, 4.0) \rightarrow good$
  - $[4.0, 5.0] \rightarrow high$

For presentation purposes, the above mapping is also applied to composite criteria as we regard that qualitative values better represent evaluation results in the eyes of the prospective reader. Please also note that due to paper length restriction reasons, the evaluation of all individual criteria is not shown (please follow the URL in the last paragraph of Sect. 2 to view the complete results).

Table 2. Overall evaluation results

MCMP	C1 – Cloud orchestration support	C2 – Cloud application support	C3 – Platform intelligence
Cisco Cloud Center Suite	Good	Medium	Medium
Rackware Hybrid Cloud Platform	Good	Very low	Low
Morpheus Data	Good	Medium	Low
CloudBolt	Good	Low	Low
Google Anthos	Good	Medium	Medium
Cloudify	Good	Medium	Low
Melodic	Good	Medium	Good

4.1   Overall Results

Table 2 depicts the evaluation results at the global level, indicating that Melodic is the best MCMP as it reaches a good score level for two out of three dimensions. Melodic is then followed by Google Anthos and Cisco Cloud Center Suite, which have attained medium score levels for two dimensions and a good level for one. Finally, Rackware Hybrid Cloud Platform seems to be the least performant, focusing mainly on supporting just the first from the three dimensions.

4.2   Cloud Orchestration Support

Table 3 depicts the overall results for this dimension which are quite encouraging as all MCMPs seem to attain a good score level. Further, there is some evaluation uniformity as most MCMPs seem to attain the same score for each criterion in the second hierarchy level (the intermediate one). Exceptions to this rule can be observed in the last three criteria of that level.

Table 3. Cloud orchestration support evaluation results

MCMP	C1.1	C1.2	C1.3	C1.4	C1.5	C1.6
Cisco Cloud Center Suite	Good	Good	Yes	Good	Good	No
Rackware Hybrid Cloud Platform	High	Good	Yes	Medium	Good	No
Morpheus Data	High	Good	Yes	Medium	Good	No
CloudBolt	High	Good	Yes	Medium	Good	No
Google Anthos	High	Good	Yes	Good	Good	No
Cloudify	High	Good	Yes	Medium	Good	Low
Melodic	High	Good	Yes	Medium	High	No

In particular, for the service support, Google Anthos and Cisco Cloud Center Suite attained a good score due to their ability to support a multitude of services at the platform level. This makes them ideal for applications requiring multi-cloud support crossing multiple abstraction levels. Melodic is distinguished in the automation criterion as it can derive and execute automatically an application deployment plan. All other MCMPs can just execute a user-supplied plan. Much improvement is needed for the standards support as only one MCMP just supports one standard, the TOSCA [6] cloud application modelling language.

Finally, we should remark the high support level for the first dimension criterion, which, in conjunction with the second one, highlights the main focus of MCMPs towards supporting the infrastructure level over a great diversity of cloud providers. In addition, cross-cloud support (not visible in Table 3) should be also highlighted. As such, we can conclude that the support level for this dimension is satisfactory but there is a need for further improvement in some criteria, especially the fourth and sixth ones (service support & standards).

4.3 Cloud Application Support

Table 4 depicts the overall results for this dimension which can be regarded as moderate such that much improvement is needed. This also unveils the current focus of MCMPs on supporting cloud orchestration and not providing any kind of additional support to cloud applications. Compared to the first dimension, there is also a high diversity of evaluation results per criterion.

Table 4. Cloud application support evaluation results

MCMP	C2.1	C2.2	C2.3	C2.4	C2.5	C2.6
Cisco Cloud Center Suite	Good	Low	Medium	High	Very low	Medium
Rackware Hybrid Cloud Platform	Low	Low	Medium	No	No	No
Morpheus Data	Medium	Low	Low	Medium	Very low	High
CloudBolt	Medium	Low	Low	Medium	Very low	Low
Google Anthos	Medium	Low	Good	No	Good	High
Cloudify	Good	Low	Low	Medium	Very low	High
Melodic	High	Low	Medium	Medium	Very low	Low

Concerning the dimension criteria in the intermediate level, the worst performance is over the lifecycle management and the containerisation ones. For the first, this result seems logical as the MCMP focus is mainly on a few activities in the lifecycle (the deployment and provisioning ones). For the second, the result highlights that MCMPs expect that devops exploit already existing, external tools while Docker is the current container form & technology widely adopted. This indicates that other container forms, more suitable for high-performance computing (HPC) like Singularity [7], are not currently supported.

We now concentrate on the rest of the criteria where usually one MCMP prevails. For the modelling support, Melodic achieves the highest possible score as it adopts CAMEL [8], a rich multi-cloud application modelling language, covering multiple aspects related to the application lifecycle. Melodic obtains the highest score for all modelling support criteria apart from the policy modelling one as CAMEL concentrates on defining application-specific policies. More details about the way CAMEL covers multi-cloud computing can be found in [9].

Google Anthos obtains the highest score in data management as it features data creation and secure data migration while exhibiting a medium data source diversity. On the other hand, Cisco Cloud Center Suite achieves the highest score in workflow support as it enables both to edit management workflows and execute application workflows by using specific (PaaS-based) workflow engines.

Finally, it seems that CI/CD support has been well recognised as multiple MCMPs supply CI/CD capabilities to devops. This then enables to rapidly deploy new versions of multi-cloud applications to achieve fast time-to-market, an essential characteristic to survive in a very competitive business world.

4.4 Platform Intelligence

Melodic prevails in this dimension (see Table 5). This is due to its core ability to support the continuous optimisation of multi-cloud applications at the global level which presupposes appropriate support also to application monitoring and event management as the cornerstones for adaptive application provisioning. The rest of the MCMPs only support application component scaling. Melodic is superior also in data management where it supports maintaining metadata about the data manipulated by applications while it is the only MCMP accounting for (big) data features and optimisation objectives during application deployment reasoning. Lastly, Melodic is the only MCMP allowing the complete, mathematical specification of both metrics and optimisation objectives, thus covering essential measurability gaps and achieving true optimality by considering multiple optimisation objectives, spanning traditional cost & performance-oriented, data-specific and reconfiguration-specific objectives.

Table 5. Platform intelligence evaluation results

MCMP	C3.1	C3.2	C3.3	C3.4	C3.5	C3.6
Cisco Cloud Center Suite	Low	Low	Low	Medium	Good	Medium
Rackware Hybrid Cloud Platform	No	Low	Low	Low	Good	No
Morpheus Data	Low	Medium	Low	Low	No	Medium
CloudBolt	No	Low	Low	Medium	No	Medium
Google Anthos	No	Medium	Low	Good	Good	No
Cloudify	No	Medium	Low	Good	Medium	No
Melodic	High	Medium	Medium	Good	High	Medium

We now concentrate on the criteria requiring more improvement than the rest. In the monitoring (composite) criterion, the medium level reached by some MCMPs is related to the inability to support system metrics on all abstraction levels and the automatic derivation of metric configuration knowledge. From these MCMPs, Melodic is distinguished as it enables specifying any metric kind due to the use of a rich mathematical language while Google Anthos as it enables incorporating user sensors in a cloud application's monitoring infrastructure.

For the runtime adaptation, no MCMP supports adaptation based on higher-abstraction-level actions. However, Melodic is distinguished as it supports global reconfiguration while Google Anthos prevails in terms of scaling support as it features both vertical and horizontal scaling of containerised components.

Finally, more than half of the MCMPs can dynamically discover cloud service offerings via cloud-specific APIs. However, they cannot also derive these services' non-functional profile. While the latter could have been an important knowledge to assist in selecting the right cloud services for a multi-cloud application.

5   Conclusions and Challenges

Due to the advantages that multi-cloud computing offers, various multi-cloud management platforms (MCMPs) have been developed, each with its own advantages and weaknesses. This paper attempted to review all these MCMPs based on a hierarchical criteria framework covering the dimensions of cloud orchestration support, cloud application support and platform intelligence. The review relied on a two-level aggregation approach over the assessment of individual criteria at the lowest hierarchy level. In this aggregation, equal weights were given to the criteria to signify their equal relative importance. This can be altered to better reflect the individual preferences of different users.

The evaluation results clearly showed that there is one MCMP that prevails, namely Melodic, providing the unique feature in terms of platform intelligence of continuous, global multi-objective application optimisation. They also showed which are those criteria requiring better support across all MCMPs, like those of monitoring and runtime adaptation as well as application lifecycle support.

We believe that the next challenges will further boost MCMPs' adoption.

BPaaS Management. MCMPs focus on traditional multi-tier applications. However, business processes (BPs) are currently moving to the cloud and require complete management support. Prototypes like CloudSocket [2,10] demonstrate that it is feasible to support such a management across multiple clouds and levels. However, there is still a need for further automation while the known business-to-IT gap must be better closed. Apart from this, technological developments like computational capability enhancement and serverless computing make more eminent the need to support a new breed of (multi-) cloud-based BPs (so called BPaaSes) which are adaptive and flexible as well as incorporate a mixture of different tasks kinds (service-, function-, user- and analytics-based).

Polymorphic Applications. As indicated in Sect. 3, components might have cloud-specific configurations in one form but could also appear in different forms (e.g., micro-services, functions). Thus, the configuration diversity is quite large. Further, different component forms might exhibit different service levels when encountering the same workload. This requires not only to specify but also select and configure the right form of a component depending on user requirements. Such a selection could be also conducted either at design or even at runtime, leading to the era of polymorphic components and applications. In our view, this represents the next breed of multi-cloud applications which will be adaptive to both their context and requirements, whenever these change.

High-Performance Multi-Cloud Computing. Traditional HPC infrastructures lead to long turnaround delays, especially in cases of high load. Recent work [11] identified that cloud computing resources can be used instead to attain a similar service level with a reduced cost and turnaround time. To further satisfy the ever increasing thirst for more computing power for heavy analytics tasks, the need to move HPC workloads in the cloud is recognized by some providers who rush to supply specialised and high-performant resources (e.g., GPUs and virtualised FPGAs) plus ultra-fast networks to provide suitable compute and networking support for HPC applications. This trend must be well covered by MCMPs to provide the right abstraction means enabling to properly select HPC-compatible resources that best fit application requirements. This also requires to properly specify this resources kind by the MCMPs' modelling languages [9] to support their matching with component requirements. Besides, MCMPs must support different container forms, like Singularity [7], stated as superior to Docker container forms, especially for HPC applications.

Acknowledgements. This work has received funding from European Union's Horizon 2020 programme under grant agreement No. 731664 (MELODIC).

References

1. Petcu, D.: Multi-cloud: expectations and current approaches. In: MultiCloud, Prague, Czech Republic, pp. 1–6. ACM (2013)
2. Kritikos, K., Zeginis, C., Griesinger, F., Seybold, D., Domaschka, J.: A cross-layer BPaaS adaptation framework. In: FiCloud, Prague, Czech Republic, pp. 241–248. IEEE Computer Society (2017)
3. Goodman, L.A.: Snowball sampling. Ann. Math. Statist. **32**(1), 148–170 (1961)
4. Nelson, L.E., O'Donell, G., Caldwell, J., Reese, A.: The Forrester Wave^{TM}: hybrid cloud management, Q2 2018. Technical report, Forrester research (2018)
5. Cheung, M., Fletcher, C., Byrne, P., Smith, D.: Magic quadrant for cloud management platforms. Technical report G00369275, Gartner (2019)
6. Rutkowski, M., Boutier, L., Lauwers, C.: Topology and orchestration specification for cloud applications (TOSCA). Technical report V1.2, Organization for the Advancement of Structured Information Standards (OASIS), January 2019
7. Kurtzer, G.M., Sochat, V., Bauer, M.W.: Singularity: Scientific containers for mobility of compute. PLoS ONE **12**(5), e0177459 (2017)
8. Bergmayr, A., et al.: A systematic review of cloud modeling languages. ACM Comput. Surv. **51**(1), 22:1–22:38 (2018)
9. Kritikos, K., Skrzypek, P.: Are cloud modelling languages ready for multi-cloud? In: 12th International Conference on Utility and Cloud Computing Companion (UCC 2019 Companion), Auckland, New Zealand. IEEE/ACM (2019)
10. Woitsch, R., Utz, W.: Business process as a service model based business and IT cloud alignment as a cloud offering, October 2015. In: ES. IEEE (2015)
11. Netto, M.A.S., Calheiros, R.N., Rodrigues, E.R., Cunha, R.L.F., Buyya, R.: HPC cloud for scientific and business applications: taxonomy, vision, and research challenges. ACM Comput. Surv. **51**(1), 8:1–8:29 (2018)

Identification of Comparison Key Elements and Their Relationships for Cloud Service Selection

Anis Ahmed Nacer[(✉)], Olivier Perrin, and François Charoy

Université de Lorraine, CNRS, Inria, LORIA, 54000 Nancy, France
anis.ahmed-nacer@inria.fr, {olivier.perrin,francois.charoy}@loria.fr

Abstract. Nowadays, the cloud computing industry is enjoying an exponential growth, where several cloud service providers compete to be one of the market leaders. Usually, providers offering similar services use different non-functional attributes to describe them. Thus, given the heterogeneity and diversity of services descriptions, the selection process of the appropriate cloud service becomes challenging. Architects no longer know what criteria to use to make the suitable cloud services selection. In this paper, we highlight the challenge of identifying key elements of comparisons and their relationship for selecting cloud services. Further, we propose a methodology to solve this issue based on real data available from service providers and benchmark work. Our methodology is validated based on two case studies of cloud relational databases and cloud queuing services.

Keywords: Cloud computing · Cloud service selection · Microservices

1 Introduction

Nowadays, cloud service providers present their services as Add-ons plans that are described according to a set of Non-Functional Attributes (NFAs). NFAs are settings that describe how a service is configured. They can influence Non-Functional Requirements (NFRs) such as performance, security and availability. The competition between the providers and the lack of standard have led them to describe their services differently to attract consumers. Service plans descriptions are different, incomplete, and use different designation for the same NFA. Further, these descriptions do not specify the relationship or impact between the comparisons' key elements (NFAs and NFRs). Thus, Choosing the most appropriate service to meet the NFR of architects becomes a challenging task. The selection of the most appropriate cloud service depends heavily on the choice of comparisons' key elements and their relationships. The comparisons' key elements of service plans are a set of NRFs and NFAs. In practice, incorrect selection of comparisons' key elements and their relationships results in an incorrect service evaluation. Therefore, comparisons' key elements and their relationships must be carefully described at the outset of the assessment.

A. Brogi et al. (Eds.): ESOCC 2020, LNCS 12054, pp. 74–82, 2020.
https://doi.org/10.1007/978-3-030-44769-4_6

The main challenge when selecting cloud services is to determine what are NFRs and NFAs that should be considered and how NFAs influence NFRs. In this paper, we propose a method that relies on architect input and service analysis. It consists of the following steps: (1) Understand the architects' requirements and how they reason regarding the choice of service plans for their applications. To do so, we propose to conduct semi-structured interviews with architects; (2) Identify the key elements of the comparison that meet the architects' requirements and the relationship between them. For that we propose to review service provider plans, works on cloud service benchmarks and literature reviews (3) Ensure the completeness of the list of key elements for comparison and their relationship. To do so we propose to conduct an empirical study with the architects. The outcomes of our methodology are the identification of a set of NFAs, NFRs and their relationships that we can use to evaluate cloud services.

The paper is organized as follows: Sect. 2 describes the proposed methodology for selecting the comparisons' key elements and their relationships to the selection of cloud services. Section 3 presents the validation of our methodology Sects. 4 and 5 present respectively the related work and the conclusion.

2 Proposed Method

An important step in selecting cloud services is to identify NFR, NFA and their relationships. Figure 1 gives an overview of the proposed methodology.

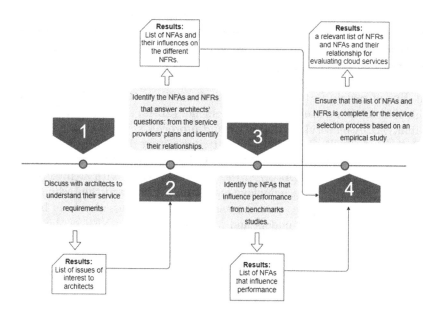

Fig. 1. Methodology for identifying NFAs and NFRs and their relationships for cloud service selection problems

2.1   Identification of Architects' Requirements

As a primary step, we organized interviews with some architects to clarify their minimum requirements and expectations from the different services. We asked them about their overall service requirements through open-ended questions like "what questions should they answer to choose the best plans from cloud service providers for their applications?" From these interviews, we have compiled a list of questions that architects consider when choosing cloud services, including the following as examples: how to predict capacity? Are performance specifications aligned with architects' expectations for cloud services? Do service plans provide replication and fail-over support?

The aim of this study is twofold: (1) group common issues for the generic evaluation of different services offered by different providers; and (2) establish the NFR that are used to assess services. The questions are grouped according to their influence on these requirements.

2.2   Identification of Attributes from Service Plans

As a second step, we need to identify the attributes that help to evaluate and match cloudware service plans to architect's requirements. Depending on plans, service provider indicates the presence or absence of some operational configuration. Evaluating plans on an absolute scale remains difficult. We identified attributes associated to service plans from providers that give access to their services on Heroku, IBM Cloud and Azure. We classified them into 4 categories, which are as follows: **(1) Capacity attributes** that provide information about the performance and the capacity of the service. We can use them to calibrate the plan according to the requirements of the application; **(2) Functional attributes** that give information about the functional coverage of the service. A database service for instance may include supplementary functions, including monitoring of certain features or auditing of functions; **(3) Service attributes** provide information on service level agreements (SLAs) such as SLA on support availability, SLA on service availability and protocols supported by the service; **(4) Technical attributes** include the attributes that describe how the service is deployed or operated. They have different impact on NFR of the service. To determine the impact of NFAs on NFRs, we first discussed with architects about their experiences with service deployment. Also, we reviewed the technical documentation of cloud services to understand why a NFA was advertised by cloud providers. By this way, we understand its influence on the NFR of the service. Determining the rate of influence of NFAs on NFRs is difficult. It depends on factors whose information is not available from the service providers. This includes the deployment of the provider's architecture: the number of nodes on which the service is deployed and the technologies used to develop the service. In addition, the influence of NFAs on NFRs depends on the nature of the applications for which the service is intended. Due to these difficulties, we only indicate the positive, neutral or negative impact on the technical attribute $(+, =, -)$. Table 1 gives an example of a database service's technical attributes and their impact on NFRs.

Table 1. Example of the influence of certain NFAs on NFRs for relational cloud database services

Attributes	Performance	Availability	Reliability	Security	Scalability
RAM	+	=	=	=	=
IOPS	+	=	=	=	=
Backup	−	+	+	=	=
Rollback	=	+	=	=	=
Replication	−	+	+	=	=

2.3 Identification of Attributes Based on Benchmark Works

All NFRs, except performance, can be assessed from the NFAs supplied by cloud service providers. Performance should be considered as a particular NFR. The only way to identify the attributes that have an impact on this NFR, is to refer to benchmarks. In order to understand the attributes that influence service performance, we reviewed previous benchmarking work[1] that compares the performance of different cloud services for different use cases, under different constraints and experience configurations. This study is interesting but incomplete because most benchmarking works do not provide all the attributes that influence performance in their experiments. In experiments for the same use case, with the same constraints and experimental configurations, we observed that the performance results are different. We do not know if this is due to external factors undeclared attributes or technical inaccuracies. To complete our study, we reviewed previous work that focused on a structured analysis of the fundamental principles of variation and predictability of service provider performance.

2.4 Selection of NFAs and NFRs from an Empirical Study

To ensure the completeness and the relevance of the collected technical attributes, we propose to conduct an empirical study. The aim is to understand how architects decide the types of components to develop a new application, and the criteria that guide their choices. We are particularly interested in core components (database, messaging, caching, indexing, monitoring...) that can be deployed as servers or consumed as services in the cloud. We conducted a semi structured interview, as done in [1], on a general perception of services with seven software architects. All of them have more than four years of experience in cloud computing environments and have participated in several projects covering different application areas such as data engineering, software/systems development, engineering systems and test infrastructure. Individual interviews were performed. Each lasted around one hour. The interviews are recorded, transcribed and synthesized. The architects' responses are assessed on the basis of their technical knowledge and experience. The survey for this study is built on

---

[1] https://www.2ndwatch.com/blog/benchmarking-amazon-aurora/.

37 questions divided into three parts: questions on the architect's experience, questions on the overall application and questions on each service/component[2]. For example, when asked: "Why do you want to move from IBM's provider database service to Amazon for your application?" Architects A1, A2, A3, A4 and A6 replied: "IBM does not provide Virtual Private Cloud (VPC) for its services and this motivates us to switch to Amazon services" and architects A5 and A7 replied: "We consider VPC important but not important enough to migrate our service to another cloud service provider". These responses conclude that the NFA "VPC" is necessary for the architects' application. Therefore, VPC can be an important NFA for cloud service evaluation according to the architects' application requirements. We asked the same types of questions about service selection and collected the NFA that were missing for service evaluation, ensuring at the same time that the list of NFA we had collected was complete for service evaluation. To summarize, we filtered the NFA that were collected in the previous steps and retained only the ones that are relevant to the evaluation of services. In addition, we identify missing attributes that could not be collected in the previous steps. Using our methodology, we aim to identify a relevant list of NFAs, NFRs and their relationships for which cloud services will be evaluated.

3   Empirical Validation of the Method

To validate the approach described in Sect. 2, we conducted two case studies: SQL database services and queue services. We examine these services on the basis of actual configuration data available from service providers and benchmarking works. Due to space limitation, only the first use case (SQL database) is presented. The second use case is shared here [3]. In the rest of this section, we apply our methodology to identify the key elements of the comparison and their relationships to the SQL cloud service.

 – **Identification of Architects' Requirements:** For this step, we focus on questions raised in Subsect. 2.1. The questions are grouped according to their influence on the two NFRs reliability and availability. Regarding availability, architects raised a set of questions such as: What are the regions available for service? Are they adequate in terms of legal and regulatory requirements? Do service plans provide replication and fail over support? For reliability, the architects raised a set of questions such as: What is the frequency/severity of failures for the service? What is the mean time between failures (MTBF)? What is the mean time to repair the system (MTTR)? Note that the findings of this study are generic and can be reused for all types of services. The full results of this study are described in[4].

---

[2] https://docs.google.com/document/d/11LTsFJCTSqNlX5DJPYgdU9NRW8IFyd6e GiRimiY2JeQ/view.

[3] https://drive.google.com/file/d/1tBouKaagH8lMJdoYDPDri7U7Oo_iHUSY/view? ths=true.

[4] https://drive.google.com/file/d/1s7xy3u-voLkO9XKo3K5s2yqdHgaHYfFi/view? usp=sharingforacompleteanddetailedlistofthequestionsofthisstudy.

– **Result of Identification of NFAs and their influence on NFRs:**
Many SQL database service solutions are available and are deployed by different cloud service providers. The interesting attributes of these services are the following: **(1)** *The capacity attributes:* the only ones that can be identified are: **(i)** Storage capacity in Gb; **(ii)** IOPS that corresponds to the underlying disk performance; **(iii)** The maximum simultaneous connection to the database; and **(iv)** The row limit. **(2)** *The functional attributes*: include the monitoring and the audit. **(3)** *The technical attributes:* are more diverse and heterogeneous and they may have different impact on NFA. As explained previously, with the exception of performance, for which additional benchmarking may be required, there are only two ways to determine the impact of NFAs on cloud services NFRs: use the expertise of the architects who deployed the service or consult the technical documentation[5,6,7]. Given the difficulty of determining the level of influence of the NFA on NFRs (explained in Sect. 2.2), we present in Table 2 the technical attributes with the estimated positive, neutral or negative impact of NFR (+, =, −). At this stage this is all we can say about this impact.

Table 2. Influences of NFAs on NFRs for relational cloud database services

Attributes	Performance	Availability	Reliability	Security	Scalability
RAM	+	=	=	=	=
IOPS	+	=	=	=	=
SSD	+	=	=	=	=
Server cores	+	=	=	=	=
Backup	−	+	+	=	=
Rollback	=	+	=	=	=
Replication	−	+	+	=	=
Single tenant	+	=	=	+	=
Multi tenants	−	=	−	+	=
Encryption	=	=	=	+	=
VPC	=	=	=	+	=
Multi region	=	+	+	=	=
Scaling auto increase	=	=	=	=	+
Scaling not supported	=	=	=	=	−
Scaling converted to other storage types	=	=	=	=	+
Read replicas	−	=	=	=	+

---

[5] https://docs.oracle.com/cloud/latest/mysql-cloud/UOMCS/UOMCS.pdf/.
[6] https://cloud.google.com/sql/docs/mysql/.
[7] https://medium.com/@lakshmanLD/comparison-of-mysql-across-aws-azure-and-gcp-19af2d208d9a.

– Result of identification of attributes based on benchmarks: Cloud SQL services run on providers' virtual machines. These virtual machines have a direct impact on the SQL services that run on them. Therefore, NFAs that influence the performance of virtual machines also influence the performance of SQL services. So we reviewed previous work [7] that conducted a large-scale literature review to collect and codify existing research on the predictability of public IaaS cloud performance. We identified the following attributes are relevant to assess the performance of cloud SQL services: **(1)** the CPU model, the hardware heterogeneity and the tenancy model; **(2)** temporal and geographic (region) factors; **(3)** the number of nodes and the number of containers on which the service is deployed. To complete our study, we reviewed previous benchmarking work that has been done directly on cloud SQL services [2,6]. We collected the following attributes in addition to those we previously identified on the performance of cloud SQL services: **(1)** user connections are a resource that can limit performance; **(2)** replication and failover significantly reduce service performance; **(3)** the location of the data center influences performance; **(4)** number of read replicas improves performance of SQL cloud database services.

– Result of selection of NFAs and NFRs from an empirical study We carried out an empirical study with the architects on cloud SQL database services. A set of responses are collected. For example, to the question: "Why did you choose the High Availability (HA) option for your service when it costs about twice as much as a regular instance? architects A1, A2, A5 and A6 replied: "The MySQL service is a business service in our application. It should be very available. This is the critical part of the application. A failure of this service will cause the failure of the entire application. A fail over is necessary to maintain this service available when the instance is "blocked". It has happened that the primary instance is "blocked" and that a restart of the instance takes up to 30 min (supplier ticket). To avoid these downtimes, we have opted for the HA option" and architects A4, A3 and A7 replied: "A complete failure of a zone is probably very rare, so HA is an important option, but not so important as to be indispensable." We asked several questions about the selection of cloud SQL database services and ensured that the list of NFAs previously collected was relevant to our study. Based on previous studies and the architects answers, a relevant list of NFAs and their influences on NFRs was developed (as shown in Table 2) to select SQL cloud services based on the application requirements of the architects.

4   Related Work

Several approaches have been proposed to select the best service provider plans. These approaches use NFAs to evaluate cloud services. In this section, we examine the NFAs used in these approaches. We identified two main approaches, non-benchmark-based and benchmark-based. On one hand the Non-benchmark-based approaches [5,9,10] use different attributes such as: availability rate, execution time, instance starting time and mean time between failures (MTBF).

These attributes are difficult to express and can be addressed in several ways. Thus using them to solve the cloud service selection problem is of little relevance. On the other hand, several benchmark-based studies have been conducted. In [4], Smart CloudBench, a generic benchmarking tool allows to compare the offers available on the IaaS cloud market and monitor their performance. However, it is limited to IaaS and does not consider more heterogeneous middleware services. In [8], CloudCmp, a benchmarking tool is presented for cost comparison and performance measures of many services between different providers. In [3], a benchmarking methodology is applied to only four cloud storage service offers for specific workloads. The shortcoming of these approaches lies in a consideration of performance and price only, without considering other NFRs such as security, availability, reliability or security.

5   Conclusion

In this paper, we proposed a methodology for identifying key elements of comparisons and their relationship for cloud service selection. It is based on actual data available from service providers and benchmarks. First, we conducted a survey among architects to understand their requirements for selecting cloud services. Further, we identified issues that interest architects and we ranked them according to their influence on NFRs. Then, we identified the attributes of the service provider plans that answer the architects' questions and their influence on the NFRs from the technical documentation. Moreover, we reviewed the work on cloud benchmarking to collect the attributes that influence performance. Finally, we conducted an empirical study to ensure that the list of attributes we identified was complete and to add those that were missing. As a future work, we will use the results of this study to assess cloud services and cloud service composition by application type.

References

1. Ameller, D., Ayala, C., Cabot, J., Franch, X.: Non-functional requirements in architectural decision making. IEEE Softw. **30**(2), 61–67 (2012)
2. Bernstein, P.A., et al.: Adapting microsoft SQL server for cloud computing. In: IEEE 27th International Conference on Data Engineering, pp. 1255–1263. IEEE (2011)
3. Bocchi, E., Mellia, M., Sarni, S.: Cloud storage service benchmarking: methodologies and experimentations. In: IEEE 3rd International Conference on Cloud Networking (CloudNet), pp. 395–400. IEEE (2014)
4. Chhetri, M.B., Chichin, S., Vo, Q.B., Kowalczyk, R.: Smart CloudBench–a framework for evaluating cloud infrastructure performance. Inf. Syst. Front. **18**(3), 413–428 (2016)
5. Karim, R., Ding, C., Miri, A.: An end-to-end QoS mapping approach for cloud service selection. In: IEEE Ninth World Congress on Services (SERVICES), pp. 341–348. IEEE (2013)

6. Lang, W., Bertsch, F., DeWitt, D.J., Ellis, N.: Microsoft Azure SQL database telemetry. In: Proceedings of the Sixth ACM Symposium on Cloud Computing, pp. 189–194. ACM (2015)
7. Leitner, P., Cito, J.: Patterns in the chaos–a study of performance variation and predictability in public IaaS clouds. ACM Trans. Internet Technol. (TOIT) **16**(3), 15 (2016)
8. Li, A., Yang, X., Kandula, S., Zhang, M.: CloudCmp: comparing public cloud providers. In: Proceedings of the 10th ACM SIGCOMM Conference on Internet Measurement, pp. 1–14. ACM (2010)
9. Wagle, S.S., Guzek, M., Bouvry, P., Bisdorff, R.: An evaluation model for selecting cloud services from commercially available cloud providers. In: IEEE 7th International Conference on Cloud Computing Technology and Science (CloudCom), pp. 107–114. IEEE (2015)
10. Zheng, X., Martin, P., Brohman, K., Da Xu, L.: CLOUDQUAL: a quality model for cloud services. IEEE Trans. Ind. Inf. **10**(2), 1527–1536 (2014)

Deployment and Workflows

Deployable Self-contained Workflow Models

Benjamin Weder[(✉)], Uwe Breitenbücher, Kálmán Képes, Frank Leymann,
and Michael Zimmermann

Institute for Architecture of Application Systems, University of Stuttgart,
Universitätsstraße 38, 70569 Stuttgart, Germany
{benjamin.weder,uwe.breitenbuecher,kalman.kepes,frank.leymann,
michael.zimmermann}@iaas.uni-stuttgart.de

Abstract. Service composition is a popular approach for building software applications from several individual services. Using imperative workflow technologies, service compositions can be specified as workflow models comprising activities that are implemented, e.g., by service calls or scripts. While scripts are typically included in the workflow model itself and can be executed directly by the workflow engine, the required services must be deployed in a separate step. Moreover, to enable their invocation, an additional step is required to configure the workflow model regarding the endpoints of the deployed services, i.e., IP-address, port, etc. However, a manual deployment of services and configuration of the workflow model are complex, time-consuming, and error-prone tasks. In this paper, we present an approach that enables defining service compositions in a self-contained manner using imperative workflow technology. For this, the workflow models can be packaged with all necessary deployment models and software artifacts that implement the required services. As a result, the service deployment in the target environment where the workflow is executed as well as the configuration of the workflow with the endpoint information of the services can be automated completely. We validate the technical feasibility of our approach by a prototypical implementation based on the TOSCA standard and OpenTOSCA.

Keywords: Service composition · Workflow technology · Service deployment automation · Configuration automation

1   Introduction

A popular approach for building applications by combining several individual services is called *service composition*, which can reduce the time and cost to develop new services or applications significantly [7,13]. Service compositions can be specified using imperative workflow languages, such as the *Business Process Execution Language (BPEL)* [14], to benefit from their robustness and features like automatic recovery [12]. Imperative workflow models usually comprise activities that can be executed in the workflow engine, like script calls, and invocations

A. Brogi et al. (Eds.): ESOCC 2020, LNCS 12054, pp. 85–96, 2020.
https://doi.org/10.1007/978-3-030-44769-4_7

of services that run in the environment. The endpoints of available services can be retrieved using a *service registry*. Then, the services have to be bound to the workflow, which means the workflow is configured with the required information to access the services, such as the used protocols or the service endpoints [13].

However, for the successful binding, the required services must be running and accessible by the workflow [18]. Services that are provided over the internet are usually always on and can be accessed from any place if they are not protected by security mechanisms, like firewalls [8,12]. Thus, in general, the binding is feasible independent of the execution environment, e.g., the network of the workflow engine executing the workflow. However, if a workflow requires a service that is not publicly available, the service binding, and therefore, the workflow execution fails. Hence, the missing services have to be deployed by the user to execute the workflow successfully. However, a manual determination of the services that are required, as well as the deployment of these services, is a complex, time-consuming, and error-prone task and not suited for non-technical users [2]. Additionally, the service binding with the deployed services has to be performed by the user, or the service has to be registered correctly with the service registry. An error in the configuration, like a wrong IP-address, leads to the failure of the overall workflow. Furthermore, if a service is migrated, e.g., to another virtual machine, the workflow configuration and the service registry have to be updated correspondingly. Otherwise, the service is no longer accessible, and the workflow execution fails. Therefore, this process leads to a lot of manual work, which is error-prone and should be automated as far as possible.

Many services are not offered over the internet, and therefore, the user of the workflow is in charge of deploying these services. Furthermore, there may also be technical reasons to deploy a service that is available over the internet close to the workflow engine executing the workflow, e.g., to reduce the latency of the service interactions or the required network bandwidth. An example is a workflow processing big data, which would overload the network if the used services are deployed outside the local environment. Thus, to enable the execution of such workflows, the required services must be deployed in the target environment by the user before the workflow execution. However, this leads to the previously described problems, such as erroneous configurations due to human errors.

In this paper, we tackle these challenges by an approach, which allows packaging imperative workflows with all necessary deployment models to deploy the required services of the workflow as a self-contained archive. It consists of the workflow model and a set of deployment models for the required services, which are attached to the activities of the workflow that invoke the services. Additionally, our approach addresses the automatic deployment of all required services in the target environment. Finally, the approach includes the automatic configuration of the workflow with the endpoint information of the deployed services, and therefore, enables defining imperative workflows in a self-contained manner without additional manual tasks to set up required services in the environment.

2   Fundamentals and Problem Statement

In this section, we introduce fundamentals about service composition approaches, imperative workflow technologies, and the deployment of services. Furthermore, we present the problem statement which underlies our approach.

2.1   Service Composition

The creation of new applications by combining existing services is denoted as *service composition* [11]. Service composition can reduce development time and cost significantly as existing functionality is reused instead of implementing it again. In *static service composition*, the required service functionalities and the order in which they have to be invoked are specified at the design time of the service composition [3]. Furthermore, the concrete service implementation must be selected for each required functionality, and the service composition has to be configured to invoke them, which is referred to as *binding* [13]. The binding includes the configuration of the required protocol to invoke the service, the message format, and the endpoint, i.e., the IP address and port of the service. The available services can be retrieved using a *service registry*, which provides binding information for running services to a requester [9]. Thereby, the selection and binding of services during the development of the service composition is called *static binding*. In contrast, the binding at runtime is referred to as *dynamic binding*, which allows to dynamically select a suited service based on non-functional requirements. In this paper, we focus on the static binding of services.

2.2   Imperative Workflow Technology

Service compositions can be specified using *imperative workflow languages*, such as the *Business Process Execution Language (BPEL)* [14]. An imperative workflow consists of a predefined set of activities that have to be executed to achieve the goals of the workflow [5]. Activities can be divided into different categories, e.g., activities that invoke web services or activities that require an human action. The different activities are connected by *control flow* and *data flow edges* [12]. Control flow edges specify a partial order in which the activities of the workflow have to be executed. In contrast, data flow edges define which parts of the output data of an activity must be transferred to which other activities. Two benefits of using workflow technologies are scalability and robustness [5]. Another advantage is the comprehensive error handling mechanisms implemented in most workflow languages and engines. These mechanisms, e.g., allow executing activities in a transactional manner and role changes back in case of an error. Thus, workflows can be executed robustly and provide high-availability to the user.

Due to these advantages, workflows are essential for the implementation of long-running *business processes* [12]. Such business processes have to be executed (i) reliably, (ii) robustly, (iii) in parallel, and (iv) provide high-availability to the user to achieve the maximum business value. The implementation of programs, e.g., written in programming languages such as Java or C, that fulfill these

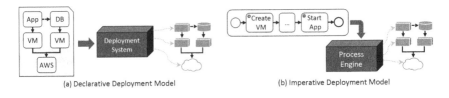

(a) Declarative Deployment Model   (b) Imperative Deployment Model

Fig. 1. Deployment model approaches.

properties is a complex and time-consuming task, as they have to be designed specifically with these non-functional properties in mind. In contrast, workflow management systems are general-purpose systems and provide the needed properties directly to the user without the need to implement or adapt them for a certain use case. Hence, they ease the development of workflows implementing business processes [5]. Therefore, workflow technology is of vital importance for the implementation and execution of long-running business processes.

2.3   Service Deployment

For our approach, we distinguish between *provided services*, that are offered by a provider over a network, e.g., the internet, and *self-hosted services*, for which the required software artifacts for the deployment are available, but for which the user is in charge of deploying them. Provided services are *"always-on"*, which means the user can directly use them and is not in charge of creating or deleting them [12]. Examples of this kind of service are Google Maps, Dropbox, or Spotify. In contrast, self-hosted services do not always run on the infrastructure of some provider, and thus, must be deployed by the user before using them in a workflow. All utilized services must be *available* to execute a workflow successfully. This means the services have to respond to requests and return correct results [12]. We focus on self-hosted services in our approach as the user is in charge of deploying them and keeping them available as long as they are needed.

However, the deployment of the required self-hosted services is a complex, time-consuming, and error-prone task [2]. The infrastructure, such as a virtual machine, has to be prepared, the dependencies of the service have to be installed, and the software artifacts of the service have to be transferred to the prepared infrastructure. Furthermore, the service must be configured with the required certificates, and the needed authentication has to be set up. Additionally, the workflow models have to be configured using the endpoint information of the deployed services to access them during runtime [12]. Therefore, a lot of manual work has to be done, and this process should be automated as far as possible.

In recent years several technologies for automating the deployment and management of applications have been developed, such as *Terraform*[1] or *Kubernetes*[2] [20]. Using these technologies, applications are described as reusable

---

[1] https://terraform.io.
[2] https://kubernetes.io.

deployment models, which can be used to instantiate the application fully automatically. Depending on the modeling approach, deployment models can be divided into two classes, as shown in Fig. 1: *declarative* and *imperative deployment models* [6]. A declarative deployment model describes the structure of an application, including all software and hardware components and their relations. In contrast, imperative deployment models express the deployment process in a procedural manner and contain all activities that have to be executed to deploy the application, as well as the execution order of these activities. Such imperative deployment models can be defined using workflow languages such as BPEL.

Thus, deployment automation technologies can be utilized to deploy required self-hosted services automatically in the target environment. However, the deployment automation technologies are not integrated with workflows and do not update the endpoint information of the activities invoking the services. Hence, the user has to trigger the deployment of the services using a deployment system, retrieve the endpoints from the deployed services, and configure the workflow according to the endpoints. As outlined previously, this process is complex and time-consuming for non-technical users and can lead to configuration errors.

2.4   Problem Statement

As described in the previous subsections, workflow technology is essential for the execution of long-running business processes. However, some of the used services are usually not available over the internet and have to be deployed by the user. Hence, (i) the deployment models for the required self-hosted services have to be determined first. This is complex if there are repositories with lots of deployment models, as it is unclear for non-technical users how to search and select appropriate deployment models. Additionally, (ii) the determined deployment models must be transferred into the target environment for the workflow execution. Further, (iii) required services have to be deployed by passing the corresponding deployment models to a deployment system. Finally, (iv) the services have to be bound to the workflow to access them on runtime. Hence, a lot of complex and time-consuming work has to be performed to prepare the target environment and the workflow for the execution and this process should be automated. Therefore, the resulting research question for this work can be formulated as follows: *"How can business processes be modeled in a self-contained manner and be deployed in the target environment fully automatically including all required services?"*

3   Self-contained Workflow Models

To enable packaging and deploying workflow models that require services that are not provided with the "always-on" property over the network, a self-contained packaging format is needed. Without such a packaging format, the required self-hosted services of a workflow have to be determined manually and deployed

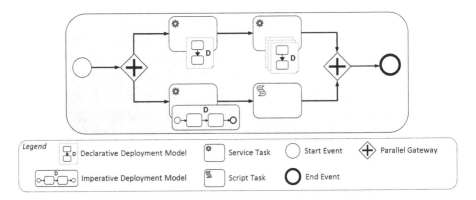

Fig. 2. Our new modeling approach: self-contained imperative workflow models.

in the environment to execute the workflow successfully. Thus, our goal is to develop a packaging format that enables bundling all required information.

The conceptual structure of a *self-contained workflow model* is depicted in Fig. 2. It contains the workflow which can be modeled, e.g., using a standardized workflow language such as BPEL. In the example, the workflow starts, performs two sequences of two activities in parallel, and terminates afterward. However, in contrast to existing workflow archives, deployment models can be added and linked by the activities in the self-contained workflow model. For example, the activity on the top-left references a declarative deployment model. This deployment model can be used to deploy the service that is invoked by the activity. If multiple deployment models for services with the same functionality exist, they can all be linked by the invoking activities (see top-right activity). E.g., one deployment model could deploy the service on a private cloud, while the other could use a local workstation. Further, different deployment models can implement the same service providing various non-functional properties, like response time or security. Hence, a selection based on non-functional requirements of the user or available hardware in the target environment can be performed.

In addition to declarative deployment models, imperative deployment models can be referenced by activities of the self-contained workflow model too (see bottom-left activity). While declarative deployment models simplify common and non-complex application deployments and require only limited technical expertise, imperative deployment models can be modified arbitrarily [6]. Hence, they are better suited for complex deployments with a lot of custom-tailored components. Therefore, our approach allows utilizing both kinds of deployment models to deploy a required service to be generally applicable.

Finally, a self-contained workflow model can also contain activities that do not require the deployment of a service, and thus, have no reference to a service deployment model. For example, an activity that is implemented by a script can be executed within the workflow engine and has no external dependency on a service (see bottom-right activity). Additionally, some activities have to be per-

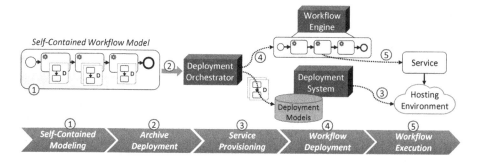

Fig. 3. Overview of the approach for self-contained imperative workflow models.

formed by humans, such as the physical set up of a device. Hence, depending on the required software tools to perform the human task, deployment models may be referenced. Further, activities can invoke provided services that are accessible over the network and do not have to be deployed before the workflow execution.

Self-contained workflow models enable to define imperative workflows implementing service compositions in a self-contained manner with all required service deployment models. Hence, the required services do not have to be determined and transferred into the target environment by the user, which can be a complex task if there are many deployment models available. However, the user is still in charge of deploying the services and configuring the workflow with the endpoints. Therefore, an approach to automate these tasks is required.

4 Automatic Service Deployment

After transferring the self-contained workflow model into the target environment, the required services must be deployed by using the included service deployment models. Furthermore, the endpoints of the deployed services have to be retrieved, and the services have to be bound to the workflow using this endpoint information. In this section, we present an approach to automate these tasks.

Figure 3 gives an overview of our approach. It covers all steps from the definition of the self-contained workflow model to the workflow execution. In the first step, the user models his workflow utilizing a suited modeling tool. The modeling tool presents the available service deployment models to the user, and therefore, allows referencing them within activities of the workflow. After finishing the modeling, the workflow is packaged as a self-contained workflow model. Subsequently, the self-contained workflow model can be transferred into the target environment for the workflow execution without the need to transmit additional files. In the target environment, it is passed to the *deployment orchestrator*, which handles the upload of the deployment models to a suitable deployment system (step 2). Thereby, the required deployment system depends on the kind of deployment models that are referenced by the activities. E.g., if they are imperative or declarative and based on a standard, such as TOSCA [15], or a proprietary format. However, the deployment orchestrator can use any deployment system by providing a plugin system to enable easy extensibility.

Before deploying the services, the deployment orchestrator has to select one of the referenced service deployment models per service if multiple alternatives are available. Therefore, the available computing infrastructure can be registered at the deployment orchestrator by a system administrator. This information can be used to exclude deployment models that utilize infrastructure that is not available in the target environment. In case, that no deployment models remain, the deployment must be aborted and the user has to be informed. If multiple alternative deployment models still exist, the selection can be continued by comparing the non-functional requirements, that can be specified by the user, with the non-functional properties of the different deployment models [21].

After selecting the service deployment models, the deployment orchestrator triggers the deployment of all required self-hosted services (step 3). For the creation of the services, different input parameters, such as user name and password for the deployment on a private cloud, can be required. These input parameters have to be provided by the user in step 3. Alternatively, all parameters can already be included in the deployment models that are contained in the self-contained workflow model. This eases the instantiation of the workflow model. However, it can reduce the portability if, e.g., a deployment model using a locally installed hypervisor is part of the self-contained workflow model. Therefore, the endpoint of the hypervisor should be provided by the user after transferring the archive into the target environment. After deploying the services, they are bound to the workflow by the deployment orchestrator. Subsequently, the correctly configured workflow can be deployed into the workflow engine (step 4). Finally, the workflow engine executes the workflow, and the activities access the deployed services (step 5). Thus, the workflow can be executed with no manual task except the upload of the self-contained workflow model to the deployment orchestrator in the target environment despite the usage of self-hosted service.

5   Prototype

This section presents the prototypical implementation of our approach. Due to its wide distribution, the workflow language BPEL and the open-source workflow engine *Apache ODE*[3] were selected to model and execute the workflows. For the specification of the service deployment models, the *Topology and Orchestration Specification for Cloud Applications (TOSCA)* [15] is used. TOSCA is an OASIS standard, which allows describing cloud applications in a vendor-neutral way, and therefore, eases portability and interoperability of modeled applications. The prototype is based on the open-source TOSCA modeling tool *Winery*[4]. We extended Winery to enable the modeling of BPEL-based service compositions and the attachment of declarative service deployment models to

---

[3] https://github.com/apache/ode.
[4] https://github.com/OpenTOSCA/winery.

the activities. The resulting workflow can be packaged by Winery into a self-contained workflow archive. Furthermore, the services and the workflow can be deployed automatically using the workflow engine Apache ODE and the *Open-TOSCA Container*[5], an open-source TOSCA-compliant runtime, which is part of the *OpenTOSCA ecosystem* [1]. After the service deployment is successful, the services can be bound to the workflow by Winery. Therefore, the required services can be deployed and the workflow can be configured fully automatically. The created enhancements are plug-in based and can easily be extended to support other workflow engines or deployment systems.

6 Related Work

Research works from different research areas focus on the development of self-contained archives or packaging formats. The TOSCA [15] standard can be used to define cloud applications in a portable and self-contained manner. For this, all required information for the application deployment is packaged in a *Cloud Service Archive (CSAR)*, which can be executed by any TOSCA-compliant runtime. Qasha et al. [16] provide a framework for scientific workflow reproducibility and portability in the cloud. For this, they propose to use TOSCA to define scientific workflows together with the specification of the hosting environment. Hence, the resulting CSAR can be used by a TOSCA runtime to automatically deploy the required services and to enact the workflow. However, every workflow activity, its execution environment, and control or data connections between different activities have to be modeled using TOSCA. This can lead to a cluttered model that gets incomprehensive. Furthermore, benefits from classical workflow languages and engines, like widely known graphical notations or automatic scaling, can not be reused directly and have to be provided additionally.

Different approaches use *virtual machine images* to provide workflows in a portable and reproducible manner [10,17]. This means, they create virtual machine images from the running services, which can then be utilized to execute the workflow in other environments. For this, new virtual machines are created from each required image. However, the virtual machine images often depend on provider-specific extensions, which are used to improve the performance, and therefore, the portability is reduced. Additionally, services running on other infrastructures, like local workstations, are not considered. Another problem is the size of the virtual machine images that impedes their transmission.

Several scientific workflow management systems provide capabilities to submit tasks to available computing resources and to set up required services automatically when they are invoked by a workflow. *Pegasus* [4] separates the description of the scientific workflow from the execution environment to allow the specification of portable workflows. Additionally, it enables the runtime optimization of workflows regarding the performance or reliability by selecting appropriate

---

[5] https://github.com/OpenTOSCA/container.

computing resources for the given requirements. Thus, Pegasus contains a *mapper* component that searches and assigns computational resources to activities of the abstract workflow provided by the user. However, Pegasus is only capable to use existing resources and prepares them by transferring files or needed executables. In contrast to our approach, it is not possible to deploy required services using arbitrary deployment models employing Pegasus.

Kepler [19] is an open-source scientific workflow management system, that was extended to enable the usage of EC2 resources within workflows. Therefore, it is possible to deploy services on cloud resources in scientific workflows. However, this extension is provider-specific and not suited for services that should be hosted on different infrastructure. Furthermore, every task, including the deployment of virtual machines, the setup of needed programs and the copying of data, has to be modeled within the workflow. This can quickly lead to a cluttered model that gets incomprehensive and decreases the reusability.

Vukojevic-Haupt et al. [18] introduce an approach for the on-demand deployment of services that are required by a workflow. This means the services are deployed when they are invoked by the workflow and decommissioned afterward to save computing resources. Therefore, they proposed the extension of an enterprise service bus to enable the deployment of services. However, they assume that all required services are available as so-called *service packages* in a local service repository. The service packages include all artifacts needed to deploy the services, and therefore, correspond to deployment models in our approach. Hence, in contrast to our approach, the workflow archives are not self-contained, and new service packages must be registered by the service registry manually before the workflow is initiated, which reduces the portability of the workflows.

7   Conclusion

In this paper, we presented an approach (i) to specify service compositions in a self-contained manner using imperative workflow models and (ii) to support the automatic deployment of services that are required in the environment. For this, we defined self-contained imperative workflow models, which contain the workflow, and additionally, the deployment models of the required services that are attached to the corresponding activities of the workflow. Hence, the user is no longer responsible for determining the required services for a workflow, transferring the corresponding deployment models into the target environment, initiating the deployment, and configuring the workflow with the service endpoints before executing it. Instead, these time-consuming and error-prone tasks can be automated completely. Further, our approach eases the execution of the workflow in another environment, as all required software artifacts are contained in the self-contained imperative workflow model. We prototypically implemented our approach using the TOSCA standard to model declarative deployment models and BPEL as the workflow language to specify the service compositions.

Acknowledgement. This work was partially funded by the DFG project *DiStOPT* (252975529), the DFG's Excellence Initiative project *SimTech* (390740016), and by the BMWi project *Industrial Communication for Factories* – IC4F (01MA17008G).

References

1. Binz, T., et al.: OpenTOSCA – a runtime for TOSCA-based cloud applications. In: Basu, S., Pautasso, C., Zhang, L., Fu, X. (eds.) ICSOC 2013. LNCS, vol. 8274, pp. 692–695. Springer, Heidelberg (2013). https://doi.org/10.1007/978-3-642-45005-1_62

2. Breitenbücher, U., Binz, T., Képes, K., Kopp, O., Leymann, F., Wettinger, J.: Combining declarative and imperative cloud application provisioning based on TOSCA. In: International Conference on Cloud Engineering (IC2E), pp. 87–96. IEEE (2014)

3. Bucchiarone, A., Gnesi, S.: A survey on services composition languages and models. In: International Workshop on Web Services-Modeling and Testing, p. 51 (2006)

4. Deelman, E., Vahi, K., Rynge, M., Juve, G., Mayani, R., da Silva, R.F.: Pegasus in the cloud: science automation through workflow technologies. IEEE Internet Comput. **20**(1), 70–76 (2016)

5. Ellis, C.A.: Workflow technology. Comput. Support. Coop. Work Trends Softw. Ser. **7**, 29–54 (1999)

6. Endres, C., Breitenbücher, U., Falkenthal, M., Kopp, O., Leymann, F., Wettinger, J.: Declarative vs. imperative: two modeling patterns for the automated deployment of applications. In: Proceedings of the 9th International Conference on Pervasive Patterns and Applications, pp. 22–27. Xpert Publishing Services (2017)

7. Erl, T.: Service-Oriented Architecture: Concepts, Technology, and Design. Prentice Hall PTR, Upper Saddle River (2005)

8. Freelon, D.G.: ReCal: intercoder reliability calculation as a Web service. Int. J. Internet Sci. **5**(1), 20–33 (2010)

9. Gottschalk, K., Graham, S., Kreger, H., Snell, J.: Introduction to Web services architecture. IBM Syst. J. **41**(2), 170–177 (2002)

10. Jiang, F., Castillo, C., Schmitt, C., Mandal, A., Ruth, P., Baldin, I.: Enabling workflow repeatability with virtualization support. In: Proceedings of the 10th Workshop on Workflows in Support of Large-Scale Science, p. 8. ACM (2015)

11. Lemos, A.L., Daniel, F., Benatallah, B.: Web service composition: a survey of techniques and tools. ACM Comput. Surv. (CSUR) **48**(3), 33 (2016)

12. Leymann, F., Roller, D.: Production Workflow: Concepts and Techniques. Prentice Hall PTR, Upper Saddle River (2000)

13. Leymann, F., Roller, D., Schmidt, M.T.: Web services and business process management. IBM Syst. J. **41**(2), 198–211 (2002)

14. OASIS: Web Services Business Process Execution Language (WS-BPEL) Version 2.0. Organization for the Advancement of Structured Information Standards (OASIS) (2007)

15. OASIS: Topology and Orchestration Specification for Cloud Applications (TOSCA) Version 1.0. Organization for the Advancement of Structured Information Standards (OASIS) (2013)

16. Qasha, R., Cała, J., Watson, P.: A framework for scientific workflow reproducibility in the cloud. In: IEEE 12th International Conference on e-Science (e-Science), pp. 81–90. IEEE (2016)

17. Stodden, V., Leisch, F., Peng, R.D.: Implementing Reproducible Research. CRC Press, Boca Raton (2014)

18. Vukojevic-Haupt, K., Karastoyanova, D., Leymann, F.: On-demand provisioning of infrastructure, middleware and services for simulation workflows. In: Proceedings of the 6th IEEE International Conference on Service Oriented Computing and Applications, pp. 91–98. IEEE (2013)
19. Wang, J., Altintas, I.: Early cloud experiences with the Kepler scientific workflow system. Procedia Comput. Sci. **9**, 1630–1634 (2012)
20. Wurster, M., et al.: The essential deployment metamodel: a systematic review of deployment automation technologies. Softw. Intensive Cyber Phys. Syst., 1–13 (2019). https://doi.org/10.1007/s00450-019-00412-x
21. Yu, T., Lin, K.J.: Service selection algorithms for Web services with end-to-end QoS constraints. IseB **3**(2), 103–126 (2005)

Technology-Agnostic Declarative Deployment Automation of Cloud Applications

Michael Wurster[1]([✉]), Uwe Breitenbücher[1], Antonio Brogi[2],
Lukas Harzenetter[1], Frank Leymann[1], and Jacopo Soldani[2]

[1] Institute of Architecture of Application Systems, University of Stuttgart,
Stuttgart, Germany
{wurster,breitenbuecher,harzenetter,leymann}@iaas.uni-stuttgart.de
[2] Department of Computer Science, University of Pisa, Pisa, Italy
{brogi,soldani}@di.unipi.it

Abstract. Declarative approaches for automating the deployment and
configuration management of multi-component applications are on the
rise. Many deployment technologies exist, sharing the same baselines for
enacting declarative deployments, even if based on different languages
for specifying multi-component applications. The Essential Deployment
Metamodel (EDMM) Modeling and Transformation Framework allows
to specify multi-component applications in a technology-agnostic manner, and to automatically generate the technology-specific deployment
artifacts allowing to deploy an IaaS-based application. In this paper,
we propose an extension of the EDMM Modeling and Transformation
Framework to PaaS and SaaS by allowing to deploy application components on PaaS platforms or to implement them by instrumenting SaaS
services. Given that not all existing deployment technologies support
PaaS and SaaS deployments, we also propose the new EDMM Decision
Support Framework allowing us to determine which deployment technologies can be used to deploy an application specified with EDMM.

Keywords: Deployment modeling · Deployment automation · Cloud
application

1 Introduction

The widespread of cloud computing and DevOps resulted in a plethora of different deployment technologies being proposed. These aim at establishing highly
automated deployment processes, as manual deployments of complex multi-
component applications is cumbersome and error-prone [18,25]. By describing
the components and infrastructure of an application in reusable deployment
models, a repeatable end-to-end deployment automation can be established.

This is typically done by following a declarative approach, i. e., by specifying
the structure of an application and the desired state into which an application

A. Brogi et al. (Eds.): ESOCC 2020, LNCS 12054, pp. 97–112, 2020.
https://doi.org/10.1007/978-3-030-44769-4_8

or parts thereof have to be transferred [15]. The declarative approach is indeed considered the most appropriate for application deployment and configuration management [6,17,31], as also witnessed by the multitude of existing deployment technologies following such an approach, e. g., AWS CloudFormation, Chef, Juju, Kubernetes, Puppet, and Terraform, just to mention some.

At the same time, existing declarative deployment technologies differ in supported features and mechanisms, as well as in the modeling language for describing the application and its desired state. Open standards (e. g., TOSCA [23,24]) have been proposed to ensure the portability of cloud application deployments from a provider/technology to another. However, major providers and deployment technologies are currently not supporting such standards. This makes it difficult to compare technologies based on their capabilities, select a deployment technology that is suited to accomplish given requirements, and to migrate a deployment model from one technology to another.

In our previous work, we tackled the aforementioned issue by starting from most used declarative deployment technologies and by distilling their essential parts into what we called the *Essential Deployment Metamodel* (EDMM) [31]. We also implemented a concrete YAML-based language for modeling applications with EDMM. Further, we proposed the *EDMM Modeling and Transformation Framework* [30] allowing to exploit EDMM as a "normalized metamodel" to deploy the same application with different technologies: After specifying the application with EDMM, the transformation framework can automatically generate the deployment artifacts needed to deploy the application with the selected target deployment technology. Notably, by simply re-running the transformation framework with a different target deployment technology, the same application specification can be used to migrate the deployment of an application from one technology to another [30].

The EDMM Modeling and Transformation Framework, however, currently supports the deployment of multi-component applications only on virtual compute resources such as virtual machines or containers (i. e., IaaS). In this paper, we overcome this limitation by providing the following two main contributions:

1. We extend the EDMM Modeling and Transformation Framework to deploy application components also on *PaaS platforms*, as well as to exploit existing *SaaS services* to implement components.
2. We present the *EDMM Decision Support Framework* allowing us to determine which declarative deployment technologies can be used to deploy a given EDMM model.

The latter is intended to help application developers to avoid trying to deploy an application with a deployment technology not offering the needed features, e. g., Juju is intended to automate the deployment of multi-component applications over IaaS-based virtual machines, but it cannot be used to deploy application components on PaaS platforms.

The rest of the paper is organized as follows. Section 2 presents the fundamentals and motivations for our work. Section 3 introduces our approach and Sect. 4 presents the overall system architecture on which our contributions are based

on. Section 5 describes the prototypical implementation while, finally, Sect. 6 and
Sect. 7 discuss related work and draw some concluding remarks, respectively.

2 Background and Motivations

We hereafter introduce the fundamental notions and terms needed in the rest
of this paper. We also illustrate a simple yet effective example motivating our
work.

2.1 Deployment Models and Deployment Technologies

For automating the deployment of an application, *deployment models* are typically used to describe the desired result: In general, there is a distinction between
imperative deployment models and *declarative deployment models* [15]. Declarative models, in general, declare exactly *what* the desired state into which an application or parts thereof are transferred to. In contrast, imperative models define
the exact process of *how* the desired state is reached using executable workflows
or programmatic actions. Hence, a declarative deployment model specifies the
structure of components to be deployed and defines the desired state in the form
of properties or configurations for those components, but it requires a deployment
technology that interprets the model and derives the exact order of operations to
reach this state. For example, in Terraform an application developer creates a set
of files defining the cloud resources the foreseen application requires. Terraform,
when executing the application deployment, analyzes the resource definitions
and derives a workflow having exact steps and actions required to roll-out the
desired state defined by the application developer.

In industry and research, declarative deployment models are widely accepted
as the most appropriate approach for application deployment and configuration management [17]. As a result, a plethora of different technologies have
been developed following this approach such as Chef, Puppet, AWS CloudFormation, Terraform, and Kubernetes. However, application systems are often in
constant change and, besides the major effort for adapting the application itself,
the associated deployment models must be adapted using different or additional
deployment technologies. Deployment technologies are heterogeneous regarding
supported features and modeling languages, and this could result in major efforts
whenever an application and its actual deployment have to be adapted to changes
or evolutions in the application requirements. Therefore, it is crucial to postpone
as late as possible the choice of which deployment technology to use. An even
better approach for application developers is to define their application structure and desired state in a technology-agnostic manner, e.g., by exploiting a
normalized metamodel. With a normalized modeling of the application and of
its desired state, one can indeed automatically generate the deployment artifacts
needed to deploy the application using a given deployment technology.

In our previous work [31], a systematic review of widely used declarative
deployment technologies revealed the Essential Deployment Metamodel

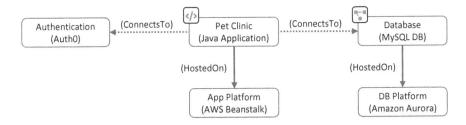

Fig. 1. Simple cloud application which can only be deployed by using a subset of one of the top-most deployment technologies.

(EDMM). EDMM provides a normalized metamodel as a technology-independent baseline for deployment automation research and provides a common understanding of declarative deployment models. EDMM comprises the essential parts supported by well-known technologies and facilitates the transformation in different concrete technologies by a semantic mapping, which avoids deployment technology lock-in.

2.2 Motivating Scenario

As a motivating scenario for our work, we consider a rather simple cloud application. Figure 1 depicts the scenario and shows a Java application, named "Pet Clinic", in the center that is hosted on *AWS Beanstalk*, the platform as a service (PaaS) offering by Amazon Web Services (AWS). This application connects to a fully managed database platform, *Amazon Aurora* which is a managed MySQL database as a service (DBaaS) offering by AWS. Both the Java application as well as the Database component have an artifact attached (cf. Fig. 1), which is, for example, a packaged JAR file in case of the Java application and a SQL file containing the actual database schema and initial data in case of the database component. The left hand side of Fig. 1 depicts a software as a service (SaaS) offering. For this scenario, we envision the usage of a managed authentication service to provide single sign-on between different applications. The Java application, therefore, needs to connect or redirect users to this authentication service to authenticate and authorize them.

Even if simple, this application cannot be deployed by various deployment technologies (and by almost all of the most popular technologies we analysed in our previous work [31]). This scenario, as it is, is only fully supported by Terraform, as Terraform provides different plugins for different cloud providers and services. Indeed, parts of the application structure are supported by other deployment technologies as well. For example, AWS CloudFormation, Ansible, and Chef are capable to deploy applications to AWS Beanstalk. However, SaaS hosted components are not widely supported—Terraform supports many popular SaaS offerings. Alternatively, custom deployment automation tools are required that are most likely offered by SaaS providers.

To fully automate the deployment, a decision support system is needed to determine which declarative deployment technologies can be used to fully deploy a given application deployment model. It is important that application developers receive early deployability feedback immediately while modeling the application. Further, to overcome the technology-specific differences, EDMM as a normalized metamodel provides a solid baseline for deployment automation research and a common understanding of declarative deployment models. The knowledge of essential parts supported by well-known technologies facilitates transformation to different deployment technologies, which avoids deployment technology lock-in.

2.3   Essential Deployment Metamodel

The EDMM was introduced as the result of a systematic review of technologies that contain the essential elements of declarative deployment models to enable the comparison and selection of appropriate technologies [31]. The EDMM enables a common understanding of declarative deployment models and, thus, eases the comparison and selection of appropriate technologies. It defines *Components* as physical, functional, or logical units of an application. Further, *Relations* are defined as directed physical, functional, or logical dependencies between exactly two components. Both can be typed using *Component Types* and *Relation Types* to express reusable entities that specify a certain semantic. Further, EDMM defines *Properties* as a way to describe the current state or prescribe the desired target state or configuration of a component or relation. Moreover, *Operations* are used in declarative deployment models to define executable procedures performed to manage a component or relation. Such operations provide hook points and are executed by deployment technologies to implement certain requirements during application deployment. Finally, the EDMM also defines *Artifacts* such that an artifact implements a component or operation and is therefore required for the execution of the application deployment as well as the final application system. The terminology of EDMM is considered as baseline in the course of this paper.

3   Transforming EDMM Models into Deployment Technology-Specific Models

In this section, we introduce our approach to transform a technology-independent application deployment model based on EDMM into a *deployment technology-specific model* (DTSM) while ensuring supportability by respective deployment technologies. As depicted in Fig. 2, the approach is structured in four steps: (1) Create EDMM Model, (2) Check Supportability with Different Technologies, (3) Transform EDMM Model into DTSM, and (4) Execute DTSM. In the following, we will provide details on each of such steps. Notably, the grey-dashed boxes represent already existing building blocks [30] that are extended in this work, while dark boxes highlight the new main contributions of this work.

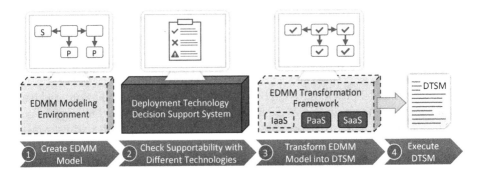

Fig. 2. Transformation of EDMM Models while ensuring their transformability to specific deployment technologies (based on [30])

3.1   Step 1: Technology-Independent Application Modeling

The modeling of the application is done in EDMM to provide a normalized and technology-independent model. The model is composed graphically by using the *EDMM Modeling Environment* that we proposed in our previous work [30]. The application developer uses the modeling environment to compose a cloud application that, for instance, has the structure as depicted in Fig. 1. The creation of certain EDMM components is based on existing types that are provided by the modeling environment. At any time, the resulting model is compliant to the EDMM in YAML specification[1] and can be exported. To improve the modeling experience and to tackle the issue that an application developer needs live feedback whether a certain deployment technology is capable of deploying the current model, the modeling environment uses the *Deployment Technology Decision Support System*, which is presented next.

3.2   Step 2: Check Deployment Technology Support

In this work, we introduce the *Deployment Technology Decision Support System* building block as shown in Fig. 2. Having this, an application developer can immediately check whether a EDMM model can be transformed into a *deployment technology-specific model* (DTSM) used by a certain deployment technology. The latter obviously holds if the EDMM model includes entities and features supported by a deployment technology. For example, the user gets immediate feedback if a modeled application is supported by Terraform, AWS CloudFormation, Juju, or Ansible, to name just a few. Hereby, the EDMM modeling environment triggers the decision support module whenever an application developer changes the EDMM model. This module consumes the current EDMM model and checks whether and to which degree the model is transformable into a DTSM of a specific deployment technology. The decision support module generates a

---

[1] https://github.com/UST-EDMM/spec-yaml.

report that is presented to application developer. Based on this report, we facilitate decision support by checking transformability into a specific deployment technology.

3.3   Step 3: Transform EDMM Model into DTSM

For transformation, the EDMM model is consumed by the *EDMM Transformation Framework* module. In this work, we build on top of the existing EDMM Transformation Framework, which we proposed in a previous work [30]. This system is already able to transform EDMM models containing virtual compute resources (IaaS), i.e., operating systems, virtual machines, or containers, and the software that needs to be deployed on them including their configuration and orchestration. To further support cloud application scenarios, we extend the module to comprise certain transformation rules for *PaaS* and *SaaS* component types such that EDMM models containing these can be transformed into respective deployment technology-specific models (DTSM). For example, there are transformation rules for AWS CloudFormation to transform possibly modeled PaaS components. Further, we provide rules, e.g., for Terraform, to transform respective SaaS components into the deployment technology's counterpart. Due to the extensibility and pluggable architecture of the EDMM Transformation Framework, this only leads to changes in the respective plugins to implement the transformation rules accordingly for PaaS and SaaS.

3.4   Step 4: Technology-Specific Deployment Execution

The output of the EDMM Transformation Framework is a deployment technology-specific model (DTSM). For example, in Terraform this will be a configuration that consists of one or more `*.tf` files referencing respective artifacts to deploy. In our approach, we deliberately output technology-specific models to facilitate DevOps activities such as infrastructure as code (IaC) in modern software development environments. By producing human- and machine-readable model files, we enable that transformed results are managed using version control system, e.g., to trigger Git-based continuous integration and delivery (CI/CD) workflows. Notably, by simply re-running the EDMM Transformation Framework targeting a different deployment technology, the same EDMM model can be used to generate the respective technology-specific deployment model [30].

4   System Architecture of the EDMM Modeling, Decision Support, and Transformation System

Figure 3 shows the overall system architecture of the proposed approach. To support the depicted approach from above, several components are required. The *Modeling Tool* is a web-based modeling environment that uses a *REST API* to retrieve and update its data. The *Types Repository* contains reusable EDMM component types that an application developer can use for modeling and provide

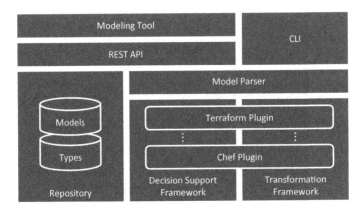

Fig. 3. System architecture supporting modeling, decision support, and transformation of EDMM models into DTSMs.

the respective technical and platform abstractions. An application developer uses these types through the *Modeling Tool* to graphically compose the structure of the EDMM model, which are stored and manged in the *Models Repository*.

To check the transformation support and facilitate decision support, the *Decision Support Framework* is introduced as depicted in Fig. 3. To transform an EDMM model the *Transformation Framework* is envisioned. Both components employ a plugin architecture that supports the integration of various deployment technologies in an extensible and pluggable way. Each plugin employs the knowledge whether a certain EDMM component is supported for transformation or not. The Decision Support Framework is able to utilize the plugins to check a given EDMM model and to produce a report what components (or component types) are not supported. Further, the plugins carry the logic and transformation rules to transform an EDMM model into a deployment technology-specific model (DTSM), which includes the creation of respective technology-specific directory structures, files, and artifacts. The *Model Parser* consumes a textual EDMM model in YAML and creates an internal data structure used by the Decision Support Framework, the Transformation Framework, and the respective plugins.

In addition, the system offers a command-line interface (CLI) that can be either used directly by the user or integrated into any automated workflow, e. g., to facilitate IaC by using it within a CI/CD pipeline. Either way, using the CLI or the web-based interface, an application developer can select the desired target deployment technology in which an EDMM model should be transformed.

5   Validation: Prototypical Implementation

In this section, we illustrate a prototypical implementation of the proposed approach and the foreseen system architecture. As mentioned before, we base our prototype on two existing components: (i) Eclipse Winery [21] as the EDMM Modeling Environment and (ii) the EDMM Transformation Framework [30].

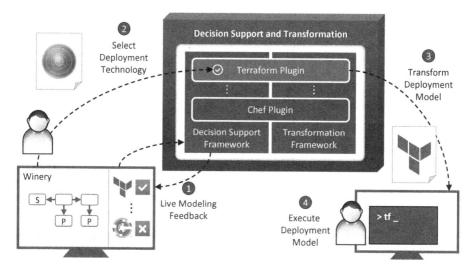

Fig. 4. Prototype flow demonstrating the modeling, decision support, and transformation of an EDMM model to Terraform.eps

5.1 Overview

Eclipse Winery is a web-based environment to graphically model TOSCA-based application topologies. It provides a *back-end* to manage component and relation types, their property definitions, operations, and artifacts. Further, it provides a *Topology Modeler* component which enables the graphical composition of application deployment models including the specification of the components' properties. Even though Winery was initially developed as TOSCA modeling environment, in previous work we showed that EDMM can be mapped to TOSCA [31].

First of all, we extended the EDMM modeling language and introduced new built-in types to respectively cover the motivation scenario depicted in Fig. 1. We extended Winery's Topology Modeler in order to provide a live checking of application models. Winery calls the *Decision Support Framework* whenever the application developer changes the EDMM model, e. g., when adding or removing components. For this purpose, the EDMM Transformation Framework was extended by the *Decision Support Framework* component. Due to the fact that the EDMM Transformation Framework employs a plugin architecture, we extended the existing plugin interface and its `checkModel()` lifecycle method to return a respective result set that highlights the components that are not supported. The communication between Winery and the EDMM Transformation Framework is achieved using REST over HTTP. In addition to the existing CLI of the EDMM Transformation Framework, we now also provide a REST API over HTTP to trigger the transformation for a certain target deployment technology.

EDMM in YAML	Transformation to Terraform

``
components:
  # other components
  # omitted for brevity
  authentication:
    type: auth0
    properties:
      domain: example.test
      identifier: ...
      scopes: user,admin
      client_id: abc
      client_secret: xyz123abc
``
	``
	resource "auth0_resource_server" "authentication" {
	  name = "authentication"
	  identifier = "..."
	  signing_alg = "RS256"
	  scopes {
	    value = "user"
	  }
	  scopes {
	    value = "admin"
	  }
	  ...
	}
	``

Fig. 5. Terraform transformation mapping.

To use the prototype[2], we created a Docker Compose configuration able to start a pre-configured and ready-to-use EDMM Modeling, Decision Support, and Transformation System. All changes and improvements in the course of this paper have been merged to the *master* branches of the respective repositories.

5.2 Modeling and Transformation Flow

In this section, we show the overall modeling, decision support, and transformation flow of our implemented prototype. The flow is explained based on a modeling example that follows our motivating scenario in Fig. 1. Further, we chose Terraform to describe the flow based on a concrete deployment technology.

Application developers start the integrated EDMM Modeling, Decision Support, and Transformation System. By using the EDMM Modeling Tool, users are able to model their desired application structure. As depicted in Fig. 4, the user composes the structure by drag-and-drop desired components to the canvas. Additionally, users define respective relations between them by connecting the components. To facilitate decision support, we implemented live modeling feedback directly in the modeling environment (cf. 1 in Fig. 4). Whenever, the overall model is changed, the EDMM Decision Support Framework is triggered. All available plugins of the Decision Support and Transformation Framework are queried to check if the current model contains unsupported components. The modeling environments retrieves the result and presents it to the application developer. For example, a model that reflects the scenario depicted in Fig. 4, can be transformed into "Terraform" but not into "Chef". If a model is supported by one or more deployment technologies, application developer can export the model according to the EDMM in YAML specification. From here, the user executes the transformation, i. e., using the EDMM CLI, and selects the desired and supported deployment technology (cf. 2 in Fig. 4). The output of the system is the transformed output according to the need a corresponding deployment technology requires. For example, in case of Terraform, it will be a

---

[2] https://github.com/UST-EDMM.

ready to use working directory containing Terraform configuration files (cf. 3 in Fig. 4). Lastly, the application developer is able to execute the actual deployment using the tools and interfaces provided by the deployment technology. For instance, Terraform provides a CLI to "apply" the generated configuration. At this point, application developers can use their well-known development environments and tools to deploy and manage their applications (cf. 4 in Fig. 4). For example, the generated deployment artifacts can be versioned in revision control systems, such as Git, to facilitate the use of automated CI/CD pipelines.

We executed the modeling and transformation flow according to our motivation scenario from Sect. 2.2 (the full EDMM modeling example in YAML is available online[3] on GitHub). In Fig. 5, we show an excerpt a modeled EDMM-based SaaS component and its mapping to the actual Terraform resource. In such cases, the system generates a respective `auth0_resource_server` resource that maps to the corresponding properties. For this special case, the Terraform plugin comprises a special transformation rule to split the comma-separated list of the EDMM property `scopes` into separate `scopes` blocks.

6 Related Work

The problem of automating the deployment of multi-component applications on cloud platform is well-known [29], with most of existing approaches being declarative [6]. The OASIS standard TOSCA [23,24] is one of the most known approaches in this direction, as it provides a standardized language for specifying multi-component application in a portable way. Specified applications can then be deployed on cloud infrastructures, provided that the latter support the declarative processing of TOSCA application specifications, e. g., by featuring the OpenTOSCA runtime [7]. Our approach differs from TOSCA, as we aim at automatically generating the deployment artifacts needed to deploy an application with an existing technology as it is.

Similar considerations apply to other approach à la TOSCA, e. g., CAMEL [1], MODAClouds [12], Panarello et al. [26], SeaClouds [8] and trans-cloud [9], just to mention some. Starting from a vendor-agnostic specification of a multi-component application, all such approaches enable its deployment on heterogeneous clouds. This is done by relying on additional components offered by the targeted clouds or on ad-hoc middleware platforms processing the application specification to deploy their components on heterogeneous clouds. Our approach also starts from agnostic representations of multi-component applications, but it rather automatically generates different deployment artifacts for different deployment technologies, in order to directly utilize them to deploy applications on heterogeneous clouds.

In this perspective, closer approaches to ours are those by Di Cosmo et al. [10,11] and by Guillén et al. [16], which both share our baseline idea of generating concrete deployment artifacts from a vendor-agnostic specification of a multi-component application and of its desired configuration. Di Cosmo et al.

---

[3] http://bit.ly/3akWSYR.

indeed propose a solution for automatically synthesizing a concrete deployment for a multi-component application in a cloud environment, based on a high-level specification of the application and its desired state. Their solution is however targeting OpenStack cloud deployments, while we target 13 different production-ready deployment technologies, each allowing to deploy applications on various different cloud infrastructures [30].

Guillén et al. [16] instead present a framework for developing multi-service application that are decoupled from the architecture, services, and libraries provided by cloud vendors. Based on additional metadata indicating application requirements, the framework generates cloud compliant software artifacts that are deployed in each cloud platform. This approach is even closer to ours, as the same application can be deployed differently by re-running the framework and instructing it to target different clouds. The approach by Guillén et al. however differs from ours since it is intended to process applications whose sources are available to the framework, while our approach only considers the application specification and the final packaged software artifact. This allows us to process a wider set of applications, as we allow developers to reuse *black-box* third-party software or SaaS services to implement the components of an applications. Similar considerations apply to the solution proposed by Alipour and Liu [3], who exploit model-to-model transformation to obtain a cloud specific application deployment from a vendor-independent application.

Other solutions worth mentioning are OAM [22], Kompose [28] and Compose Object [13]. The OAM has recently been proposed to allow developers and operators to separately describe containerized applications with a vendor-agnostic representation. It indeed allows developers to describe what containerized components do and how they should be configured, while operators can complete application specifications by configuring runtime environments. Obtained application specifications can then be run on Kubernetes with Rudr[4]. Our approach can be used for the same purposes, and it can be used not only for running containerized applications on Kubernetes, but also for running other types of applications on other deployment technologies. Similar considerations apply to Kompose and Compose Object, both enabling the deployment of containerized applications on Kubernetes. Kompose does so by automatically generating a Kubernetes deployment for containerized applications specified in Docker Compose, while Compose Object is a Kubernetes plugin for directly running such a kind of applications on Kubernetes clusters.

It is worth noting that our approach of transforming EDMM models to deployment artifacts is essentially a M2M (Model-to-Model) transformation [20]. We could have hence implemented our approach by suitably configuring existing frameworks, e. g., ATL [19], QVTd [14], or ADOxx [2], which already come with tooling for graphical modeling and transformation. However, we decided to implement our solution as a lightweight command-line tool, as it offers a convenient way to be integrated in CI/CD pipelines and supporting DevOps [5].

---

[4] https://github.com/oam-dev/rudr.

It is also worth noting that our approach is inspired by the work by Papazoglou and van den Heuvel [27], who firstly outlined the possibility of *blueprinting* cloud-based application deployments, i. e., specifying the deployment of multi-component applications in a reusable way, and to exploit such specifications to automate application deployments. Such a foundational idea is the rationale behind our EDMM modeling and transformation framework. Our framework was also inspired by Andrikopoulos et al. [4], who firstly investigated the commonalities among existing cloud modeling languages and collected them in the so-called GENTL topology language. In our previous work [31] we followed a similar approach for obtaining the EDMM itself, which we then exploit in this and former work to develop the EDMM modeling and transformation framework.

In summary, to the best of our knowledge, ours is the first approach automatically generating the artifacts needed to process multi-component applications using different existing deployment technologies by also allowing to reuse third-party software and SaaS services to implement some components of an application. It does so by starting from the widely accepted idea of specifying an application in a technology-agnostic way, without requiring cloud providers to support additional runtimes, and by piggybacking on existing, production-ready deployment technology to actually enact application deployments.

7   Conclusions and Future Work

The EDMM modeling and transformation framework [30,31] allows to deploy a multi-component application using different, existing declarative deployment technologies. It indeed features a YAML-based language distilling the essentials of existing technologies, which allows to describe a multi-component application and its desired state. Deploying an application or migrating from a deployment to another then only requires to feed the EDMM transformation framework with the application specification. By selecting the target deployment technology, the transformation framework will automatically generate the deployment artifacts needed to deploy the specified application using such technology. This currently comes at the price of only exploiting IaaS-based virtual machines or containers as compute nodes where to deploy the components of an application.

In this paper, we presented an extension of the EDMM Modeling and Transformation Framework allowing to deploy application components on PaaS platforms and to exploit existing SaaS services to implement components of an application. We also proposed a decision support system allowing to determine which declarative deployment technologies can actually be used to deploy an application specified with EDMM, as some existing technology may not be offering all features needed to deploy the specified application (e. g., Juju and CFEngine are not supporting the deployment application components on PaaS platforms). To illustrate the helpfulness of our extension, we also shown how it was exploited on a running example, which, despite simple, would have not be addressed by the original EDMM Modeling and Transformation Framework.

The contributions in this paper present a first step towards cloud-native application deployments using EDMM. However, in future work, it needs to be analyzed which general features a declarative deployment technology has to support to deploy *arbitrary* cloud-native applications comprising, e. g., FaaS components and arbitrary other managed services such as message queues. Therefore, we will first analyze the requirements on deployment technologies to support deploying arbitrary cloud-native applications and integrate required mechanisms and plugins afterwards into our system. Further, we plan to extend the intelligence of the decision support system by allowing to measure the *distance* from an application specification to its deployment on a given technology, e. g., in terms of the least amount of adaptation updates that must be applied to the application to allow its deployment on such technology. We also plan to include an adaptation recommender in the decision support system, capable of indicating to the application developer the changes to apply to an application to allow its deployment on a desired technology, e. g., indicating to replace the PaaS platform used to host some components with a IaaS-based software stack, so as to enable the deployment of an application on Juju and CFEngine.

Acknowledgements. This work is partially funded by the EU project *RADON* (825040), the DFG project *SustainLife* (379522012), and the projects *AMaCA* (POR-FSE) and *DECLware* (University of Pisa, PRA_2018_66).

References

1. Achilleos, A.P., et al.: The cloud application modelling and execution language. J. Cloud Comput. **8**(1), 1–25 (2019). https://doi.org/10.1186/s13677-019-0138-7
2. ADOxx: ADOxx.org (2020). https://www.adoxx.org. Accessed 13 Feb 2020
3. Alipour, H., Liu, Y.: Model driven deployment of auto-scaling services on multiple clouds. In: 2018 IEEE International Conference on Software Architecture Companion (ICSA-C), pp. 93–96 (2018)
4. Andrikopoulos, V., Reuter, A., Gómez Sáez, S., Leymann, F.: A GENTL approach for cloud application topologies. In: Villari, M., Zimmermann, W., Lau, K.-K. (eds.) ESOCC 2014. LNCS, vol. 8745, pp. 148–159. Springer, Heidelberg (2014). https://doi.org/10.1007/978-3-662-44879-3_11
5. Belmont, J.M.: Hands-On Continuous Integration and Delivery, 1st edn. Packt Publishing, Birmingham (2018)
6. Bergmayr, A., et al.: A systematic review of cloud modeling languages. ACM Comput. Surv. **51**(1), 1–38 (2018)
7. Binz, T., et al.: OpenTOSCA – a runtime for TOSCA-based cloud applications. In: Basu, S., Pautasso, C., Zhang, L., Fu, X. (eds.) ICSOC 2013. LNCS, vol. 8274, pp. 692–695. Springer, Heidelberg (2013). https://doi.org/10.1007/978-3-642-45005-1_62
8. Brogi, A., et al.: EU project seaclouds - adaptive management of service-based applications across multiple clouds. In: Proceedings of the 4th International Conference on Cloud Computing and Services Science (CLOSER 2014), pp. 758–763. SciTePress (2014)
9. Carrasco, J., Durán, F., Pimentel, E.: Trans-cloud: CAMP/TOSCA-based bidimensional cross-cloud. Comput. Stand. Interfaces **58**, 167–179 (2018)

10. Di Cosmo, R., Eiche, A., Mauro, J., Zacchiroli, S., Zavattaro, G., Zwolakowski, J.: Automatic deployment of services in the cloud with Aeolus Blender. In: Barros, A., Grigori, D., Narendra, N.C., Dam, H.K. (eds.) ICSOC 2015. LNCS, vol. 9435, pp. 397–411. Springer, Heidelberg (2015). https://doi.org/10.1007/978-3-662-48616-0_28

11. Di Cosmo, R., et al.: Automated synthesis and deployment of cloud applications. In: Proceedings of the 29th ACM/IEEE International Conference on Automated Software Engineering, pp. 211–222. ACM (2014)

12. Di Nitto, E., Matthews, P., Petcu, D., Solberg, A. (eds.): Model-Driven Development and Operation of Multi-Cloud Applications: The MODAClouds Approach. SAST. Springer, Cham (2017). https://doi.org/10.1007/978-3-319-46031-4

13. Docker Inc: Compose Object (2020). https://github.com/docker/compose-on-kubernetes. Accessed 13 Feb 2020

14. Eclipse Foundation: Eclipse QVTd (QVT Declarative) (2020). https://projects.eclipse.org/projects/modeling.mmt.qvtd. Accessed 13 Feb 2020

15. Endres, C., Breitenbücher, U., Falkenthal, M., Kopp, O., Leymann, F., Wettinger, J.: Declarative vs. imperative: two modeling patterns for the automated deployment of applications. In: Proceedings of the 9th International Conference on Pervasive Patterns and Applications (PATTERNS), pp. 22–27. Xpert Publishing Services (2017)

16. Guillén, J., Miranda, J., Murillo, J.M., Canal, C.: A service-oriented framework for developing cross cloud migratable software. J. Syst. Softw. **86**(9), 2294–2308 (2013)

17. Herry, H., Anderson, P., Wickler, G.: Automated planning for configuration changes. In: Proceedings of the 25th International Conference on Large Installation System Administration (LISA 2011), pp. 57–68. USENIX (2011)

18. Humble, J., Farley, D.: Continuous Delivery: Reliable Software Releases Through Build, Test, and Deployment Automation. Addison-Wesley, Boston (2010)

19. Jouault, F., Allilaire, F., Bézivin, J., Kurtev, I.: ATL: a model transformation tool. Sci. Comput. Program. **72**(1), 31–39 (2008)

20. Kahani, N., Bagherzadeh, M., Cordy, J.R., Dingel, J., Varró, D.: Survey and classification of model transformation tools. Softw. Syst. Model. **18**(4), 2361–2397 (2018). https://doi.org/10.1007/s10270-018-0665-6

21. Kopp, O., Binz, T., Breitenbücher, U., Leymann, F.: Winery – a modeling tool for TOSCA-based cloud applications. In: Basu, S., Pautasso, C., Zhang, L., Fu, X. (eds.) ICSOC 2013. LNCS, vol. 8274, pp. 700–704. Springer, Heidelberg (2013). https://doi.org/10.1007/978-3-642-45005-1_64

22. Microsoft and Alibaba Cloud: Open Application Model (2020). https://oam.dev. Accessed 13 Feb 2020

23. OASIS: Topology and Orchestration Specification for Cloud Applications (TOSCA) Version 1.0. Organization for the Advancement of Structured Information Standards (OASIS) (2013)

24. OASIS: TOSCA Simple Profile in YAML Version 1.2. Organization for the Advancement of Structured Information Standards (OASIS) (2019)

25. Oppenheimer, D., Ganapathi, A., Patterson, D.A.: Why do internet services fail, and what can be done about it? In: Proceedings of the 4th Conference on USENIX Symposium on Internet Technologies and Systems (USITS 2003). USENIX (2003)

26. Panarello, A., Breitenbücher, U., Leymann, F., Puliafito, A., Zimmermann, M.: Automating the deployment of multi-cloud applications in federated cloud environments. In: Proceedings of the 10th EAI International Conference on Performance Evaluation Methodologies and Tools, pp. 194–201. Institute for Computer Sciences, Social-Informatics and Telecommunications Engineering (ICST) (2017)
27. Papazoglou, M.P., van den Heuvel, W.J.: Blueprinting the Cloud. IEEE Internet Comput. **15**(6), 74–79 (2011)
28. The Kubenetes Authors: Kompose (2020). https://kompose.io. Accessed 13 Feb 2020
29. Wettinger, J., Andrikopoulos, V., Leymann, F., Strauch, S.: Middleware-oriented deployment automation for cloud applications. IEEE Trans. Cloud Comput. **6**(4), 1054–1066 (2018)
30. Wurster, M., et al.: The EDMM modeling and transformation system. In: Service-Oriented Computing – ICSOC 2019 Workshops. Springer, December 2019
31. Wurster, M., et al.: The essential deployment metamodel: a systematic review of deployment automation technologies. SICS Softw.-Intensive Cyber-Phys. Syst. (2019). https://doi.org/10.1007/s00450-019-00412-x

Blockchain-Based Healthcare Workflows in Federated Hospital Clouds

Armando Ruggeri[1], Maria Fazio[1,2(✉)], Antonio Celesti[1,3], and Massimo Villari[1]

[1] MIFT Department, University of Messina, Messina, Italy
{armruggeri,mfazio,acelesti,mvillari}@unime.it
[2] IRCCS Centro Neurolesi "Bonino-Pulejo", Messina, Italy
maria.fazio@irccsme.it
[3] INdAM - GNCS Group, Rome, Italy

Abstract. Nowadays, security is one of the biggest concerns against the wide adoption of on-demand Cloud services. Specifically, one of the major challenges in many application domains is the certification of exchanged data. For these reasons, since the advent of bitcoin and smart contracts respectively in 2009 and 2015, healthcare has been one of the major sectors in which Blockchain has been studied. In this paper, by exploiting the intrinsic security feature of the Blockchain technology, we propose a Software as a Service (SaaS) that enables a hospital Cloud to establish a federation with other ones in order to arrange a virtual healthcare team including doctors coming from different federated hospitals that cooperate in order to carry out a healthcare workflow. Experiments conducted in a prototype implemented by means of the Ethereum platform show that the overhead introduced by Blockchain is acceptable considering the obvious gained advantages in terms of security.

Keywords: Blockchain · Smart contract · Healthcare · Cloud · SaaS · Hospital · Federation

1 Introduction

The demographic growth of the last century combined with the increased life expectancy and shortage of specialized medical personnel in Europe [1,2] has made the access to proper medical treatments one of the major concerns of the last decade. The recent advancements brought by the Cloud computing paradigm have been only partially taken in consideration by hospitals and more in general medical centers so far, in spite of a considerable number of scientific initiatives in eHealth [3]. In particular, a crucial aspect that have slowed the "Cloudisation" of hospitals has regarded security of exchanged data. It is essential that shared pieces of healthcare data are certified and their integrity guaranteed in order to prevent that pieces of clinical information are either intentionally or accidentally altered.

In recent years different solutions have been proposed to solve such an issue: among these, the Blockchain technology, thanks to its intrinsic features of data

© IFIP International Federation for Information Processing 2020
Published by Springer Nature Switzerland AG 2020
A. Brogi et al. (Eds.): ESOCC 2020, LNCS 12054, pp. 113–121, 2020.
https://doi.org/10.1007/978-3-030-44769-4_9

non-repudiation and immutability, has aroused a great interest in both scientific and industrial communities. Founded in 2009 as the technology behind Bitcoin [4], it has completely revolutionized traditional encryption-based security systems, introducing a new approach able to apply hash-based encryption in which information is saved on blocks and each block is linked to the previous one via a hash coding. One of the major applications of Blockchain regards smart contract, i.e., a computer protocol aimed at to digitally facilitate, verify, and enforce the negotiation of an agreement between subjects without the need of a certification third party.

Blockchain technologies have been increasingly recognized as a technology able to address existing information access problems in different applications domains including healthcare. In fact, it can potentially enhance the perception of safety around medical operators improving access to healthcare services that are guaranteed by a greater transparency, security and privacy, traceability and efficiency.

In this paper, by exploiting the intrinsic security feature of the Blockchain technology, we propose a clinical workflow that:

- enables to create a virtual healthcare team including doctors belonging to different federated hospitals;
- enables to share patients' electronic health records among virtual healthcare team members preserving sensitive data;
- adopts smart contracts in order to make the transactions related to applied therapies trackable and irreversible;
- enables security in electronic medical records when they are accessed by patients and medical professionals;
- guarantees the authenticity of whole federated healthcare workflow.

In general, the proposed solution allows tracking the treatment of patients that can take place in different federated hospitals from the hospitalization to the dismissal, supporting the whole medical personnel in planning treatments. Moreover, we discuss a Software as a Service (SaaS) that allows to apply the workflow.

The remainder of this paper is organized as follows. A brief overview of most recent initiatives about the adoption of Blockchain in healthcare is provided in Sect. 2. Motivations are discussed in Sect. 3. The design of the SaaS is presented in Sect. 4, whereas its implementation adopting Flak, MongoDB and Ethereum is described in Sect. 5. Experiments demonstrating that the overhead introduced by Blockchain is acceptable considering the obvious gained advantages in terms of security are discussed in Sect. 6. In the end, conclusions and light to the future are discussed in Sect. 7.

2   Related Work

In recent years numerous research studies have been conducted in healthcare domain with particular attention to the application of the Blockchain technology [5].

Blockchain can drastically improve the security of hospital information systems as discussed in many recent scientific works [6–9]. However, up to now, most of scientific initiatives are either theoretical or at an early stage and it is not always clear which protocols and frameworks should be used in order to carry out system implementation that can be deployed in real healthcare environments.

Blockchain has been increasingly recognized as a tool able to address existing open information access issues [10]. In fact, it is possible to improve access to health services by using the Blockchain technology in order to achieve greater transparency, security and privacy, traceability and efficiency. In this regard, a solution adopting Blockchain with the purpose to guarantee authorized access to the patients' medical information is discussed in [11]. In particular, mechanisms to preserve both patient's identity and the integrity of his/her clinical history is proposed.

Another application of Blockchain regards the supply chain in the pharmaceutical sector and the development of measures against counterfeit drugs. While the development of new drugs involves substantial costs related to studies in order to evaluate the safety and updating of the drug, the use of smart contracts guarantees informed consent procedures and allows in certifying the quality of data [12].

Differently from the above mentioned most recent scientific initiatives, this paper describes a practical implementation of how Blockchain can be used to improve medical analysis treatments empowering collaboration among a group of federated hospitals.

3   Motivation

This paper aims at recommending new approaches able to harmonize health procedures with new technologies in order to guarantee patients' safety and therapeutic certification, verifying that every doctor's choice is immutably recorded, with the purpose to guarantee and track that all hospital protocols have been scrupulously followed. Furthermore, the proposed system was designed and implemented in order support a virtual healthcare team including a selected group of doctors in order to make a clear picture about the patient's clinical status especially in a critical condition. The anonymized patient's health data and clinical analyses are shared among doctors participating in the federation of hospitals while the patient's data are never shared.

Figure 1 describes a scenario where patient's clinical data is shared across participants to a federation of hospitals for cooperation and knowledge sharing, and the data exchanged is certified on a private Blockchain where all participants are known and trusted.

Specifically, the proposed healthcare workflow adopted in the proposed system includes the following phases:

1. **Hospitalization**: patient reaches the hospital and personal details, date and type of visit are recorded;

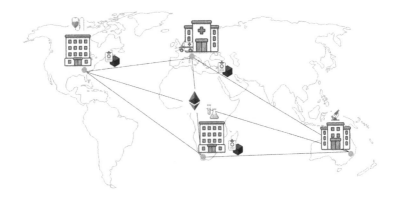

Fig. 1. Federation of hospitals: clinical data is shared across participants for cooperation

2. **Analysis**: patient follows the procedures to ascertain the nature of the disease (e.g., blood tests, clinical examinations, possible CT scans, RX laboratory tests, etc) and the results of the analyzes are saved on a Cloud storage space inside the hospital Cloud managed on a dedicated directory for the patient identified by a visit identification code;
3. **MD evaluation**: doctor analyzes the results of clinical analysis and prepares a report with the therapy to be followed;
4. **Federated teleconference**: a selected pool of doctors belonging to the hospital federation is invited to participate to a virtual healthcare team in a teleconference in order to clarify the patient's clinical situation. The patient's health data and clinical analysis are shared with the other doctors belonging to the virtual healthcare team; patient's details are never shared;
5. **Drug administration**: the hospitalized patient is constantly monitored by nurses who apply treatments based on therapeutic indications; each treatment is recorded.

4   System Design

Once the virtual healthcare team has identified the disease, it writes a prescription for the treatment indicating the disease itself to cure and a drug description including dosage and mode of use. It is important to guarantee that only authorized doctors are allowed to create a new prescription or to update an existing one because a wrong diagnosis can lead to a worsening of clinical condition or death and so it becomes mandatory to know who created a new electronic health record.

The system was designed as a Software as a Service (SaaS) in order to store: (i) patient's electronic health records; (ii) treatments for specific diseases resulting from medical examinations. The objective of the whole system is to harmonize health procedures by means of the following technologies:

- **Blockchain engine**: to use the features of a decentralized and distributed certification system with the technology offered by the development and coding of smart contract;
- **Cloud storage**: to use an open-source and open-architecture file hosting service for file sharing managed with authorizations to archive all the files required to support the analysis of the nature of the disease such as blood tests, CT scans and laboratory tests;
- **NoSQL database**: to exploit the potential of a document-oriented database to store and manage patient data and diseases through tags for a fast and efficient search and to store blockchain transaction hashes and links to files stored in Cloud Storage.

5   Implementation

The SaaS was designed in order in order to apply the previously described healthcare workflow supporting a virtual healthcare team whose members are doctors belonging to different federated hospitals. Figure 2 shows the main software components used to implement the SaaS.

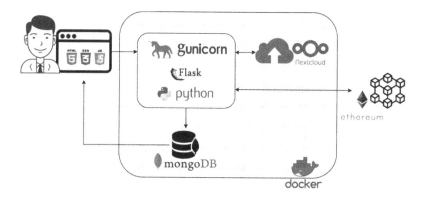

Fig. 2. SaaS software components.

A graphical web interface implemented with HTML5, CSS and JavaScript serves as an entry point of the SaaS. All requests coming from patients and doctors flow through such an interface and are elaborated by a server built in Python3 leveraging Flask as Web Server Gateway Interface (WSGI) and Gunicorn to handle multiple requests with a production-ready setup. All the components are configured as Docker containers in order to take the advantages of the virtualizaiton technology allowing service portability, resiliency and automatic updates that are typical of a Cloud Infrastructure as a Service (IaaS).

The Python web server provides a front-end that allows retrieving all existing patients' information (such as personal details, disease and pharmaceutic codes, links to documentation and Blockchain hash verification); adding new patients; and submit new treatments specifying all the required pieces of information. Specifically, a web page is dedicated to register a new patient, saving his/her primary personal information, and a separate web page is dedicated to the registration of a new treatment. It is possible to select the medical examination date, patient and doctor who does the registration to be chosen from the patients already registered and available in the database.

Since patients' sensitive data must be anonymized and health records and treatments must be trackable and irreversible, related pieces of information where stored combining a NoSQL DataBase Management System (DBMS) with a Blockchain system. Therefore, all pieces of information are stored in the MongoDB NoSQL DBMS and in the Ethereum private network through a smart contract developed in solidity. It has been chosen to use Ethereum with a private network installation considering what has been reported in Blockbench [13] highlighting the impossibility for Hyperledger Fabric, i.e., an alternative Blockchain platform, to scale above 16 nodes, which results in an important limitation for the scope of this scientific work which aims at creating a trusted and federated network among multiple hospital Clouds, and considering that Ethereum is more mature in terms of its code-base, user-base and developer community.

The smart contract accepts the input parameters such as anonymized patient id and doctor id, disease and pharmaceutic codes and stores these pieces of information in a simple data structure. The hash code resulting from the mining of each transaction is stored in the MongoDB database and can be used for verification using services like etherscan.io.

All the clinical documentation produced is uploaded in a local instance of NextCloud storage using a folder per treatment which does not contain any patient's personal data rather than the patient's anonymized identification number in order to be compliant with the General Data Protection Regulation (GDPR). Every change in the files or content of the folder will be tracked making it possible to keep a history of the documentation and its modifications.

This service is capable of detecting any modification occurred to files or folder using a listener called *External script*. It is then possible to store the fingerprint and timestamp of each modification in the database thus making it possible to track the history of the treatment. This is important to guarantee the system overall anti-tampering feature.

6   Performance Assessment

Experiments were focused on Blockchain mechanism of our SaaS implementation in order to asses the performance of the certified treatment prescription system. In particular, the system assessment has been conducted analysing the total execution time required to perform a varying number of transactions, i.e., treatment registrations through Ethereum in combination with a varying number of accounts of doctors. The testbed was arranged considering a server with following hardware/software configuration: Intel® Xeon® E3-12xx v2 @ 2.7GHz, 4 core CPU, 4 GB RAM running Ubuntu Server 18.04.

All analyses have been performed by sending transactions to the server varying the number of total and simultaneous requests. Specifically, each request invokes a new treatment registration and an Ethereum transaction mining for that. Experiments were conducted considering 100, 250 and 500 transactions and 25, 50 and 100 accounts. Each test has been repeated 30 times considering 95% confidence intervals.

To simulate a real private instance of Ethereum Blockchain, all tests have been performed using Ropsten Ethereum public test network, leveraging 300+ available nodes with a real server load status. It must be considered that Ethereum Blockchain Ropsten environment is based on Proof of Work (PoW) consensus protocol which makes difficult to obtain scalability and system speed.

Figure 3(a) describes a new treatment registration request without sending transactions to Ethereum Blockchain. This demonstrates how the server scales as the execution time is consistent for simultaneous requests (25, 50, 100) in spite of the total number of requests. Figure 3(b) shows an expected degradation of the system as compared to the requests made without Ethereum Blockchain mining and to the total number of sent transactions. This is the worst-case scenario based on the number of accounts as one account can only send one transaction at a time due to the nonce preventing replay attacks.

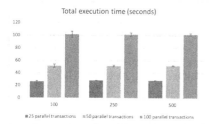

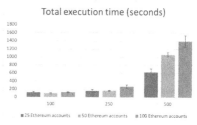

(a) Test execution without Blockchain mining.

(b) Test execution with Blockchain mining.

Fig. 3. Total execution time variation.

7   Conclusion and Future Work

This project demonstrates how Blockchain can be used in the healthcare environment to improve hospital workflow guaranteeing the authenticity of stored data. Experimental results highlight that the performance of the certified treatment prescription system introduce an acceptable overhead in terms of response time considering the obvious advantages introduced by the Blockchain technology.

Definitely, the Blockchain technology is destined to evolve in the near future improving system capabilities and robustness, and public test instances with different consensus protocols will be made available with benefits on performance and scalability.

In future developments, this work can be extended integrating a comprehensive healthcare scenario with different involved organizations, such as pharmaceutical companies registering in the Blockchain all the phases of drug production until sealing of final package and shipment, Thus, when patient buys a prescribed medicine it is possible to link the patient with the medicine box, which would mean an important step towards the end of drugs' falsification and an important assurance for the end-user who can be identified in case a specific drug package has been recalled.

Acknowledgment. This work has been partially supported by the TALISMAN Italian PON project and by the Italian Healthcare Ministry founded project Young Researcher (under 40 years) entitled "Do Severe acquired brain injury patients benefit from Telerehabilitation? A Cost-effectiveness analysis study" - GR-2016-02361306.

References

1. Hassenteufel, P., Schweyer, F.X., Gerlinger, T., Henkel, R., Lückenbach, C., Reiter, R.: The role of professional groups in policy change: Physician's organizations and the issue of local medical provision shortages in France and Germany. European Policy Analysis (2019)
2. Dubas-Jakóbczyk, K., Domagała, A., Mikos, M.: Impact of the doctor deficit on hospital management in Poland: a mixed-method study. Int. J. Health Plann. Manag. **34**, 187–195 (2019)
3. Jha, A.K., et al.: How common are electronic health records in the United States? A summary of the evidence. Health Aff. **25**, W496–W507 (2006). PMID: 17035341
4. Nakamoto, S.: Bitcoin: a peer-to-peer electronic cash system (2009)
5. Griggs, K., Ossipova, O., Kohlios, C., Baccarini, A., Howson, E., Hayajneh, T.: Healthcare blockchain system using smart contracts for secure automated remote patient monitoring. J. Med. Syst. **42**(7), 130 (2018)
6. Chakraborty, S., Aich, S., Kim, H.: A secure healthcare system design framework using blockchain technology. In: 2019 21st International Conference on Advanced Communication Technology (ICACT), pp. 260–264 (2019)
7. Dasaklis, T.K., Casino, F., Patsakis, C.: Blockchain meets smart health: towards next generation healthcare services. In: 2018 9th International Conference on Information, Intelligence, Systems and Applications (IISA), pp. 1–8 (2018)
8. Srivastava, G., Crichigno, J., Dhar, S.: A light and secure healthcare blockchain for IoT medical devices. In: 2019 IEEE Canadian Conference of Electrical and Computer Engineering (CCECE), pp. 1–5 (2019)
9. Hossein, K.M., Esmaeili, M.E., Dargahi, T., khonsari, A.: Blockchain-based privacy-preserving healthcare architecture. In: 2019 IEEE Canadian Conference of Electrical and Computer Engineering (CCECE), pp. 1–4 (2019)
10. Zhang, P., White, J., Schmidt, D., Lenz, G., Rosenbloom, S.: FHIRchain: applying blockchain to securely and scalably share clinical data. Comput. Struct. Biotechnol. J. **16**, 267–278 (2018)
11. Ramani, V., Kumar, T., Bracken, A., Liyanage, M., Ylianttila, M.: Secure and efficient data accessibility in blockchain based healthcare systems. In: 2018 IEEE Global Communications Conference (GLOBECOM), pp. 206–212 (2018)

12. Razak, O.: Revolutionizing pharma – one blockchain use case at a time (2018)
13. Dinh, T.T.A., Wang, J., Chen, G., Liu, R., Ooi, B.C., Tan, K.L.: BLOCKBENCH: a framework for analyzing private blockchains. In: Proceedings of the 2017 ACM International Conference on Management of Data, Association for Computing Machinery, pp. 1085–1100 (2017)

Monitoring

Monitoring Behavioral Compliance with Architectural Patterns Based on Complex Event Processing

Christoph Krieger[1]([✉]), Uwe Breitenbücher[1], Michael Falkenthal[1],
Frank Leymann[1], Vladimir Yussupov[1], and Uwe Zdun[2]

[1] Institute of Architecture of Application Systems, University of Stuttgart,
Stuttgart, Germany
{krieger,breitenbuecher,falkenthal,leymann,yussupov}@iaas.uni-stuttgart.de
[2] Faculty of Computer Science, University of Vienna, Vienna, Austria
uwe.zdun@univie.ac.at

Abstract. Architectural patterns assist in the process of architectural decision making as they capture architectural aspects of proven solutions. In many cases, the chosen patterns have system-wide implications on non-functional requirements such as availability, performance, and resilience. Ensuring compliance with the selected patterns is of vital importance to avoid architectural drift between the implementation and its desired architecture. Most of the patterns not only capture structural but also significant behavioral architectural aspects that need to be checked. In case all properties of the system are known before runtime, static compliance checks of application code and configuration files might be sufficient. However, in case aspects of the system dynamically evolve, e.g., due to manual reconfiguration, compliance with the architectural patterns also needs to be monitored during runtime. In this paper, we propose to link compliance rules to architectural patterns that specify behavioral aspects of the patterns based on runtime events using stream queries. These queries serve as input for a complex event processing component to automatically monitor architecture compliance of a running system. To validate the practical feasibility, we applied the approach to a set of architectural patterns in the domain of distributed systems and prototypically implemented a compliance monitor.

Keywords: Architecture compliance · Architectural patterns ·
Behavioral compliance monitoring · Complex event processing

1 Introduction

While designing complex software systems, various architectural decisions need to be made by software architects and later implemented in code by software developers. Architectural patterns can assist in the process of architectural decision making and documentation, as they capture structural and behavioral

A. Brogi et al. (Eds.): ESOCC 2020, LNCS 12054, pp. 125–140, 2020.
https://doi.org/10.1007/978-3-030-44769-4_10

architectural aspects of proven solutions that are documented in a generic and technology-independent way [9,22,23]. An example of an architectural pattern in the domain of distributed systems is the *Circuit Breaker* pattern [13]. This pattern describes how to avoid cascading failures in case of network or remote services failures by wrapping remote function calls with a proxy that monitors failures and reacts in a similar way as an electrical circuit breaker.

However, the correct realization of the architectural decisions is often not ensured during the entire life-cycle of a software system. Reasons for this are inadequate implementation by application developers, non-compliant deployment of application components, and also operator errors during manual configuration of the running system. As a consequence, the software system drifts apart from the original design specification, which is commonly referred to as *architectural drift* [16]. This is particularly problematic in the case of the chosen architectural patterns as they are concerned with essential aspects of the software architecture that often have system-wide implications on quality aspects such as availability, performance, and resilience. For example, a non-compliant realization of the aforementioned Circuit Breaker pattern can lead to cascading failures of services which harm the reliability of the overall system. Thus, architectural compliance checks are needed to ensure the correct implementation, deployment, and configuration of architectural aspects described by the chosen patterns. In case behavioral aspects of the system dynamically evolve during runtime, architectural compliance can not be guaranteed by simply checking the application code and configuration files during design-time. For example, operator errors during configuration of a running system may cause behavioral deviation from the intended architecture. In such cases, it is of vital importance to not just check architectural compliance during design-time but also monitor the compliance during run-time.

Therefore, the research question of this work is: "How can we automatically monitor a system's architectural compliance based on behavioral aspects described in architectural patterns?". To tackle this issue, we present an approach for architectural compliance monitoring based on complex event processing. We propose to specify behavioral aspects described by architectural patterns as so-called *Pattern Compliance Rules* that serve as input for an *architectural compliance monitoring system* to monitor the compliance of an application with the specified patterns. Thereby, we show how behavioral compliance aspects described in architectural patterns can be specified based on events using stream query languages and how the runtime events can be automatically monitored while the system executes. Moreover, to validate the practical feasibility of the presented approach, we applied the concept to a set of architectural patterns for designing distributed systems and prototypically implemented a compliance monitor using Esper.

2   Fundamentals and Motivation

In this section, we describe fundamentals required for understanding this paper. Moreover, we introduce a motivating scenario that is used throughout the paper to explain the presented approach.

2.1   Patterns and Design Decisions

Patterns describe proven solutions for problems that frequently reoccur in a certain context [2]. Patterns are documented in an abstract way and typically follow a well-defined structure comprising a *pattern's name*, a *problem description*, details about the *context* in which they can be applied, and a proven *solution*. In the domain of software architecture, various *pattern languages* exist that describe proven solutions for designing application architectures. For example, the *Circuit Breaker* pattern [13] tackles the problem of cascading failures in distributed systems when networks or remote services fail. Here, function calls to remote services are wrapped with a proxy that monitors failures and reacts similarly as electrical circuit breakers. In case a given threshold of consecutive failures is exceeded, the circuit breaker trips and for a specified timeout period all attempts to invoke the remote service will fail immediately. Another architecture pattern useful for distributed applications is the *Watchdog* pattern [7] that describes how failing application components can be detected and replaced automatically to ensure high availability. Thus, using such patterns significantly helps in the architectural decision making as problems at hand can be solved by using proven solutions. Moreover, as patterns provide developers with information about the rationale and consequences of a solution, they can be used to assist the documentation of *architectural design decisions* (ADD) [21].

2.2   Motivating Scenario

In this section, we introduce a motivating scenario that is used throughout the paper to motivate and explain our approach. When designing microservice-based applications, development teams are faced with the complexity of a distributed system and need to make various design decisions to build fault tolerant services. Patterns provide an effective way to help making and documenting such important design decisions as they capture architectural aspects of proven solutions together with their rationale and consequences. The following are common pattern-based design decisions made in practice to design highly available microservice-based applications (see e.g. [8]):

ADD01: To prevent the application from excessive load, caused by malicious or misconfigured clients, the *Rate Limiting* pattern [18] needs to be implemented that enforces a request limit of four requests per second for each client.

ADD02: To prevent cascading failures, the *Circuit Breaker* pattern [13] needs to be implemented for all remote function calls. A circuit breaker needs to trip in case three consecutive calls of the remote function fail. The specified timeout for an open circuit breaker is five seconds.

ADD03: To ensure sufficient availability, the *Watchdog* pattern [7] should be applied to detect and replace failed application component instances.

The implementation and configuration of the documented architectural patterns is done manually by software developers which is error-prone, meaning that parts of the patterns may be misconceived, accidentally overlooked, or even intentionally ignored due to time pressure. Such configuration and implementation errors can have an implication on the overall resilience and availability of the system. For example, behavioral non-compliance of circuit breakers, e.g., to the specified threshold of consecutive failures defined in the aforementioned ADD, can lead to cascading failures and eventually jeopardize the whole application. Just as critical for ensuring availability of the application is the correct implementation of the Watchdog pattern. A watchdog is often implemented by simply configuring an existing monitoring component. As an example, in case of virtual machines running on Amazon EC2, an auto scaling group can be configured that specifies a minimum number of virtual machine instances in that group. By replacing failed component instances, Amazon's EC2 Auto Scaling ensures that the group never goes below the specified minimum. However, creating such configurations or reconfiguring existing ones can become a complex and error-prone task which often results in non-compliant system behavior [14]. Thus, architecture compliance checks are needed to ensure the correct implementation, deployment, and configuration of a system's architectural aspects [20]. In case all application components, their relationships, and architectural decisions to be implemented are known before runtime of the application, checking compliance using static analysis might be enough. However, in case behavioral aspects of the system can be dynamically reconfigured during runtime the compliance can no longer be guaranteed by static compliance checks alone. For such applications, it is of vital importance to not just check architectural compliance during design-time but also monitor the compliance during run-time. In this paper, we propose to specify behavioral aspect of architectural patterns based on run-time events which can be used to automatically monitor architecture compliance.

2.3 Complex Event Processing

Complex Event Processing (CEP) is a set of techniques and tools for analyzing and controlling complex series of interrelated events, e.g., produced by distributed systems [11]. This technique can be used to monitor behavioral architecture compliance aspects of a system based on runtime events. *Stream query languages*, are used to configure CEP engines to observe live data streams of events and aggregate so-called low-level events into complex (high-level) events to enable discovery of event patterns having semantic significance in a specific context [12]. For example, a typical low-level event is a network event, such as an HTTP request sent by a service or the response to that request. While a single request provides no significant behavioral information, multiple ones observed in particular order and time can provide more insights into the system behavior and help to recognize non-compliant behavior. One frequently used Stream

Query Language is Esper Event Processing Language (EPL) which is included as a part of Esper's open source CEP engine [4]. Statements in Esper EPL have an SQL-like syntax containing standard query clauses such as *SELECT*, *FROM*, and *WHERE*. In this context, event streams represent data sources, whereas events serve as the basic unit of data. Moreover, Esper EPL provides multiple event pattern operators and time windows to facilitate querying of event data. For example, Listing 1.1 shows an EPL statement that can be used to analyze network events emitted by a running application to detect HTTP responses that exceed a response time of 1 second. The statement demonstrates the idea of emitting a high-level ResponseTimeout event in case a HttpRequest event is not followed by a corresponding HttpResponse event within a time window of 1 second. For a complete overview of the Esper EPL, we refer to the documentation provided by Esper [4].

```
1   insert into ResponseTimeout
2   from pattern [every a=HttpRequest −> not b=HttpResponse(a.sender = b.receiver)
3   and timer:within(1 sec)];
```

Listing 1.1. An example of an EPL statement for analyzing a stream of HTTP events.

3   An Approach for Monitoring Behavioral Compliance with Architectural Patterns

The main idea of our approach is to introduce so called Pattern Compliance Rules which serve as configuration code for monitoring behavioral compliance with architectural patterns. A Pattern Compliance Rule (PCR) contains a set of stream query language statements that specify behavioral aspects of an architectural pattern based on runtime events which can be automatically monitored while a system executes. The overall concept of our approach is shown in Fig. 1. There, Pattern Compliance Rules are managed in a *Pattern Compliance Rule Repository*. Similar to the patterns itself, the PCRs managed in the repository are application-agnostic which has the advantage that existing PCRs can be reused, hence reducing the required effort for the creation of compliance monitoring code. In addition, *Instrumentation Templates* are associated with each Pattern Compliance Rule providing program or configuration code that can be used for the instrumentation of a monitored application to emit the necessary runtime events. Thereby, each Instrumentation Template targets a specific technology, e.g., programming language and instrumentation mechanism. Based on the architectural patterns that should be monitored, a set of corresponding Pattern Compliance Rules are selected from the repository and bound to application-specific details of architectural design decisions. The resulting *application-specific PCRs* serve as configuration code for a complex event processing engine of a specialized software component, called a *Pattern Compliance Monitor*. Moreover, the Instrumentation Templates associated with the chosen PCRs can be used as a basis for the instrumentation of the monitored application to create the necessary runtime

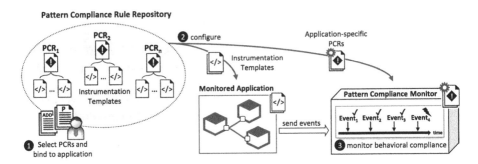

Fig. 1. Conceptual overview of the approach for monitoring behavioral compliance with architectural patterns.

events. Each event represents the occurrence of an activity within the monitored application. For example, an event may represent a request sent between application components and contain information about the source and target of the request. While the application executes, the runtime events are continuously sent to the Pattern Compliance Monitor. There, the stream of events is observed to monitor compliance with the expected behavior described by the Pattern Compliance Rules.

3.1   Method

Figure 2 depicts a step-wise method for the configuration of the monitoring environment. The method consists of five steps, namely (i) identifying architectural patterns to be implemented in an application, (ii) selecting the corresponding Pattern Compliance Rules from the Pattern Compliance Rule Repository, (iii) optionally creating Pattern Compliance Rules that are not already contained in the repository, (iv) binding the selected PCRs to application-specific details, and (v) using the resulting application-specific PCRs as configuration code for behavioral architecture compliance monitoring and instrument the monitored application to emit the necessary runtime events. In the following, we describe every step in more detail and exemplify the method based on the Rate Limiting pattern described in the motivating scenario.

Step 1: Identify Patterns. In the first step, the architectural documentation, which is created during the system design phase, is analysed to identify a set of architectural patterns that need to be realized by the implementation and deployment of the application. For example, in case of the motivating scenario presented in Sect. 2.2, the three architectural patterns Rate Limiting, Circuit Breaker, and Watchdog can be identified by analysing the documentation of ADD01, ADD02, and ADD03. Other data sources potentially containing pattern descriptions could be design diagrams or other formats of architecture documentation. The resulting set of identified patterns is then passed as an input to the next step.

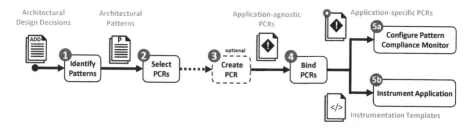

Fig. 2. An overview of the step-wise method for the configuration of the monitoring environment.

Steps 2 and 3: Select or Create PCRs. In the second step, for each identified pattern a corresponding PCR is chosen from the PCR Repository as shown in Fig. 2. The PCRs managed in the repository are so-called *application-agnostic PCRs*, meaning that instead of application-specific implementation details, they contain placeholders in the form of variables. This has the main advantage that PCRs managed in the repository can be reused, hence reducing the required effort for the creation of monitoring code. Optionally, in case a corresponding PCR for one of the identified architectural patterns does not already exist, a new one is created and added to the repository. For example, in the case of the Rate Limiting pattern, an application-agnostic Rate-Limiting PCR is selected or created that describes the expected behavior of application components implementing this pattern based on runtime events. The pattern states that the number of requests that can be made by a client should be restricted to a defined limit. Listing 1.2 depicts an exemplary Rate-Limiting PCR described using the Esper EPL. There, variables are marked in bold. The PCR describes an event pattern of HTTP requests that violates the behavior described by the Rate Limiting pattern. There, each request made by a client is represented by an *HttpRequest* event containing the *source* the request originates from, e.g. the client's IP address, and the *responseCode* returned by the server. The EPL statement (line 3–7) observes the stream of HttpRequest events per client and selects the aggregation of events as a *RateLimitViolation* in case the number of accepted HTTP requests observed in a given time interval exceeds a predefined limit. The request limit and the time interval for rate-limiting are defined as variables and can be bound to concrete values based on application-specific details.

```
1   create schema HttpRequest(source, responseCode)
2
3   @Name('Rate Limiting Violation')
4   insert into RateLimitViolation
5   select count(*) from HttpRequest#time_batch(interval sec)
6   where responseCode = '200'
7   group by source having count(*) > requestLimit;
```

Listing 1.2. An exemplary application-agnostic PCR for the Rate Limiting pattern defined using the Esper EPL.

Step 4: Bind PCRs. In the fourth step, the application-agnostic PCRs are bound to application-specific details to (i) align them with application-specific design decisions and (ii) to serve as executable configuration code for the Pattern Compliance Monitor shown in Fig. 2. This means all variables, contained in a rule, are replaced with application-specific data, e.g., documented in architectural design decisions. For example, to align the Rate Limiting PCR with the architectural design decision ADD01 documented in the motivating scenario, the *requestLimit* is defined as four requests and the *interval* is set to one second.

Step 5: Configure Monitoring Environment. In step 5, the set of previously created application-specific PCRs are used as configuration code for the Pattern Compliance Monitor as shown in Fig. 1. Also, depending on the type of events defined in the selected PCRs, the components of the monitored application need to be instrumented to emit the necessary runtime events into the stream observed by the Pattern Compliance Monitor. For example, in case of the Rate Limiting PCR, each HTTP request needs to be reported as an event that comprise an identifier of the client that sent the request, e.g., an IP address or access token and the response code of the request. The instrumentation can be achieved by different mechanisms depending on technology specific details of the monitored application. Thereby, Instrumentation Templates linked to the selected PCRs can be used to reduce the instrumentation effort. For example, to instrument a Java application using Aspect-oriented Programming [10], a template can be used that implements the functionality for emitting a certain event type in an aspect written in Java's aspect-oriented extension AspectJ. Aspects can be easily added to the existing code of the to be monitored application without modifying the application code itself. As another example, in case a service mesh infrastructure layer is used, a template can be used that provides configuration code for the service mesh to create a log entry for each request sent between application components. The logs can then be aggregated and sent to the Pattern Compliance Monitor.

3.2 System Architecture

The system architecture of the Pattern Compliance Monitor is depicted in Fig. 3. A Web UI provides access to the functionality of the Pattern Compliance Monitor. The business logic layer comprises the five major components *CEP Engine*, *Violation Subscriber*, *Event Handler*, *PCR Manager*, and *Instrumentation Template Manager*. The CEP Engine implements a complex event processing engine that can be configured based on Stream Query Language statements to analyze a series of events. The PCR Manager is responsible for retrieving application-agnostic Pattern Compliance Rules stored in the *Pattern Compliance Rule repository*, binding them to application-specific details as described in Sect. 3.1, and configuring the CEP Engine using the resulting application-specific Pattern Compliance Rules. The Event Handler provides the functionality for consuming events from a given destination, e.g., a message queue, and adding them

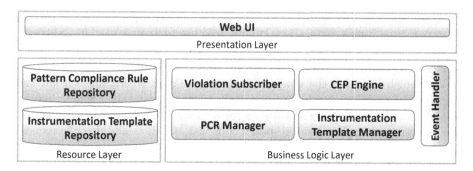

Fig. 3. The system architecture of the Pattern Compliance Monitor

to the event stream analyzed by the CEP Engine. The Violation Subscriber subscribes to the Pattern Compliance Rules used as configuration for the CEP engine and receives updates about compliance violations detected by the engine. The Instrumentation Template Manager is used to manage Instrumentation Templates stored in the *Instrumentation Template Repository* and to retrieve a set of Instrumentation Templates based on the chosen Pattern Compliance Rules and technology-specific details of the application to be monitored.

4 Applying the Approach to the Motivating Scenario

In this section, the presented approach is applied to the motivating scenario described in Sect. 2.2. We will discuss how the behavioral aspects contained in the textual description of the patterns Circuit Breaker and Watchdog can be specified as application-agnostic PCRs using EPL statements that serve as configuration code for architecture compliance monitoring. We point out that the application-agnostic PCR for the Rate Limiting pattern is described in Sect. 3.1. Furthermore, we will discuss how we validated our approach of architecture compliance monitoring using the created Pattern Compliance Rules. We describe how we prototypically implemented the Pattern Compliance Monitor and instrumented a microservice-based application to be monitored to emit the necessary runtime events.

4.1 Circuit Breaker

The Circuit Breaker is a common architectural pattern used in microservice-based applications. It describes how to avoid cascading failures by wrapping functions that call remote services with a proxy that monitors failures and reacts similarly to an electrical circuit. The pattern states that when the number of consecutive failures crosses a given threshold the circuit breaker needs to trip and for the duration of a timeout period all attempts to invoke the function will fail immediately [13]. Conversely, the Circuit Breaker pattern is violated in case, even though the number of consecutive failed attempts to call a remote service is exceeded, the defined timeout is ignored and calls to the remote service are still executed. An application-agnostic Circuit Breaker PCR that describes this violation using EPL statements is shown in Listing 1.3. There, each call to a remote service is represented by an *HttpRequest* event containing the event properties *source*, which identifies the wrapped function the request originates from, and *responseCode*, which provides the returned response code of the request (line 1). In our example, we distinguish between the response code 200, which means that the request has succeeded and response code 503, which means that the request failed due to unavailability of the remote service. First, to monitor the behavior of each circuit breaker in an application separately, the HttpRequest events in the observed event stream are partitioned based on their source (line 3). Referring to this partition, a complex event called *FailureRateExcessEvent* is emitted if there is a consecutive sequence of failed HTTP requests that exceed the threshold defined by the variable *failureThreshold* (line 5–7). In other words, the event is emitted in case the defined threshold of consecutive failures for a particular remote function call is exceeded. Finally, a violation statement is defined indicating a non-compliant behavior of a circuit breaker (line 9–12). The violation is emitted if a FailureRateExcessEvent is followed by a HttpRequest event within the period defined by the variable *timeout*. This means that even though the number of consecutive failed attempts to call a remote service is exceeded, the defined timeout is ignored and calls to the remote service are still executed. Hence, the behavior described by the Circuit Breaker pattern is violated. The concrete timeout and failure threshold for the rule can be set based on application-specific decisions. For example, in the case of the architectural design decision (ADD02), described in the motivating scenario, the failure threshold is set to three and the timeout is specified as five seconds.

```
1    create schema HttpRequest(source, responseCode)
2
3    create context SegmentedByCB partition by source from HttpRequest;
4
5    context SegmentedByCB insert into FailureRateExcessEvent
6    select * from HttpRequest#length(failureThreshold + 1)
7    where statusCode = "503" having count(*) > failureThreshold;
8
9    @Name('Timeout Violation')
10   select b.id as circuitBreakerId from pattern
11   [every (a = FailureRateExcessEvent −> b=HttpRequest(id = a.id)
12   where timer:within(timeout msec))];
```

Listing 1.3. An exemplary application-agnostic PCR for the Circuit Breaker pattern.

4.2 Watchdog

The Watchdog pattern describes a component that detects and replaces failing application component instances automatically to ensure sufficient availability of the application [7]. The pattern states that failing application component instances have to be replaced in case of failures. One possible information source for detecting failures are periodic heartbeats sent by the instances that verify proper functioning. Listing 1.4 depicts an application-agnostic Watchdog PCR that analyzes the periodic heartbeats sent by application components to monitor if failing application components are detected and replaced. Each Heartbeat sent by an application component is represented by a *Heartbeat* event, containing the event properties *id*, which identifies the running instance of an application component that sent the heartbeat, and *groupId*, which defines a logical grouping of running instances to identify replicas of a component instance (line 1). The second statement (line 3–4) defines an *InstanceCount* event to count the amount of uniquely identifiable running instances for a given replica group, i.e., the current number of replicas of a component instance. To filter out terminated instances, the statement only counts events that are emitted less than five seconds ago. The next definition statement (6–7) emits a *DecreaseCountEvent* if there is a sequence of two InstanceCount events where the first event contains a higher number as the second event. In other words, every time the amount of running instances in a replica group is decreased, a DecreaseCountEvent is emitted. Similar, an *IncreaseCountEvent* is defined which is emitted every time the amount of running instances is increased (line 9–10). Finally, a violation statement is defined (line 12–14), emitting an event that indicates a non-compliant behavior of the Watchdog component. This event is emitted if a DecreaseCountEvent is not followed by an IncreaseCountEvent within a given time threshold, i.e., failed component instances are not replaced within a certain time. The variables *monitoredGroupId* and *timeThreshold* allow customization of the statements and can be defined based on application-specific data, e.g., contained in architectural design decisions.

```
1   create schema Heartbeat(id, groupId)
2
3   insert into InstanceCount select count(*) as number
4   from Heartbeat(groupId = monitoredGroupId).std:unique(id)#time_batch(5 sec);
5
6   insert into DecreaseCountEvent select a.number as number
7   from pattern [every a=InstanceCount -> b=InstanceCount(a.number > b.number)];
8
9   insert into IncreaseCountEvent select a.number as number
10  from pattern [every a=InstanceCount -> b=InstanceCount(a.number < b.number)];
11
12  @Name('Watchdog Violation')
13  select * from pattern [every DecreaseCountEvent ->
14  not IncreaseCountEvent and timer:interval(timeThreshold msec)];
```

Listing 1.4. An exemplary application-agnostic PCR for the Watchdog pattern.

4.3 Prototypical Implementation

For the validation of our approach, we prototypically implemented the system architecture of the Pattern Compliance Monitor described in Sect. 3.2 using Java and Esper[1]. We used the message broker software RabbitMQ[2] as a messaging layer. The application to be monitored can send events as messages to the broker.

The Event Handler component of the Pattern Compliance Monitor listens for new messages sent to the broker and adds them to the event stream observed by the CEP Engine. For the test setup, we have created Pattern Compliance Rules for the three patterns Rate Limiting, Watchdog, and Circuit Breaker as described in Sects. 3 and 4. We have evaluated the feasibility of architecture compliance monitoring using the created Pattern Compliance Rules based on both, automated unit tests simulating a synthetic data set of events and a manual test based on a prototypical implementation of a microservice application using Java. We used Java's aspect-oriented extension AspectJ for realizing unified logging of run-time events without modifying the application code itself. We created aspects for logging the run-time events described by the Pattern Compliance Rules, which were then woven into the application code. Advices in the aspects implemented the logging functionality and pointcuts associated with the advices defined the execution points at which the they should run. For example, Listing 1.5 shows an excerpt of the aspect that implements unified logging of HTTP requests as events. The aspect defines an *@AfterThrowing* advice that generates a log entry for a failed HTTP request in case a method of the application's REST client does not complete normally and an HttpStatusCodeException is thrown. Similarly, an *@AfterReturning* advice was implemented in the aspect that generates a log entry for each succeeded HTTP request.

```
1  @AfterThrowing(pointcut = "execution(restclient.*.*(..))", throwing = "exception")
2  void after(HttpStatusCodeException exception) throws Throwable {
3    generateHttpRequestEvent(exception);
4  }
```

Listing 1.5. Excerpt of the Aspect implemented to provide unified logging of HTTP requests.

We used Logback as a logging framework and added a configuration for pushing all logs necessary for monitoring to the RabbitMQ message broker. For the deployment, we packaged each application component as a docker[3] container image. Docker Swarm was used to deploy the application as a multi-container docker application and scale services of the application during runtime. During runtime of the application we caused compliance violations by manually changing the behavioral aspects of the application that are concerned with the realization of architectural aspects described by the aforementioned patterns.

5 Related Work

Different works are concerned with behavioral compliance checking or monitoring of software systems. Mulo et al. [12] propose a compliance monitoring

---

[1] https://github.com/ckrieger/ADDComplianceChecking.
[2] https://www.rabbitmq.com/.
[3] https://www.docker.com/.

approach for verifying that business processes adhere to specified compliance controls. They provide a DSL that can be used to define compliance monitoring directives based on business activities and translate them into an event-based sequence that serve as compliance monitoring code. Similar to our work, complex event processing is used to implement the approach. However, their work focus on compliance concerns in the context of laws and regulations, whereas our work is concerned with checking behavioral compliance with architectural patterns. Ackermann et al. [1] compare UML sequence diagrams, which describe the intended interaction of components in a software system, against the actual behavior implemented in the system to construct a behavioral reflexion model that shows potential drift between the desired behavior of a system and the actual implementation. In contrast to ours, their work does not focus on constraints described by architectural patterns. Wendehals et al. [19] present an approach to recognize behavioral aspects of object-oriented design patterns in legacy systems by instrumenting relevant method calls and monitoring them at runtime. In contrast to our work, they use finite automata to describe behavioral aspects of the patterns. Moreover, their work focus on the detection of design patterns in object-oriented software, whereas, our work focus on architectural patterns that are relevant in the domain of distributed cloud applications. Breitenbücher [3] proposes the formalization of management patterns, e.g., patterns for the management of cloud applications, to allow their automated execution for individual applications. In contrast to ours, this work is not concerned with automated compliance monitoring but with the automated execution of the management steps described in the patterns. Saatkamp et al. [17] propose to formalize the knowledge contained in architecture and design patterns to automatically detect problems in restructured topology-based deployment models. The formalization and automated detection are based on the logic programming language Prolog. This approach is concerned with structural problem detection during design time of deployment models. In contrast, our work monitors behavioral compliance during the runtime of an application. Fahland et al. [5] provide a formalization of Enterprise Integration Patterns based on Coloured Petri Nets. Similar work is presented by Ritter et al. [15]. They propose a new formalism called timed db-nets to formally describe Enterprise Integration Patterns. Both works are exclusively concerned with the formalization of Enterprise Integration Patterns, whereas our work describes a general approach to define behavioral directives described in architectural patterns. Related in the broader sense is the work by Falkenthal et al. [6]. They introduce the concept of Solution Implementations as concrete implementations of patterns. Selection Criteria added to the relations between Solution Implementations and patterns allow to determine the most appropriate implementation for a specific use case. The concept of Solution Implementations can be used to provide a set of reusable compliant pattern implementations.

6   Conclusion and Future Work

Monitoring the system for architectural compliance helps to quickly detect inconsistencies between the intended behavior and its actual implementation. In this paper, we proposed to apply behavioral directives described by architectural patterns as input for architecture compliance monitoring of an application. For this, we presented (1) how stream query languages can be used to specify the intended behavior described in architectural patterns using runtime events, (2) how the resulting rules can be transformed into application-specific, machine-processable instructions, (3) and how a system can be automatically monitored for behavioral compliance violations using such rules. We applied the presented rule configuration approach to the Rate Limiting, Circuit Breaker, and Watchdog pattern. Further, for validating the feasibility of our approach, we prototypically implemented a Pattern Compliance Monitor based on Esper's complex event processing engine. The presented approach is not limited to the discussed patterns and can be extended to monitor compliance with other architectural patterns. However, one possible limitation to this is that some architectural patterns might comprise insufficient behavior or the described behavioral directives cannot be sufficiently expressed using stream query languages. In future work, we plan to investigate different pattern languages to identify suitable architectural patterns for extending the presented approach. Another limitation is that the approach presumes knowledge about stream query languages, e.g., the Esper EPL. Translating the intended behavior described in patterns into EPL statements can become a complex and non-trivial task. It is left for future work to ease this process, e.g., by developing a domain-specific language and tool support for the creation of Pattern Compliance Rules.

Acknowledgments. This work was partially funded by the DFG project ADDCompliance (636503), the European Union's Horizon 2020 research and innovation project RADON (825040), FWF (Austrian Science Fund) project ADDCompliance: I 2885-N33, and FFG (Austrian Research Promotion Agency) project DECO, no. 846707.

References

1. Ackermann, C., et al.: Towards behavioral reflexion models. In: Software Reliability Engineering, ISSRE 2009, pp. 175–184. IEEE, November 2009
2. Alexander, C., et al.: A Pattern Language: Towns, Buildings, Construction. Oxford University Press, Oxford (1977)
3. Breitenbücher, U.: Eine musterbasierte Methode zur Automatisierung des Anwendungsmanagements. Dissertation, Universität Stuttgart, Fakultät Informatik, Elektrotechnik und Informationstechnik (2016)
4. EsperTech: Esper (2019). http://www.espertech.com/esper/
5. Fahland, D., Gierds, C.: Analyzing and completing middleware designs for enterprise integration using coloured petri nets. In: Salinesi, C., Norrie, M.C., Pastor, Ó. (eds.) CAiSE 2013. LNCS, vol. 7908, pp. 400–416. Springer, Heidelberg (2013). https://doi.org/10.1007/978-3-642-38709-8_26

6. Falkenthal, M., et al.: From pattern languages to solution implementations. In: Proceedings of the 6th International Conferences on Pervasive Patterns and Applications (PATTERNS 2014), pp. 12–21. Xpert Publishing Services, May 2014

7. Fehling, C., et al.: Cloud Computing Patterns: Fundamentals to Design, Build, and Manage Cloud Applications. Springer, Heidelberg (2014). https://doi.org/10.1007/978-3-7091-1568-8

8. Hackernoon: Designing a microservices architecture for failure (2017). hackernoon.com/designing-a-microservices-architecture-for-failure-a57f34ded646

9. Harrison, N., et al.: Using patterns to capture architectural decisions. Software **24**(4), 38–45 (2007)

10. Kiczales, G., et al.: Aspect-oriented programming. In: Akşit, M., Matsuoka, S. (eds.) ECOOP 1997. LNCS, vol. 1241, pp. 220–242. Springer, Heidelberg (1997). https://doi.org/10.1007/BFb0053381

11. Luckham, D.: The power of events: an introduction to complex event processing in distributed enterprise systems. In: Bassiliades, N., Governatori, G., Paschke, A. (eds.) RuleML 2008. LNCS, vol. 5321, p. 3. Springer, Heidelberg (2008). https://doi.org/10.1007/978-3-540-88808-6_2

12. Mulo, E., et al.: Domain-specific language for event-based compliance monitoring in process-driven SOAs. SOCA **7**(1), 59–73 (2013). https://doi.org/10.1007/s11761-012-0121-3

13. Nygard, M.T.: Release It!: Design and Deploy Production-ready Software. Pragmatic Bookshelf, Raleigh (2007)

14. Oppenheimer, D.: The importance of understanding distributed system configuration. In: Proceedings of the 2003 Conference on Human Factors in Computer Systems Workshop. Citeseer (2003)

15. Ritter, D., et al.: Formalizing application integration patterns. In: 2018 IEEE 22nd International Enterprise Distributed Object Computing Conference (EDOC), pp. 11–20. IEEE (2018)

16. Rosik, J., et al.: Assessing architectural drift in commercial software development: a case study. Softw. Pract. Exp. **41**(1), 63–86 (2011)

17. Saatkamp, K., Breitenbücher, U., Kopp, O., Leymann, F.: An approach to automatically detect problems in restructured deployment models based on formalizing architecture and design patterns. SICS Softw.-Intensiv. Cyber-Phys. Syst. **34**, 85–97 (2019). https://doi.org/10.1007/s00450-019-00397-7

18. Stocker, M., et al.: Interface quality patterns - communicating and improving the quality of microservices APIs. In: 23rd European Conference on Pattern Languages of Programs 2018, July 2018

19. Wendehals, L., Orso, A.: Recognizing behavioral patterns at runtime using finite automata. In: Proceedings of the 2006 International Workshop on Dynamic Systems Analysis, pp. 33–40. ACM, May 2006

20. Zdun, U., Navarro, E., Leymann, F.: Ensuring and assessing architecture conformance to microservice decomposition patterns. In: Maximilien, M., Vallecillo, A., Wang, J., Oriol, M. (eds.) ICSOC 2017. LNCS, vol. 10601, pp. 411–429. Springer, Cham (2017). https://doi.org/10.1007/978-3-319-69035-3_29

21. Zimmermann, O., et al.: The role of architectural decisions in model-driven service-oriented architecture construction. In: Proceedings of the OOPSLA 2006 Workshop on Best Practices and Methodologies in Service-Oriented Architectures. Unipub (2006)

22. Zimmermann, O., Gschwind, T., Küster, J., Leymann, F., Schuster, N.: Reusable architectural decision models for enterprise application development. In: Overhage, S., Szyperski, C.A., Reussner, R., Stafford, J.A. (eds.) QoSA 2007. LNCS, vol. 4880, pp. 15–32. Springer, Heidelberg (2007). https://doi.org/10.1007/978-3-540-77619-2_2

23. Zimmermann, O., et al.: Combining pattern languages and reusable architectural decision models into a comprehensive and comprehensible design method. In: Seventh Working IEEE/IFIP Conference on Software Architecture (WICSA 2008), pp. 157–166. IEEE, February 2008

Towards Real-Time Monitoring of Data Centers Using Edge Computing

Brian Setz$^{(\boxtimes)}$ and Marco Aiello

Department of Service Computing, University of Stuttgart, Stuttgart, Germany
{brian.setz,marco.aiello}@uni-stuttgart.de

Abstract. Introducing the Internet of Things paradigm to data centers enables real-time monitoring on a scale that has not been seen before. Real-time monitoring promises to reduce the data center's operational costs and increase energy savings. As data centers can house over a hundred thousand servers, the potential number of data points that can be collected every minute is in the order of hundreds of millions. In this work-in-progress paper, we stipulate about the impact that real-time monitoring of data centers has on the network infrastructure, and demonstrate that the impact is indeed significant enough to disrupt the data center's network. We therefore propose a preliminary solution based on edge computing that minimizes the load on the network when performing real-time monitoring of a data center.

Keywords: Data centers · Real-time monitoring · Edge computing

1 Introduction

Data centers form the backbone of the modern Internet, it is their computational resources that enable many of the services that are present on the World Wide Web today. Modern data centers are massive in size, covering areas of tens of thousands square meters, housing many thousands of individual server racks [3]. It is therefore not surprising that data centers are responsible for almost 3% of the energy consumption in the United States [9]. Monitoring data centers assists in improving the energy efficiency by discovering comatose or zombie servers. These comatose servers are performing no useful work, yet still consume energy. It is estimated that up to 30% of servers are comatose [10]. Monitoring is also critical in preventing outages, which can have a wide-spread global effect [14]. Preventing outages is also critical for upholding the Quality of Service as is specified in the Service Level Agreements. Furthermore, monitoring also aids the expansion planning process of data centers by predicting future cooling and space requirements as the data center grows.

The presented research is funded by the Netherlands Organisation for Scientific Research (NWO) in the framework of the Indo-Dutch Science Industry Collaboration programme with project NextGenSmart DC (629.002.102).

© IFIP International Federation for Information Processing 2020
Published by Springer Nature Switzerland AG 2020
A. Brogi et al. (Eds.): ESOCC 2020, LNCS 12054, pp. 141–148, 2020.
https://doi.org/10.1007/978-3-030-44769-4_11

The emergence of the Internet of Things (IoT) paradigm enables monitoring of data centers at a scale that was not possible in the past. A wide variety of hardware and virtual sensors can be utilized to collect different types of data, which in turn can be used to evaluate dozens of sustainability and performance metrics [12]. As a result, the amount of data that can be collected in this environment is of massive proportions: a data center of 100 000 servers, each of which report 50 distinct metrics every second, would result in 300 000 000 data points every minute. Collecting data at such fine granularities enables the real time monitoring of the data center in its entirety. However, if this data would be collected at the high frequencies required for real-time monitoring, a different problem arises: the quantity of transmitted data would be sufficiently large to negatively impact the data center's network infrastructure.

The question we pose in this work is: *how can we leverage a data center's network infrastructure to efficiently monitor a data center in real time by utilizing the edge computing paradigm?* With the goal of answering this question, we first analyse the common network architectures found in data centers. Next, we look at the potential data sources that can be found in a data center in order to determine the size of the raw data and the required network throughput. This is followed by a preliminary design of an edge-based data collection platform that takes advantage of a data center's network infrastructure to reduce the load on the network. Finally, we discuss the results we have obtained thus far, as well as the steps we have planned for our future research.

The remainder of this paper is organised as follows. Section 2 introduces the related work, followed by a description of data center network architectures in Sect. 3. An analysis of the data that can possibly be collected in a data center is made in Sect. 4. Next, in Sect. 5 the proposed edge-based architecture is introduced. Followed by the conclusion in Sect. 6. We note that, since this is a work-in-progress paper, there is no evaluation section.

2   Related Work

Real-time monitoring is a technique that has become more popular in several domains with the emergence of the Internet of Things. In smart grids, for example, real-time monitoring promises to assist in the prevention of severe safety accidents by automatically identifying threats. The authors of [6] identified that real-time monitoring of smart grids would cause an increase in data that would be too large to handle using the traditional cloud computing paradigm. In their solution they introduce edge computing as a key component of their real time monitoring solution, reducing the network load by more than 50%.

In our previous work, a data set of 2.5 billion data points was collected from a data center [11]. A total of 13 different data types were collected from more than 160 servers every 10 s. The type of data collected includes CPU temperature and utilization, network utilization, air temperatures, power consumption, and more. The data is used to train models that can estimate the status of a server. This work provides a glimpse into the potential amount of data that can be collected in a data center.

The authors of [8] developed a method for real-time monitoring of data centers using an IoT approach. The data is environmental data, such as the temperature and the humidity level. These values are collected every 10 s, a total of 1.4 million data points were collected. Their IoT platform is based on a simple web service which accepts data collected by the custom-built sensors. The monitoring takes place on the level of individual racks.

In the work of [7], an approach is proposed for monitoring a data center in real time using low-power wireless sensors. The collected data includes temperature, humidity, airflow, air pressure, water pressure, security status, vibrations, and the state of the fire systems. The need for collecting data from servers for monitoring purposes is also recognized. The authors envision that some type of IoT platform is required for the collection, processing, storage, and management of the data. The envisioned platform is not designed or implemented.

In [5], the authors describe the role that edge computing has in the Internet of Things. They propose a layered model in which millions of IoT devices connected to thousands of edge gateways, which in turn connect to hundreds of cloud data centers. The authors also recognise the need for data abstraction, which uses edge gateways to reduce the volume of the raw data before sending it to the data center. However, deciding the extent by which the data should be reduced is an open problem, according to the authors.

The related work shows that some effort has been made to introduce hardware sensors and virtual sensors to data centers. The type of data that has been collected thus far is limited, however. In this work, an architecture is described that allows the collection of a much wider variety of data. None of the related work consider the increased network load when introducing real time monitoring to data centers.

3   Data Center Network Infrastructure

Data centers are facilities containing large amounts of computational, storage, and networking resources. These resources are mounted in 19-inch racks, which are metal enclosures with standardized dimensions. The capacity of a rack is expressed in Rack Units (U), and determines the quantity of equipment it can house. The standard full height rack is 42U tall. Rack equipment such as servers and switches often occupy between 1U to 4U of space, with blade server enclosures consuming up to 10U of space. Efficiently connecting all the rack equipment to the network can be a challenge, and the design of the data center network affects the networking efficiency at which the connected equipment operates.

The most widely used network architecture in data centers is the *3-layer data center network architecture* [2], shown in Fig. 1. As the name suggests, this architecture consists of 3 distinct layers: a core layer at the top, an aggregation layer in the middle, and an access layer at the bottom. Equipment, such as servers, that require network access are connected to the access layer, usually with 1 or 10 Gigabit links. The access layer is commonly implemented as a network switch located at the top of a rack (ToR switch) or at the end of a row of racks (EoR switch). The aggregation layer aggregates the different ToR and EoR switches, to enable network connectivity between racks. The links between ToR and EoR switches are commonly 10 or 40 Gigabit. The aggregation layer switches all connect to the core layer, these links can often be up to 100 Gigabit. The core layer is responsible for providing uplinks to the Internet.

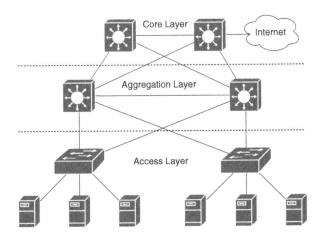

Fig. 1. An example of a 3-layer data center network architecture.

There are also other network architectures currently in use in data center, such as Facebook's data center fabric approach [4]. This approach is similar to approaches taken by Google and eBay. The notion of a server pod is introduced, which is essentially a standalone cluster consisting of racks and servers, containing up to 48 ToR switches and 4 special fabric switches. These fabric switches are responsible for interconnecting the servers in a single pod. To connect different pods, a network spine is introduced consisting of up to 48 spine switches per spine plane. This approach is highly scalable, as computational resources can be increased by introducing more pods, and the network capacity can be increased by introducing more spine planes.

Another approach is the Fat Tree data center network [1]. This approach is similar in design to the 3-layer approach, but provides guarantees regarding the available bandwidth for each server in a rack. This is done by carefully planning the numbers of switches in each layer, and increasing the number of links between individual switches the higher up the hierarchy they are. Any horizontal slice in the network graph has the same amount of bandwidth available.

Despite the significant differences between the available data center network architectures, they all contain an access layer with ToR and EoR switches in one form or another. As we show later in our proposed architecture, these ToR switches are excellent candidates to become edge gateways due to their proximity to the servers that are being monitored.

4   Impact on Network Load

To understand the significance of the additional load that is associated with real time monitoring of a data center, a number of steps have to be taken. First, the number of servers per rack and the number of racks per data center have to be identified. Next, the data types that can be collected from a server have to be investigated, as well as their data size. And finally, the load on the network that is generated by real time monitoring has to be calculated.

The number of servers that can be placed inside a rack is not only limited by the size of the servers, but also by the data center's cooling capacity and power limitations. A standard full height rack offers space for up to 40 servers, leaving 2U for other equipment. In practice this number is between 25 to 35 servers per rack. Using blade servers, the density of a rack can be increased much further. A typical high performance 10U blade server enclosure contains 16 servers. This increases the density to 64 servers per rack. There are also 3U blade servers enclosures for low performance blade servers that house 20 blade servers. This results in a maximum density of 260 servers per rack. In all cases at least 2U are left for the ToR switch and a Keyboard Video Mouse switch.

The largest data center in the world is China's Range International Information Group data center, covering over 500 000 m². More commonly, data centers are between 10 000 and 20 000 m² in size. For example, Google's Dallas data center is 18 000 m² and contains 9090 server racks [3]. Applying the previously determined server density numbers, it can be extrapolated that a data center containing 9090 server racks can house anywhere between 318 000 and 2 363 400 servers. A report from Gartner estimates that Google had around 2.5 million servers in July 2016, spread across 13 data centers, which equates to around 192 000 servers per data center [13].

There are two categories of sensors required to monitor a data center: hardware sensors and virtual sensors. The hardware sensors are used to monitor the temperature and humidity, as well as power consumption. These measurements can be made on a global level for the whole data center, as well as on individual server level. Virtual sensors are software-based sensors, they can be agents interacting with the operating system to gather information about the CPU, memory, networking interfaces, storage devices, and more. There are software agents available that can collect and publish this type of data, popular solutions include: Telegraf, StatsD, collectd, Zabbix, Prometheus, and Nagios.

In this work, Telegraf is used to represent the virtual sensors, because of its popularity and its ability to integrate with a multitude of platforms. Telegraf is a plugin-based software solution for collecting and transmitting a wide variety of data. It consists of four plugin types: input plugins, processor plugins, aggregator plugins, and output plugins. Input plugins collect data from the system, processor plugins transform the data, aggregator plugins aggregate the data, and output plugins transmit the data to other systems. Only the input plugins that collect generic system information are included in our experiments.

To determine the bandwidth required to monitor the generic metrics measured by Telegraf, experiments are performed using a real server. The server is a Dell PowerEdge R7425 with dual AMD EPYC 7551 32-core processors, 512 GB of RAM, and six 960 GB Intel S4510 SSD's. The operating system is Proxmox, a Debian-based virtualization environment. Telegraf is installed on the operating system and configured to collect the selected metrics. MQTT, a lightweight publish-subscribe network protocol, is configured as the output plugin. An MQTT broker is deployed on a second host. Wireshark, a network packet analyser, is also installed on this second host in order to monitor the network usage. The traces produced by Wireshark are analysed to calculate the required bandwidth for real time monitoring of a data center. An overview of the setup is shown in Fig. 2.

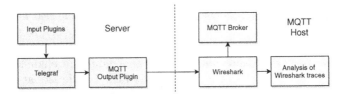

Fig. 2. Setup to analyse the bandwidth usage when performing real time monitoring.

To determine the load on the infrastructure, network packets were collected for a duration of 600 s. During this period, 185 400 messages were sent to the MQTT broker. In total, 55.3 megabytes of data were transmitted, an average of 92.2 kB/s. While seemingly insignificant for one server, however when we extrapolate this and use Google's Dallas data center and a rack density of 25 servers per rack as an example, the total bandwidth would equal 25 servers per rack × 9090 racks × 92.2 kB/s = 167.62 Gbit/s. In practice this number is conservative, as the servers per rack density is ever increasing, and data centers are becoming ever larger.

5   Proposed Edge-Based Architecture

One method to reduce the overall load on a data center's network is bringing the computations closer to the source of the data. This reduces the amount of hops required for the data to reach their destination, and in turn limits the load to the access layer instead of overloading the aggregation and core layers. The architecture we propose is shown in Fig. 3. As each rack as a ToR switch, the goal is to leverage the computational power of the switch to turn it into an edge gateway. Every edge gateway is responsible for processing and analysing the data of their rack only. Therfore, the edge gateway would only have to handle the network traffic of a limited amount of servers. The network load for the gateway ranges between 18 Mbit/s and 47 Mbit/s, for 25 servers and 64 servers per rack respectively. At these loads the impact on the switch itself is minimal.

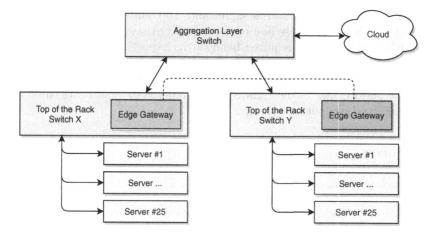

Fig. 3. Proposed edge-based architecture using Top of the Rack switches.

Because edge gateways are close to the source of the data, the network latency is also greatly reduced. This is crucial for real-time monitoring, as the data center operator should be informed as soon as possible about critical events. The edge gateway can also be used to automatically interact with the servers. For example, when a server is overheating, the gateway could inform the server to reduce the load, or even lower the frequency at which the CPU cores are operating. This allows the edge gateways to act as autonomous agents. The proposed architecture also improves the scalability of the data center. As the data center grows and more racks are placed and filled with servers, the impact that monitoring these new servers has will be minimized as the majority of the data remains at the ToR switch. It also possible for multiple racks to be clustered together, such that the edge gateways of these racks communicate with each other in a peer-to-peer fashion. Another benefit of this approach concerns the privacy. In case a rack is dedicated to processing sensitive data, the edge gateway will ensure that monitoring data collected from these sensitive servers does not leave the rack. Or, when the data does have to be transmitted outside the rack, it is anonymised and privacy sensitive data is removed before it is sent across the network.

Using edge computing instead of traditional cloud computing to perform real-time monitoring in data centers has a number of benefits. From reducing the network load, to increasing the responsiveness, enabling autonomous control, as well as improved scalability and privacy. These advantages come at the cost of increased deployment complexity, and more complex ToR switches.

6   Conclusion

Real-time monitoring of a data center comes at a cost: the increase in network traffic is significant enough to influence the performance of a data center. We estimated the additional load that is placed on a data center's network, and have shown that the additional load is significant. To counteract this problem, we proposed an architecture based on edge computing that enables real-time monitoring while reducing the required bandwidth, leveraging the network infrastructure of the data center by relying on ToR switches. In our future work, we aim to implement the proposed architecture and perform a quantitative evaluation of the performance of the architecture, compared to monitoring based on a traditional cloud computing approach.

References

1. Al-Fares, M., Loukissas, A., Vahdat, A.: A scalable, commodity data center network architecture. SIGCOMM Comput. Commun. Rev. **38**(4), 63–74 (2008)
2. Barroso, L.A., Clidaras, J., Hölzle, U.: The datacenter as a computer: an introduction to the design of warehouse-scale machines (2013)
3. Chen, T., Gao, X., Chen, G.: The features, hardware, and architectures of data center networks: a survey. J. Parallel Distrib. Comput. **96**, 45–74 (2016)
4. Farrington, N., Andreyev, A.: Facebook's data center network architecture, pp. 49–50 (2013)
5. Hassan, N., Gillani, S., Ahmed, E., Yaqoob, I., Imran, M.: The role of edge computing in Internet of Things. IEEE Commun. Mag. **56**(11), 110–115 (2018)
6. Huang, Y., Lu, Y., Wang, F., Fan, X., Liu, J., Leung, V.C.M.: An edge computing framework for real-time monitoring in smart grid. In: 2018 IEEE International Conference on Industrial Internet (ICII), pp. 99–108, October 2018
7. Levy, M., Hallstrom, J.O.: A new approach to data center infrastructure monitoring and management (DCIMM). In: 2017 IEEE 7th Annual Computing and Communication Workshop and Conference (CCWC), pp. 1–6, January 2017
8. Medina-Santiago, A., et al.: Adaptive model IoT for monitoring in data centers. IEEE Access **8**, 5622–5634 (2020)
9. Mills, M.P.: The cloud begins with coal-an overview of the electricity used by the global digital ecosystem. Technical report, Digital Power Group (2013)
10. Ngoko, Y., Cérin, C.: Reducing the number of comatose servers: automatic tuning as an opportunistic cloud-service. In: 2017 IEEE International Conference on Services Computing (SCC), pp. 487–490, June 2017
11. Setz, B., Rao, G.S.V., Lazovik, A., Aiello, M.: A data-driven approach to monitoring colocation data centers. In: 2019 IEEE International Conference on Big Data Intelligence and Computing (2019, to appear)
12. Vemula, D., Setz, B., Rao, G.S.V., Gangadharan, G.R., Aiello, M.: Metrics for sustainable data centers. IEEE Trans. Sustain. Comput. **PP**(99), 1 (2017)
13. Zaman, S.K., Khan, A.U.R., Shuja, J., Maqsood, T., Mustafa, S., Rehman, F.: A systems overview of commercial data centers: initial energy and cost analysis. Int. J. Inf. Technol. Web Eng. **14**, 42–65 (2019)
14. Zeck, A., Bouroudjian, J.: Real-world experience with a multicloud exchange. IEEE Cloud Comput. **4**(4), 6–11 (2017)

Modeling Users' Performance: Predictive Analytics in an IoT Cloud Monitoring System

Rosa Di Salvo[1](✉), Antonino Galletta[1], Orlando Marco Belcore[2], and Massimo Villari[1]

[1] MIFT Department, University of Messina, Messina, Italy
{rdisalvo,angalletta,mvillari}@unime.it
[2] Department of Engineering, University of Messina, Messina, Italy
obelcore@unime.it

Abstract. We exploit the feasibility of predictive modeling combined with the support given by a suitably defined IoT Cloud Infrastructure in the attempt of assessing and reporting relative performances for user-specific settings during a bike trial. The matter is addressed by introducing a suitable dynamical system whose state variables are the so-called origin-destination (OD) flow deviations obtained from prior estimates based on historical data recorded by means of mobile sensors directly installed in each bike through a fast real-time processing of big traffic data. We then use the Kalman filter theory in order to dynamically update an assignment matrix in such a context and gain information about usual routes and distances. This leads us to a dynamical ranking system for the users of the bike trial community making the award procedure more transparent.

1 Introduction

In last years, Smart Cities are becoming more and more popular. There are several definitions of Smart Cities: according to Giffinger et al. [1] a city becomes smart only if the performance indicators improve for several interconnected areas, such as economy, people, governance, environment, living and mobility; according to [2] and [3], e-health is a sub-area of the ICT strategies of smart cities. Smart mobility is emerging as a solution for many issues related to air and noise pollution, traffic congestion [4], transport and goods distribution slowness. In order to boost in this direction several initiatives have been proposed from local municipalities such as: (i) discounts on the purchase of season tickets for public transport; (ii) car pooling; (iii) free loan for the use of bikes, etc. In this paper, considering as starting point the project "A scuola e a lavoro con il TPL", an Italian project funded by the ministry of the environment, we propose a model to quantify and predict the use of bikes in order to assign penalties or awards to users based on their behaviour. Aim of the paper is therefore to define a forecasting system based on real information as accurate as possible to be used

© IFIP International Federation for Information Processing 2020
Published by Springer Nature Switzerland AG 2020
A. Brogi et al. (Eds.): ESOCC 2020, LNCS 12054, pp. 149–158, 2020.
https://doi.org/10.1007/978-3-030-44769-4_12

for evaluating the level of activity of trail users on usual routes by monitoring behavior consistencies or progresses towards a more bike-friendly attitude compared to previous habits. More specifically, we proposed a system that, starting from the analysis of usual routes and distances (gathered by means of IoT sensors installed on bikes), by using Kalman filtering techniques inside a discrete-time dynamical system formulation let us to properly simulate traffic flows. In view of the growing development of Smart City technologies, the IoT Cloud system for traffic monitoring described in this paper accounts for real-time information and provides prompt availability of a rich source of data to be exploited within a Kalman filtering approach in order to improve real-time path predictions and properly simulate traffic flows.

The remainder of the paper is organised as follows: Sect. 2 describes related works. Background and basic technologies are described in Sect. 3. Motivation are discussed in Sect. 4, proposed reference architecture and algorithms are discussed in Sect. 5. Finally, conclusions and our future directions are summarised in Sect. 6.

2   Related Work

It is well-known how the use of statistical methods in predicting specific parameters offers the opportunity to analyse huge amount of data and optimise a wide set of resources. In particular, a vast number of contributions dealing with the process of modelling traffic characteristics and developing short-term traffic forecasting algorithms have been proposed and presented in the literature (see [5] for a critical discussion concerning the selection of the proper methodological approach). Moreover, in the last few years, numerous research studies have been conducted in order to address the relevant issue of collecting traffic data coming from sensors installed on roads and possibly sending alert messages to users. IoT Cloud systems with connected vehicles integrated with mobile sensors for traffic monitoring aimed at big traffic data processing, that is vehicular Cloud computing, actually assume a relevant role in road traffic management [6]. In [7], where an IoT Cloud system for traffic monitoring and alert notification based on OpenGTS and MongoDB is described, it turns out how the need to resort to big data and Internet issues appears as a necessary requirement when dealing with data recovery and data processing related to sensing systems in urban scenarios. This matter becomes especially important because of the exponentially increasing of information to be stored and dynamically recovered to control and manage vehicular traffic (see also [8] and [9] further details). In the emerging field of systems and computing paradigms for big data storage and analytics [10], the traffic monitoring approach proposed in [7] offers a flexible, scalable and inexpensive way to collect sensor data from private vehicles.

Since traffic forecasting represents in general an important learning task in the transportation domain intended as a dynamic environment, a large amount of literature has been concerned with the development of Intelligent Transportation Systems (ITS) technologies [11], as well as with producing predictions from time series models ranging from ARIMA to nonlinear multivariate modeling [12], or involving neural networks [13]. Possible frameworks for producing short-term traffic forecasting models in real-time intelligent transportation systems may be based on several methodological approaches, such as Kalman filtering [14], exponential filtering [15], non-parametric statistical methods [16], multivariate state space analyses [17] or sequential learning [18].

In this direction, kept in mind the overwhelming progress of technologies, a composite modeling approach mixing tools derived from statistical analysis and ITS services would seem to provide an appealing setting with interesting perspectives.

3   Background

The development of the theoretical framework in which we are moving begins from both the setting of elastic Cloud-based designed micro-services and the traffic flows estimation approach adopted in [19]. Thus the system developed in this paper combines the advantages of a scalable Cloud-based infrastructure with a mesoscopic approach, where the kind of considered vehicles can be suitably defined, so that it can be applied to the considered case. Among dynamic traffic assignment models, classic mesoscopic approach, where packets of users belonging to the same mode move following a path, benefits from dynamic disaggregated traffic modelling (since the packets can be at least composed by a single vehicle modeled individually) adding the possibility of using macroscopic speed-density functions. In the following a short description of the theoretical assumptions and of the procedure is given.

3.1   Estimation of Origin-Destination Flows

Several methods for analyzing and forecasting traffic counts based on other available information, such as historical information, and the issue of the off-line estimation of the OD (Origin Destination) demand matrices for link flows in a freeway network (a directed graph that represents local streets or groups of streets), are deeply analyzed in [20]. In transportation systems, the modelization of assignment problems allows to simulate how demand and supply interact in a transportation network. Starting from origin-destination demand flows, the calculation of performance measures and user flows for each supply element enables the description of path choice behaviors. In particular, in the context of a simulation model of a system of real-time traveler information providing short time forecasts of time-dependent link flows in a network, the iterative application of a sequential method combining observed traffic counts with historical information represents an interesting way to perform effectively the estimation/updating of an Origin-Destination trip table for the last interval. Consider an interval h, and let d_h^H be the historical demand, while f_h and f_h^O represent the assigned and the observed link flows. Following [19], the estimated demand for the current interval, d_h^E, is obtainable by means of a generalized least square (GLS) estimator, say

$$d_h^E = \underset{d_h \geq 0}{\mathrm{argmin}}[(f_h - f_h^O)^T(f_h - f_h^O) + \theta(d_h - d_h^H)^T(d_h - d_h^H)], \qquad (1)$$

where the parameter θ is related to the weight of flows with respect to the demand.

To deal with problems of traffic simulation-assignment and dynamic network loading (DNL) map by means of assignment matrices in order to estimate Origin-Destination demand flows based on the evaluation of assigned flows, depending on the link flows f_h, the solution of a fixed-point problem is therefore required.

3.2 Prediction of Origin-Destination Flows

For solving the important and hard problem of predicting Origin-Destination (OD) tables for the forthcoming time intervals of a fixed predictive horizon either a direct or an indirect approach can be used. In the former case, statistical methods or filtering techniques are applied so that estimates of the OD matrices for the actual time slices are derived from historical data series, whereas in the later case the prediction of traffic counts for the future time intervals is estimated before the computation of the demand matrices is performed. According to the direct approach described in [19], once introduced the variables d_h^H, d_h^E, and d_h^P, representing the historical, the estimated, and the predicted demand at the interval h, the predicted OD values can be estimated by means of the law

$$d_{h+1}^P = \alpha \left[\frac{d_h^E}{d_h^H} d_{h+1}^H \right] + (1 - \alpha) d_{h+1}^H, \qquad (2)$$

where α is a smoothing parameter, whereas the ratio d_h^E / d_h^H has the meaning of taking into account possible unprecedented future events.

3.3 Dynamic Traffic Assignment

Let us divide the simulation period into subintervals and assume that all the travelling users experience the same traffic conditions. Moreover, for the sake of simplicity, we make the assumption that the length of each time interval t is the same, and we consider a uniform distribution of the departures within the intervals. The network where the users are supposed to move is represented by means of a graph, composed of nodes and arcs. From a functional point of view, each arc a, of a certain length L_a, is thought of as divided into a running and a queuing segment.

The mesoscopic approach allows the evaluation of relevant traffic indicators by grouping the vehicles into packets made up, in general, by several users having homogenous characteristics. We describe a mesoscopic model based on a packet approach (in which every packet is considered as a unique entity), providing an efficient way to carry out the dynamic traffic assignment (DTA) [21], by using the following general notation and terminology. In such a framework, the packet $P(t, k, u)$ represents in general a number of vehicles $x(t, k, u)$, belonging to class u, which depart during the same interval t and move along path k. We shall here consider the specific case where the generic packet P is made up by a single bike, that is $x(t, k, u) = 1$. Thus, the moment a new departure interval t

starts, a certain number of concurrently leaving packets (corresponding to the amount of means of transportation belonging to class u which follow path k) is generated. When the time interval t elapses, the evaluation of the outflow arc characteristics of interest for the purposes of the analysis, say queues, densities, speed, occupancy, is performed, and the obtained values are then used in view of the assignment of the outflow modalities of the points in the subsequent interval.

3.4   Kalman Filtering

The Kalman filter [22] is a recursive procedure for computing the optimal estimator within the class of linear estimators of a state vector at a certain time, based on the available (even noisy) past information. It is based on the assumption of normality of the noise and the process. Let us introduce the matrices $A_k \in \mathbb{R}^n \times \mathbb{R}^n$, connecting the state $x_{k-1} \in \mathbb{R}^n$ at the previous time step $(k-1)$ to the one at the current step (k) (*measurement sensitivity matrix*), $B_k \in \mathbb{R}^n \times \mathbb{R}^\ell$, relating some optional control input $u_k \in \mathbb{R}^\ell$ to the state, and $H_k \in \mathbb{R}^m \times \mathbb{R}^n$, establishing the relation between the state and the measurement $z_k \in \mathbb{R}^m$. According to the original formulation, the measurements are obtained at each discrete point in time k by means of the *measurement model*

$$z_k = H_k x_k + v_k, \tag{3}$$

and the Kalman filter provides an estimate of the state of the controlled process that is governed by the the linear stochastic difference equation (*system dynamic model*)

$$x_k = A_k x_{k-1} + B_k u_k + w_{k-1}, \tag{4}$$

the normally distributed independent random variables w_k and v_k (*i.e.*, $E < w_k v_j^T >= 0$ for all k and j) representing the process and the white measurement noise, respectively, say $p(w_k) \sim N(0, Q_k), p(v_k) \sim N(0, R_k)$ with Q, R covariance matrices. Once introduced the *Kalman gain matrix*

$$\bar{K}_k = P_k(-)H_k^T[H_k P_k(-)H_k^T + R_k]^{-1}, \tag{5}$$

the *state estimate observational update* at time k

$$x_k(+) = x_k(-) + \bar{K}_k[z_k - H_k x_k(-)] \tag{6}$$

returns an *a posteriori* value of the estimate $(\tilde{x}_k(+))$ from the *a priori* estimate $(\tilde{x}_k(-))$ of the state x_k of the system based on the information provided by the observation.

4   Case Study

The framework described above fits into a pilot bike trial with the aim of providing a possible tool for evaluating the users' commitment. The definition of the IoT Cloud monitoring system modeling users' performance presented in this paper makes for predictive analysis in order to address the problem of establishing a dynamical ranking system by means of an algorithm designed considering that:

- each user is assigned the same starting score (depending on the duration of the experimental phase), which represents his/her initial rating;
- the usual routes of each user and the average distances traveled during working days are estimated by employing traffic flows estimation techniques on actual geo-location data collected in real-time by a GSM/GPRS/GPS TK103 tracker based system, forwarded to a GeoJSON parsing micro-service, and then analyzed by means of an IoT Cloud system providing fast big traffic data processing;
- the users' rankings are dynamically updated as a result of the comparisons with the individual averages (once fixed a suitable tolerance).

To further clarify how the mechanism driving the reward/penalty assignments works, consider the case of a pilot trial during a fixed number of weeks, and suppose that we do expect that, at least for a certain percentage of this time interval, the user reports a regular use of the bike provided in concession. After that each individual initial score has been assigned when the trial starts, at every check, if the user did not appear to be virtuous, his/her ranking would be decreased (alternatively, his/her score would increase), on condition that in case of negative scores the user loses the lease of the bike.

5   Architectural and Algorithm Design

A suitably defined IoT Cloud Infrastructure for managing and mining sensor data, in a Smart City perspective, supports access to real-time urban data

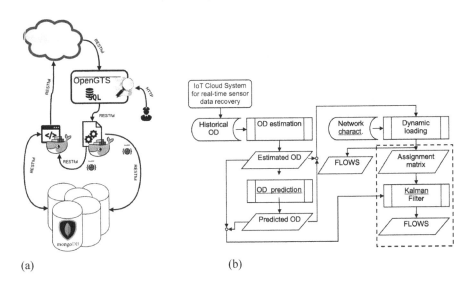

(a)   (b)

Fig. 1. (a) The IoT Cloud-based Monitoring System described in [7]. (b) A view of the functional diagram of the model.

streams by exploiting interconnections in order to effectively approach a predictive traffic analysis.

The traffic flow estimation approach used in this paper is defined as follows. Let $\mathcal{S}$ be the system made up of the N individuals which are the users of the bike trial community, say $\mathcal{S} = \{u_k\}_{k=1,...,N}$. With the aim of studying the OD flows in the five working days from Monday to Friday daily for each week, we define the state vector of the system $\mathcal{S}$ by considering the OD flows for each user recovered from the data produced by the IoT Cloud system for traffic monitoring and alert notification described in [7]. Such a kind of Cloud-based system, whose possible scheme is depicted in Fig. 1(a), is designed by considering mobile sensors based on tracker devices gathering movement data from the transportation vehicles (in our case the bikes), and proved able to elastically scale up/down its internal micro-services thanks to Docker containers and send all geo-location data (in real-time by means of a 4G network connection) to an OpenGTS server storing them in a SQL database. In addition, incoming unstructured geo-location data are forwarded to a GeoJSON parsing micro-service in order to be inserted in a MongoDB distributed database (the unstructured data guarantees a good flexibility for further data analysis and manipulation, [7]). This compact size and simple management system for tracking mobile objects, besides supporting security, positioning, monitoring, GPRS data transmission and geo-localization, suitably provides historical OD data in the initialization phase of our approach. The variables $\{d_{k,\ell}\}_{k=1,...,N,\ \ell=1,...,7}$ are thus associated to the distances traveled by each user on working ($\ell = 1,\ldots,5$) and non-working ($\ell = 6,7$) days. As a start, we focus on the users' activity during the working days and consider the mean values $\bar{d}_k$ ($\ell = 1,\ldots,5, k = 1,\ldots,N$) of the distances travelled at the end of every week of the trial.

The methodology described below allows us to achieve good results in predicting flows also for few steps ahead. During each time slice (most likely every day) the values of the Origin-Destination (OD) matrices are estimated based on the acquired information on traffic movements during the time interval just elapsed, and the prediction of the OD matrices for the subsequent time intervals within the prediction horizon are estimated. At this point, suitable assignment matrices, to be intended as fractions of the OD matrices corresponding to the leaving time intervals that are related to the flow along the given link during the current interval, are derived by using a Dynamic Network Loading (DNL) approach, and then their entries are used within a filtering framework in order to produce flow forecasts. This approach (whose scheme, shown in Fig. 1(b), refers to procedures clarified in Sect. 3) lets us to model the usual paths of the various users in order to produce an estimate of the average distances which are intended as individual standards of use during the trial. After that, the dynamic traffic assignment (DTA) is carried out by means of a mesoscopic model based on packet approach (see [21] and references therein for more in-depth details) and traffic flow forecasting is directly related to the obtained results by means of a Kalman filtering technique. In particular, once at each step the transition matrix A and an assignment matrix B are evaluated within the DTA procedure

on the basis of the speeds observed at the current and previous intervals, the
transition and *observation* equations of the filter read

$$f_{k+1}^E = A_k f_k^E + B_k u_k + w_k,$$
$$f_k^O = H_k f_k^E + v_K,$$

(7)

where the subscript k indicates the time interval we are referring to, the variables $f_k^{E/O}$ represent the estimated/observed flow, u_k is the historical variation of demand, whereas w_k and v_k are the process and the measurement errors, respectively.

To apply the Kalman filter and search for the optimal estimates, we perform the following steps: after the phase of *initialization*, in which we assign a starting value to the state vector and the covariance matrix based on the traffic data recovered and processed through vehicular Cloud computing, during the phase of *correction* we compute the Kalman gain matrix through which we update the *a priori* estimate and covariance; then, during the final phase of *prediction*, we obtain forecasts of the future state (through the correct *a posteriori estimate*) and of the covariance of the estimation error.

The application of the methods outlined above for the motivations and the reasoning set forth in Sect. 4 results in carrying out the following steps:

1. *Ranking initialization*: $r_k^{(0)} = \tilde{r}_k$ for each $k = 1, \ldots, N$;
2. *State vector initialization*: the state vector of the system is initialized by taking into account the OD data provided by a scalable Cloud-based infrastructure for the processing of big traffic data;
3. *Kalman filtering*: through the application of a discrete KF the historical series of the state vector values is filtered so as to obtain forecasts on the future states of the system;
4. *Tolerance definition*: individual tolerances are established based on the average of the distances m_k traveled by each user from the beginning of the trial: $\tau_k = \tau_k(m_k)$;
5. *Check*: every time step t, the users' ranking system is updated by adopting the rule acting as follows:
   - if $\bar{d}_k^{(t-1)} < m_k - \tau_k$, then $r_k^{(t)} = r_k^{(t-1)} - 1$;
   - if $\bar{d}_k^{(t-1)} \in [m_k - \tau_k, m_k)$, then $r_k^{(t)} = r_k^{(t-1)}$;
   - if $\bar{d}_k^{(t-1)} > m_k$, then $r_k^{(t)} = r_k^{(t-1)} + b_k$, b_k being some bonus related to the individual empowerment.

6   Conclusions and Future Work

The modeling approach described in this paper introduces a flow forecasting technique combined with an IoT Cloud Infrastructure for managing and mining sensor data in order to produce a predictive traffic analysis by taking advantage both of simulative and statistical methods. The valuable features in terms of performance of both information insertion and retrieval in MongoDB which characterize the scalable Cloud-based infrastructure used to implement an intelligent traffic monitoring system, where both OpenGTS server and micro-services were deployed by means of Docker containers, confer the implemented solution the advantage of supporting an efficient dynamic system update. Planned implementation and evaluation, immediately following the start of the trial, include the application of the IoT cloud system to storage and processing of geo-location historical data of the users of the community provided by tracker devices attached to the bikes and the use of the described dynamic network loading model for path forecast evaluation in order to obtain an efficient management of the merit ranking. Further investigations related to the application of this framework to concrete situations are planned with the goal of testing the practical application of the framework and extending the analysis and the services to more general and rich scenarios.

Acknowledgment. This work has been partially supported by the Italian project "A scuola e a lavoro con il TPL". Authors would like to thank for their valuable work Alessio Catalfamo, Francesco Martella and all partners of the project.

References

1. Giffinger, R., Gudrun, H.: Smart cities ranking: an effective instrument for the positioning of the cities. ACE Architect. City Environ. **4**(12), 7–26 (2010)
2. Al-Azzam, M., Alazzam, M.: Smart city and smart-health framework, challenges and opportunities. Int. J. Adv. Comput. Sci. Appl. **10**, 171–176 (2019)
3. Ji, Z., Ganchev, I., O'Droma, M.: A generic IoT architecture for smart cities, pp. 196–199 (2014)
4. Filocamo, B., Galletta, A., Fazio, M., Ruiz, J.A., Sotelo, M.A., Villari, M.: An innovative osmotic computing framework for self adapting city traffic in autonomous vehicle environment. In: 2018 IEEE Symposium on Computers and Communications (ISCC), pp. 01267–01270 (2018)
5. Vlahogianni, E.I., Golias, J.C., Karlaftis, M.G.: Short-term traffic forecasting: overview of objectives and methods. Transp. Rev. **24**, 533–557 (2004)
6. Ahmad, I., Noor, R.M., Ali, I., Imran, M., Vasilakos, A.: Characterizing the role of vehicular cloud computing in road traffic management. Int. J. Distrib. Sens. Netw. **13** (2017)
7. Celesti, A., Galletta, A., Carnevale, L., Fazio, M., Lay-Ekuakille, A., Villari, M.: An IoT cloud system for traffic monitoring and vehicular accidents prevention based on mobile sensor data processing. IEEE Sens. J. 18(12), 4795–4802 (2017)
8. Al-Najada, H., Mahgoub, I.: Big vehicular traffic data mining: towards accident and congestion prevention (2016)
9. Lay-Ekuakille, A., Giannoccaro, N.I., Casciaro, S., Conversano, F., Velázquez, R.: Modeling and designing a full beamformer for acoustic sensing and measurement. Int. J. Smart Sens. Intell. Syst. **10**, 718–734 (2017)
10. Fazio, M., Celesti, A., Villari, M., Puliafito, A.: The need of a hybrid storage approach for IoT in PaaS cloud federation, pp. 779–784 (2014)
11. Figueiredo, L., Jesus, I., Machado, J., Ferreira, J.R., de Carvalho, J.L.M.: Towards the development of intelligent transportation systems. In: Proceedings of 2001 IEEE Intelligent Transportation Systems, ITSC 2001 (Cat. No.01TH8585), pp. 1206–1211 (2001)

12. Armstrong, J.S. (ed.): Principles of Forecasting: A Handbook for Researchers and Practitioners. International Series in Operations Research and Management Science. Springer, Dordrecht (2001). https://doi.org/10.1007/978-0-306-47630-3
13. Zhang, P.: Time series forecasting using a hybrid ARIMA and neural network model. Neurocomputing **50**, 159–175 (2003)
14. Emami, A., Sarvi, M., Asadi Bagloee, S.: Using Kalman filter algorithm for short-term traffic flow prediction in a connected vehicle environment. J. Mod. Transp. **27**, 222–232 (2019)
15. Ross, P.: Exponential filtering of traffic data. Number 869 in Transportation Research Record. National Academy of Sciences (1982)
16. Clark, S., Grant-Muller, S., Chen, H.: Using non-parametric tests to evaluate traffic forecasting performance. J. Transp. Stat. **5**, 47–56 (2002)
17. Stathopoulos, A., Karlaftis, M.: A multivariate state space approach for urban traffic flow modeling and prediction. Transp. Res. Part C Emerg. Technol. **11**, 121–135 (2003)
18. Chen, H., Grant-Muller, S.: Use of sequential learning for short-term traffic forecasting. Transp. Res. Part C Emerg. Technol. **9**, 319–336 (2001)
19. Di Gangi, M., Croce, A.: Combining simulative and statistical approach for short time flow forecasting. In: Proceedings of ETC 2005, Transport Policy and Operations-Traffic Engoneering and Street Management-Intergrated Traffic Management II, Strasbourg, France, 18–20 September 2005 (2005)
20. Cascetta, E., Inaudi, D., Marquis, G.: Dynamic estimators of origin-destination matrices using traffic counts. Transp. Sci. **27**, 363–373 (1993)
21. Di Gangi, M.: Modeling evacuation of a transport system: application of a multi-modal mesoscopic dynamic traffic assignment model. IEEE Trans. Intell. Transp. Syst. **12**, 1157–1166 (2012)
22. Kalman, R.E.: A new approach to linear filtering and prediction problems. Trans. ASME J. Basic Eng. **82**(1), 35–45 (1960)

Data Distribution and Analytics

Multi-source Distributed System Data for AI-Powered Analytics

Sasho Nedelkoski[1]([✉]), Jasmin Bogatinovski[1], Ajay Kumar Mandapati[1], Soeren Becker[1], Jorge Cardoso[2,3], and Odej Kao[1]

[1] Technische Universität Berlin, Berlin, Germany
{nedelkoski,jasmin.bogatinovski,ajaykumar.mandapati,
soeren.becker,odej.kao}@tu-berlin.de
[2] Huawei Munich Research Center, Munich, Germany
jorge.cardoso@huawei.com
[3] Department of Informatics Engineering/CISUC, University of Coimbra,
Coimbra, Portugal

Abstract. The emerging field of Artificial Intelligence for IT Operations (AIOps) utilizes monitoring data, big data platforms, and machine learning, to automate operations and maintenance (O&M) tasks in complex IT systems. The available research data usually contain only a single source of information, often logs or metrics. The inability of the single-source data to describe precise state of the distributed systems leads to methods that fail to make effective use of the joint information, thus, producing large number of false predictions. Therefore, current data limits the possibilities for greater advances in AIOps research. To overcome these constraints, we created a complex distributed system testbed, which generates multi-source data composed of distributed traces, application logs, and metrics. This paper provides detailed descriptions of the infrastructure, testbed, experiments, and statistics of the generated data. Furthermore, it identifies how such data can be utilized as a stepping stone for the development of novel methods for O&M tasks such as anomaly detection, root cause analysis, and remediation.

The data from the testbed and its code is available at https://zenodo.org/record/3549604.

Keywords: AIOps · Distributed system · Dataset · Tracing · Metrics · Logs · Anomaly detection · Root-cause analysis

1 Introduction

AIOps refers to multi-layered technology platforms that automate and enhance IT operations by using analytics and machine learning [6]. AIOps was introduced to reduce the cost and increase the effectiveness of O&M tasks on ever-increasing complex public, private, edge, mobile, and hybrid cloud environments. The transition from mainframes, to virtual machines, to containers, and serverless computing made existing approaches and tools which rely on simple statistical

© IFIP International Federation for Information Processing 2020
Published by Springer Nature Switzerland AG 2020
A. Brogi et al. (Eds.): ESOCC 2020, LNCS 12054, pp. 161–176, 2020.
https://doi.org/10.1007/978-3-030-44769-4_13

methods obsolete due to the increasing complexity and communication patterns between services. Notable examples include Zabbix, Cacti, and Nagios [17,33].

Monitoring data is a key element of new AIOps tools and one of the cornerstones of research. The data generated by distributed IT systems can be classified into three main categories: metrics, application logs, and distributed traces [30]. *Metrics* are numeric values measured over a period of time. They describe the utilization and status of the infrastructure, typically regarding CPU, memory, disk, network throughput, and service call latency. *Application logs* enable developers to record what actions were executed at runtime by software. Service, microservices, and other systems generate logs which are composed of timestamped records with a structure and free-form text. *Distributed traces* record the workflows of services executed in response to requests, e.g., HTTP or RPC requests. The records contain information about the execution graph and performance at a (micro)service level.

Recently, various approaches – focusing on a wide range of datasets, O&M tasks, and IT systems – have been proposed. This includes variety of tasks, which extract knowledge from a specific type of data. For example, anomaly detection has been applied to metrics (numeric) [11,26,27], logs (unstructured numeric and text data) [4,7,24], and also to distributed system traces (unstructured numeric and text data) [18,19].

The existing research has mainly explored publicly available data, which usually captures only a single data source category. This limits both the development of new methods that could extract knowledge from multi-source data and their proper evaluation. The absence of data repositories capturing the three data categories from modern distributed systems prevents the development of methods for multi-source mining, knowledge extraction, semantic information learning from the naturally linked data sources. Furthermore, enables fault detection, root-cause analysis, and remediation that could give advances in the field as existing approaches typically produce a large number of false positives.

We address this issues by producing the following contributions:

- A new data of metrics, logs, and traces generated by a distributed system based on microservice architecture.
- Description of the approach developed to generate the multi-source system data and its statistics.
- Analysis of existing datasets utilized for the evaluation of AIOps algorithms, highlighting their benefits and their limitations.
- Applications of the multi-source data to develop new algorithms to support additional O&M tasks.

Specifically, during the development and data generation process, we derived the following requirements.:

R1 Originality. The data should fill the gaps in existing datasets for various AIOps tasks including anomaly detection and root-cause analysis. Moreover should open new possibilities for the development of novel methods for O&M tasks.

R2 Reusability. The data should be modular and open for and adaptable to various use cases. Next to that, the system should be easy to handle. This should allow development of single- and multi-source methods.

R3 Quality. The data should be analyzed before publishing, free of errors, and directly usable.

R3 Extendability. The testbed generating the data should allow different system configurations, fault injections, workloads, and thus data generation which suits the real production scenario of various interested parties.

2 Related Work

Metrics, logs, and traces are important data sources that are fundamental to the operation of complex distributed systems. In following we study related work for these data accordingly.

The metric data is a common way to extract useful information for describing the state of the system. However, often it is not sufficient and reliable to model the complex systems. The metrics data are obtained from monitoring of the resources such as CPU, memory, disk and network throughput and latency. A plethora of available collections of datasets containing metric data can be found in Stonybrook [31], where multiple datasets for different tasks related to anomaly detection can be found. Numenta [1] predominantly contains datasets from streaming and real-time applications, while Harvard [9], ELKI [8], LMU [15] store network intrusion data. Recently, there are multiple studies which utilize these datasets for anomaly detection, root-cause analysis, and remediation. In Subutai et al. [1], a novel anomaly detection method based on hierarchical temporal memory (HTM) is introduced. It enables anomaly detection in the streaming setting to tackle the problems of concept drift and the problem of multiple streaming sources utilizing metrics data. In Schmidt et al. [26], an unsupervised anomaly detection framework is developed and applied to real-time monitoring data in a distributed environment.

The main challenge that AIOps systems analyzing log data are facing is the unstructured nature of the logs. This problem usually requires prior and proper preprocessing and/or inclusion of domain knowledge. Often, approaches extract log key identifiers for the logs and are modeling their sequences. There exist two resources of log data for cluster systems available. The CFDR resource [3] stores links or 19 log datasets grouped in 11 data collections. The datasets cover both hardware and software logs. The second resource is the loghub data resource [35]. It consists of 16 datasets describing systems spanning across distributed systems, supercomputers, operating systems, mobile systems, server applications and standalone software. The datasets cover a different time from a few days until a few months. From the perspective of the system description, these data have weakness in providing just a single aspect of the system. In Meng et al. [16] the LogAnomlay system for detection of anomalies from logs is introduced. It utilizes a novel template2vec technique to encode the logs. Further, it extracts quantitative patterns from the logs. It uses LSTMs to detect the sequential and quantitative anomalies in the logs. In Zheng et al. [7] the DeepLog system is introduced. It tries to model the logs as natural language sequences. It allows to update the model by the operator and provides an automatic reconstruction of the workflows to enable root cause analysis.

In microservice architectures, traces are graph-like structures composed of events or spans [22]. The traces represent the system execution workflow, hence detailed information for individual services and the causal relationship to other related services can be inferred. Nedelkoski et al. [18,19] introduce novel anomaly detection methods for distributed tracing data. They proposed a multimodal neural network with long short-term memory (LSTM) to enable the learning from the sequential nature in the tracing data. They describe how the data is obtained, but the datasets are not publicly available. Azure Public dataset composes of two datasets representing two representative traces of the virtual machine of Microsoft Azure [5]. It is mostly utilized to improve resource management in large cloud platforms. Alibaba's cluster data is a collection of two datasets from real-world production [2,14,28]. In Zhen et al. [28] a novel system which automatically diagnoses stragglers for jobs is introduced. Li et al. [14] propose a deep reinforcement learning approach towards the job scheduling task. It can automatically obtain a fitness calculation method that optimizes the throughput of a set of jobs from experience. Google's collection of two tracing datasets originates from parts of Google cluster management software and systems [10].

Limitation for all the above-mentioned datasets is the absence of multi-source (view) data describing a single system. The lack of data from all observability components from one system does not allow the development of holistic systems for fault detection, root-cause analysis and remediation that consider multiple sources of data simultaneously. Our collection of data, describing the same system from the 3 perspectives of logs, metricise and traces, to the best of our knowledge, is the first of its kind. This enables building models with diverse complementary information, hence making AIOps systems to perform better [19].

3 Dataset Generator

In this section, we describe the infrastructure, experiments, workload, and the injected faults as part of the testbed for data generation. The testbed and the generated data follow the requirements stated above, as every parameter stated in following can be easily changed, satisfying part of **R2**, and **R4**.

3.1 Infrastructure

An OpenStack [29] testbed based on a microservice architecture that is running in a dockerized environment called Kolla-Ansible [13] was first deployed. OpenStack is a cloud operating system that controls large pools of computing, storage, and networking resources throughout a data-centre, all managed and provisioned through APIs with common authentication mechanisms.

The experimental testbed setup is shown in Fig. 1 and for the purpose of the generation of the data it consists of one control node named `wally-113` and four compute nodes: `wally-122`, `wally-123`, `wally-124`, and `wally-117`. It was deployed on bare-metal nodes of a cluster where each node has RAM 16 GB, 3x 1TB of disks, and 2x 1Gbit Ethernet NIC. Three hard disks were combined to a software RAID 5 for data redundancy.

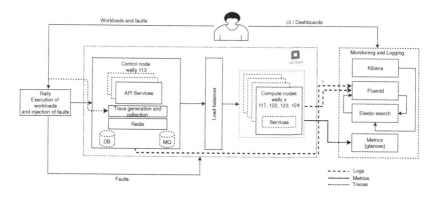

Fig. 1. Illustration of the infrastructure from where the data was generated.

3.2 Workloads and Faults Injected

To generate workloads and inject faults into the infrastructure we used Rally [25]. Rally docker image was used to create the load and inject os-faults [23] appropriately. Jasmin: We selected a list of workloads and faults that are close representatives to real production faults. The listed workloads and faults in following cover user request that is served by the main Openstack projects.

- *Create and delete server.* Jasmin: Creates and deletes a server (virtual machine). Nova project is mostly affected and present in the data. We injected a compute fault which is restarting the api container that run on the compute nodes.
- *Create and delete image.* Jasmin: The task for creating and deleting images accepts the image-location locally/ over the internet, format of the output image once created. It creates and deletes an image. The glance project of Openstack provides a service where users can upload and discover data assets that are meant to be used with other services. Here we inject the fault in the `glance-api` running on the controller node.

– *Create and delete network.* Jasmin: Rally provides task that accepts the format for creating and deletion of networks for various configurations such as multiple users and tenants. Neutron is an OpenStack project to provide networking as a service between interface devices (e.g., vNICs) managed by other Openstack services (e.g., nova, heat etc). There are various components that we focus on while injecting faults such as disrupting the below-mentioned services running in docker containers: `neutron metadata agent`, `neutron l3 agent`, `neutron dhcp agent`, `neutron openvswitch agent` and `neutron server`.

We performed two different experiments. In the first experiment, the user actions as a workload were executed in a sequential way, when one finishes then the next is started. This experiment was performed for 750, 1000, and 1000 iterations (*create and delete server*, *create and delete image*, *create and delete network*), where faults were injected every 250 iterations respectively. The fault was injected in only one iteration, however, we noticed that some of the faults take time and propagate the errors to other iterations as well. In the second experiment, the rally workloads were concurrently executed. This experiment was performed for 2000, 3000, and 6000 iterations for *create and delete server*, *create and delete image* and *create and delete network*, respectively. The faults were injected at different rates, 250 for *create and delete server* and *create and delete image* and 500 iterations for *create and delete network*. The number of the iterations for each action was chosen so that all workloads approximatelly finish in the same time. The data from the second experiment is slightly more suited for multi-source methods utilizing distributed log data, as it was generated with that as a goal. Also, HTML reports were collected which correlates all the events of creations, failures and which injections were made. This report serves as ground truth for the normal and anomalous state of the system.
Jasmin:

3.3   Data Collection

In following we describe the technologies and the methods used to collect the generated data.

Metrics. For the metrics collection across the physical nodes in the infrastructure, we utilize Glances [20], a cross-platform monitoring tool which aims to present a maximum of information into a minimal space through curses or Web-based interface. Glances is written in Python and uses the `psutil` library to get information from a system. It can adapt dynamically the displayed information depending on the terminal size. It can also work in client/server mode, also remote monitoring could be done via terminal, Web interface or API (XMLRPC and RESTful). Glances was used to gather information such as CPU, MEM and load of the machine (either controller or the compute nodes). These metrics were saved into a CSV file via the `glances-cli`.

Logs. OpenStack services use standard logging levels. For aggregating logs from all services running across the physical nodes, was used ELK (Elasticsearch, Logstash, and Kibana). Elasticsearch is a search and analytics engine which resolves the search requests. Logstash is a server-side data processing pipeline that ingests data from multiple sources simultaneously, transforms it, and then sends it to Elasticsearch. For this Fluentd, which is an open-source data collector for the unified logging layer, was utilized. It allows unifying data collection and consumption for better use and understanding of data. Kibana is a dashboard that gives the ability to the users to visualize data with charts and graphs using data that is collected by Elasticsearch. Finally, for exporting data from Elasticsearch into CSV a CLI tool, es2csv [32] was utilized. The benefit we obtain from this tool is that it can query bulk docs in multiple indices and get only selected fields, this reduces query execution time and enhances the speed of aggregating these logs that are existing on various physical nodes. We provide both, the aggregated logs as well as the raw logs to cover possible development of methods that process raw logs, such as log parsing.

Traces. OpenStack consists of multiple projects, where each project is composed of multiple services. To process user requests, e.g., creating a virtual machine, OpenStack uses multiple services from different projects. To support troubleshooting, OpenStack introduces a small but powerful library called `osprofiler` that is used by all OpenStack projects and their Python clients [21] to generate traces. It generates one trace per request, that goes through all involved services, and builds a tree of calls which captures a workflow of service invocations. To identify workflows, we monitor the following call types:

- HTTP. Captures HTTP requests, the latency of service, and projects involved.
- RPC. Represent the duration of parts of request related to different services in one project.
- DB API. The time that the request spent in the DB layer.
- Driver. In the case of nova, cinder and others we have vendor drivers.

The `osprofiler` library collects these records in a trace per request and stores them in a database (e.g., Redis). From Redis, we can query and analyze traces.

4   Dataset Description

The workloads and faults described in the previous section were executed on the testbed. As explained, the execution generated three main categories of observability data: distributed traces, metrics, and application logs. These data were recorded in concurrently in order to provide the state of the system from multiple points of view, which satisfies the **R1** for originality as no such dataset exists in previous work. In the following two sections, we describe the main attributes, properties, and statistics of each data category of the first experiment. Due to page limitations, we refer the reader to the above link in the abstract for the code for extracting the data statistics from the second experiment. All other properties hold for both experiments.

4.1   Metrics

The metrics data category contains data for the 5 physical nodes in the infrastructure. The 5 files are named metrics_wally_N, where N is either the controller node or one of the compute nodes. Each of these files has 7 features:

- now. The timestamp of the recording.
- cpu.user. Percent time spent in userspace. The user CPU time is the time spent on the processor running your program's code (or code in libraries).
- mem.used. The RAM usage of the physical host.
- load.cpucore. The number of cores of the physical host.
- load.min1, min5, min15. Linux load averages are system load averages that show the running tasks demand on the system as an average number of running plus waiting threads. This measures demand, which can be greater than what the system is currently processing.

A small sample of the metrics data for the wally113 is shown in Table 1 where we can see part of the metrics data.

Table 1. Metrics from the controller node (wally 113)

timestamp	cpu.user	mem.used (B)	load. cpucore	load. min1	load. min5	load. min15
2019-11-19 16:56:32	11.5	10221035520	8	0.8	1.02	1.18
2019-11-19 16:56:32	10.4	10221117440	8	0.8	1.02	1.18
2019-11-19 16:56:33	11.1	10222948352	8	0.8	1.02	1.18
2019-11-19 16:56:33	14.3	10223144960	8	0.8	1.02	1.18
2019-11-19 16:56:34	10.7	10222866432	8	0.8	1.02	1.18
2019-11-19 16:56:34	10.7	10223480832	8	0.8	1.02	1.18

4.2   Logs

The log files are distributed over the infrastructure and they are grouped in directories by the OpenStack projects (e.g., nova, neutron, glance, etc.) at the wally nodes. At each of the physical nodes, there are different project running. The control node has more services running and thus has more log files for the

OpenStack projects. Each project on the physical hosts has its log directory where the logs are stored. Inside each of the log directories for the projects, there are several log files. Important to note here is that even the log files are highly distributed over projects and physical nodes, they all represent the state of the system. We provide the raw log directories in this dataset along with the aggregated log file. Using the elastic search and Kibana stack we can aggregate all the logs into a central database which can serve as a starting point for the analysis.

The log entries have in total of 23 features. Not all the features are always present for all the log entries. The features: _id, _index, _score are added metadata from Kibana. The _type is fluent, the collector which is responsible for sending all the metrics and logs to Kibana. In the following, we describe the main features present in the log data.

- `hostname`. Name of the physical host (e.g., wally113)
- `user id, project domain, tenant id, request id, user domain, domain id`. Are features describing the user request to Openstack.
- `timestamp, @timestamp`. The time when the record was created.
- `log level`. Describes the level of the log entry. It can be info, error, warning, etc.
- `pid`. Process ID.
- `Payload`. Gives the most important information of the log i.e., the body of the log entry.
- `programname`. The OpenStack project that generated the log entry.
- `python module` The module responsible for generation of the log entry, and the
- `logger` Tells which project logs the event.
- `http * related fields`. Are only present if there is an HTTP call describing the endpoint, status core, version, and the method.

For the parsing of the logs, template matching, and analysis we suggest using the aggregated file described instead of the directories with raw log files, as all of the information is preserved and more structured for direct analysis. For multi-source log anomaly detection, if the aggregated file is utilized, we suggest splitting by "logger" in order to obtain entries which are grouped by their corresponding service.

4.3   Traces

The traces in the dataset are contained in 3 directories: *boot_delete, create_delete_image,* and *network_create_delete*. Each of the directories contains the scripts for running the workload and the fault injections along with the actual tracing data. These directories contain JSON files of the traces. This structure is preserved among all types of workloads (Rally actions).

Every trace has its features in the JSON entries or events. These features depend on multiple factors such as the user request, infrastructure, load balancers, and caching. An event is a vector of key-value pairs (k_i, v_i) describing the state, performance, and further characteristics of service at a given time t_i. In following we describe the main features of the events in a trace:

- host. Name of the physical host.
- name. Event name (e.g., compute_apistop).
- service. Service name (e.g., osapi_compute).
- project, Openstack project (e.g., nova).
- timestamp. The time when the event is recorded.
- trace_id. ID of the span (contains two events, e.g., compute_api-stop and compute_api-start).
- parent_id. The *parent_id* gives the ID of the parent event. This attribute can be used to represent the trace in a graph.
- base_id. ID of the trace, different events and spans with same base_id belong to one trace.

Two start and stop events (e.g., compute_apistart and compute_apistop) with the same *trace_id*. The subtraction between the stop timestamp and the start timestamp gives the duration of the span. The above features together with the duration are the most important in describing the structure, preserving the parent-child causal relationship, and the duration which represents the response time of the service invoked.

The events also contain other attributes that can be found for specific types. For example, *path, scheme, method* for HTTP calls, where the *path* and *scheme* represents the HTTP endpoint and HTTP scheme and *method* can be GET or POST. Further, the *db statement* in DB calls gives information about the SQL query, while the *function, name, args, kwargs* in RPC calls tell which function was invoked with the its corresponding arguments.

4.4   Ground Truth Labels

The workloads described along with the faults injected are both recorded in Rally HTML and JSON reports which are located at each of the directories containing trace data. These reports provide pseudo ground truth labels for the traces, metrics, and logs. They contain information for the times when the faults were injected and the resulting high level error messages. Taking the period when the anomaly was injected and merging it with the timestamps of the data files can give us true labels for the evaluation. We suggest to use the ground truth labels to evaluate algorithms and methods which are based on unsupervised learning, as in production systems injection of anomalies and access to labeled data is restricted.
Jasmin:

5   Dataset Statistics

This section provides a descriptive statistic of the datasets generated. It quantitatively describes the properties of the trace, metrics, and log datasets.

Additionally, it ensures the R3 and R2 requirements. In following, due to page limitations, we discuss the statistics for the first experiment only. The code for extracting the statistics for the second experiment is provided in the data repository.

5.1   Metrics

The number of recordings of the utilization of the resources, more specifically the CPU, memory and the load, per node varies in the range of (108900, 298251). The average number of recordings is 239127. The total number of the metric recordings is 1195637. All of the nodes have 8 CPU cores. It is important to note that the metrics data cover a time span larger than the period of execution of the experiments.

As depicted in Figs. 2 a and b, in general, the wally113 experience the greatest CPU and memory load as observed by the distribution of these two features. Furthermore, the correlation analysis of the load.min1, load.min5 and load.min15 show that they exhibit high correlation given their relatedness through time. The correlation analysis also shows quite distinct behaviour for the load.min5, load.min10, load.min15 correlations between the control node and the remaining nodes. Regarding the dependence between the cpu.user, memory.used and load.min features, no significant correlation can be identified. Roughly 3 groups of features emerge - the load.CPU, mem.used and the load.min group.

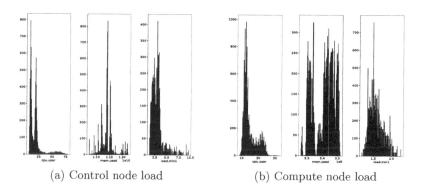

(a) Control node load   (b) Compute node load

Fig. 2. Traces: counts of services per rally action

5.2   Logs

Since the logs are semi-structured data, first we try to organize them and observe the range of interesting features that can appear in them. There are 139799

Table 2. Traces information: count of operations per workload execution.

	wsgi	db	comp. api	nova image	neutron api	neutron db	rpc
image create delete	11436	81321	0	0	0	0	0
network create delete	4692	14101	0	0	0	125321	855
boot delete	46591	125975	21572	752	313744	46642	36560

Table 3. Traces information: median time of a service per iteration

	wsgi	db	comp. api	nova image	neutron api	neutron db	rpc
image create delete	0.046	0.001	0	0	0	0	0
network create delete	0.285	0.001	0	0	0	0.001	0.001
boot delete	0.0410	0.001	0.039	0.035	0.001	0.002	0.009

log messages appearing in the sequential execution of the operations. We used Kibana to identify the different features describing them. Each log has its unique identifier referenced by the label _id. The Timestamp feature has 8 missing values. However, the timestamps provided by Kibana, stored in @timestamp contain the relevant information for the moment where the logging happened.

There are a total of 6 services recording their logs in the OpenStack logger: nova, neutron, keystone, glances, placement and cinder. Nova and neutron are services with the greatest number of logs appearing. The logs contain 3 levels of logging (INFO, WARNING and ERROR). There are 5 operation host nodes - Hostname (wally113, wally117, wally122, wally123, wally124). Most of the logs originate from the control node wally113. The python_module contains the name of the 61 modules that are logging their information into the logs with wsgi related modules being the most frequent ones (neutron_wsgi, nova.osapi_wsgi and server_wsgi). The programname refers to the program which operations are being executed. There are a total of 127654 different Payloads happened in the system and the most frequent is related to the GET operation.

For the realized HTTP calls there is information for the http status with 6 different code values, http_method with 4 possible values (GET, POST, DELETE and PUT), http_urls with a total of 3655 values and the version of the http protocol stored ins http_version. There are columns such as domain id, user domain, tenant_id, request_id, user_id, _score, _type, project_domain, Pid and domain_id that have either very large or very small variance in the number of unique values per feature. They represent start and end point in form of IP address or a result from a hash function.

5.3   Traces

Table 2 represents the total number of services for each of the traces for the three sequential operations being executed. It is given as a total sum over all the repetition of the experiment. One can be observe that there are different service invoked per operation. For example, for the `image_create_delete` operation the open stack service involved is completely on the controller node, hence the compute nodes are contacted and there is no operation related to them. The most frequently occurring invocation is split between db and wsgi. Second the operations are ordered by complexity and it can be seen that the `boot_delete_task` involves all of the 7 services.

Table 3 represents the median time of execution for each of the invoked services. The median is chosen since the distributions are skewed and the mean is not representative of the sample distribution. As it can be observed, the wsgi services are slower than the db calls since wsgi relays on http communication. It is interesting to observe that for the network create delete operation the rpc is quite small. One explanation for this is the small rate of rpc call per individual execution. This means that not all executions of this operation involve rpc calls. Since multiple workloads involve invoking different number of individual operation the times should be compared with caution.

We inject the fault in the `glance-api` running on the controller node.

6   Applications of Multi-source AIOps

While previous work has been generally done on single-source data, we believe that to develop robust, holistic approaches for anomaly detection, root-cause analysis, self-healing, resource optimization, and performance analysis a multi-source data is highly desirable.

In this section, we shortly describe possible AIOps approaches that can exploit the benefits of processing multi-source observability data.

Multi-source Anomaly Detection. The distributed logs over projects and physical hosts enable multimodal end-to-end learning and more robust log anomaly detection. Of course, this adds complexity for data integration and fusion, as the distributed logs are produced with different timestamps. Together, the distributed logs and metrics can again be combined into more complex model or network of models. Lastly, the graph-like structures of the tracing data can be incorporated to complete the robust anomaly detection where all available observability data is considered.

Root-Cause Analysis. The integration of multi-source observability data can be exploited by using some kind of Fishbone diagrams [12] to find the root-cause of problems. A method can start with simple metric-only anomaly detection, which typically provides little information about the root-causes of problems, and drill down to more complex data structures which are richer in explaining anomalies. For example, one can start by analyzing the latency of microservices endpoints. If anomalies are detected after processing metrics, one can use the timeframe when the anomaly occurred to select and analyze structural changes in traces. Traces can provide information about which servers are possibly faulty. Afterwards, application logs can be accessed to find the root-cause of problems.

Precision Increase. Ensemble learning [34] can be used to machine learning algorithm results by combining several models applied to the three correlated data sources categories. Such an approach would allow the production of algorithms with better predictive accuracy when compared to the algorithms which process single-data sources.

Feature Extension. Many machine learning algorithms rely on features, which for AIOps are individual measurable characteristics of the behaviour of IT distributed systems at a given time. By using multi-source data, the spectrum of available features to an algorithm is dramatically increased. Thus, we expect the quality of algorithms and their results to increase in the future.

7   Conclusion

AIOps systems rely on suitable observability data. We released a multi-source data containing distributed metrics, logs, and tracing data obtained from a complex distributed system based on microservice architecture. We describe in details the infrastructure, experiments performed, and the fault injection. Furthermore, we provided descriptive statistical properties of the data.

Furthermore, we motivated possible applications of this data for improvements in anomaly detection, root-cause analysis, remediation, and feature extension. We hope that this dataset will foster advances in the research of AIOps, which has been limited mainly to explored data capturing only a single data source category.

References

1. Ahmad, S., Lavin, A., Purdy, S., Agha, Z.: Unsupervised real-time anomaly detection for streaming data. Neurocomputing **262**, 134–147 (2017)
2. Alibaba trace data (2019). https://github.com/alibaba/clusterdata
3. CFDR (2019). https://www.usenix.org/cfdr-data
4. Correia, J., Ribeiro, F., Filipe, R., Arauio, F., Cardoso, J.: Response time characterization of microservice-based systems. In: 2018 IEEE 17th International Symposium on Network Computing and Applications (NCA), pp. 1–5. IEEE, New Jersey (2018)
5. Cortez, E., Bonde, A., Muzio, A., Russinovich, M., Fontoura, M., Bianchini, R.: Resource central: understanding and predicting workloads for improved resource management in large cloud platforms. In: Proceedings of the International Symposium on Operating Systems Principles (SOSP) (2017)
6. Dang, Y., Lin, Q., Huang, P.: AIOps: real-world challenges and research innovations. In: Proceedings of the 41st International Conference on Software Engineering: Companion Proceedings, pp. 4–5. IEEE Press (2019)

7. Du, M., Li, F., Zheng, G., Srikumar, V.: DeepLog: anomaly detection and diagnosis from system logs through deep learning. In: Proceedings of the 2017 ACM SIGSAC Conference on Computer and Communications Security, pp. 1285–1298. ACM, New York (2017)
8. ELKI (2019). https://elki-project.github.io/datasets/outlier
9. Goldstein, M.: Unsupervised Anomaly Detection Benchmark (2015). https://doi.org/10.7910/DVN/OPQMVF
10. Google trace data (2019). https://github.com/google/cluster-data
11. Gulenko, A., Schmidt, F., Acker, A., Wallschlager, M., Kao, O., Liu, F.: Detecting anomalous behavior of black-box services modeled with distance-based online clustering. In: 2018 IEEE 11th International Conference on Cloud Computing (CLOUD), pp. 912–915. IEEE, New Jersey (2018)
12. Ishikawa, K.: Guide to Quality Control. JUSE, Tokyo (2012)
13. Kolla-ansible's documentation. https://docs.openstack.org/kolla-ansible/latest/
14. Li, F., Hu, B.: DeepJS: job scheduling based on deep reinforcement learning in cloud data center. In: Proceedings of the 2019 4th International Conference on Big Data and Computing, pp. 48–53. ACM, New York (2019)
15. LMU (2019). https://www.dbs.ifi.lmu.de/research/outlier-evaluation/
16. Meng, W., et al.: LogAnomaly: unsupervised detection of sequential and quantitative anomalies in unstructured logs. In: Proceedings of the Twenty-Eighth International Joint Conference on Artificial Intelligence, IJCAI 2019, Macao, China, 10–16 August 2019, pp. 4739–4745 (2019)
17. Nagios enterprises. https://github.com/NagiosEnterprises
18. Nedelkoski, S., Cardoso, J., Kao, O.: Anomaly detection and classification using distributed tracing and deep learning. In: 2019 19th IEEE/ACM International Symposium on Cluster, Cloud and Grid Computing (CCGRID), pp. 241–250. IEEE, New Jersey (2019)
19. Nedelkoski, S., Cardoso, J., Kao, O.: Anomaly detection from system tracing data using multimodal deep learning. In: 2019 IEEE 12th International Conference on Cloud Computing (CLOUD), pp. 179–186. IEEE, New Jersey (2019)
20. Nicolargo: nicolargo/glances (2019). https://github.com/nicolargo/glances
21. Openstack: openstack/osprofiler. https://github.com/openstack/osprofiler
22. OpenZipkin: openzipkin/zipkin (2018). https://github.com/openzipkin/zipkin
23. Performa: os-faults. https://opendev.org/performa/os-faults
24. Pina, F., Correia, J., Filipe, R., Araujo, F., Cardoso, J.: Nonintrusive monitoring of microservice-based systems. In: 2018 IEEE 17th International Symposium on Network Computing and Applications (NCA), pp. 1–8 (2018)
25. Rally. https://rally.readthedocs.io/en/latest/
26. Schmidt, F., et al.: IFTM - unsupervised anomaly detection for virtualized network function services. In: 2018 IEEE International Conference on Web Services (ICWS), pp. 187–194. IEEE, New Jersey (2018)
27. Schmidt, F., Suri-Payer, F., Gulenko, A., Wallschläger, M., Acker, A., Kao, O.: Unsupervised anomaly event detection for cloud monitoring using online arima. In: 2018 IEEE/ACM International Conference on Utility and Cloud Computing Companion (UCC Companion), pp. 71–76. IEEE, New Jersey (2018)
28. Shen, H., Li, C.: Zeno: a straggler diagnosis system for distributed computing using machine learning. In: Yokota, R., Weiland, M., Keyes, D., Trinitis, C. (eds.) ISC High Performance 2018. LNCS, vol. 10876, pp. 144–162. Springer, Cham (2018). https://doi.org/10.1007/978-3-319-92040-5_8
29. Shrivastwa, A., Sarat, S., Jackson, K., Bunch, C., Sigler, E., Campbell, T.: OpenStack: Building a Cloud Environment. Packt Publishing, Birmingham (2016)

30. Sridharan, C.: Distributed Systems Observability: A Guide to Building Robust Systems. O'Reilly Media, Sebastopol (2018)
31. Oregon (2019). http://odds.cs.stonybrook.edu/
32. Taraslayshchuk: taraslayshchuk/es2csv (2018). https://github.com/taraslayshchuk/es2csv
33. Zabbix. https://github.com/zabbix
34. Zhang, C., Ma, Y.: Ensemble Machine Learning: Methods and Applications, 1st edn, p. 332. Springer, New York (2012). https://doi.org/10.1007/978-1-4419-9326-7
35. Zhu, J., et al.: Tools and benchmarks for automated log parsing. In: Proceedings of the 41st International Conference on Software Engineering: Software Engineering in Practice, pp. 121–130. IEEE Press, Piscataway (2019)

Blockchain- and IPFS-Based Data Distribution for the Internet of Things

Simon Krejci, Marten Sigwart, and Stefan Schulte(✉) ⓘD

Distributed Systems Group, TU Wien, Vienna, Austria
{s.krejci,m.sigwart,s.schulte}@dsg.tuwien.ac.at
https://www.dsg.tuwien.ac.at

Abstract. Distributing data in a tamper-proof and traceable way is a necessity in many Internet of Things (IoT) scenarios. Blockchain technologies are frequently named as an approach to provide such functionality. Despite this, there is a lack of concrete solutions which integrate the IoT with the blockchain for data distribution purposes.

Within this paper, we present a middleware which connects to IoT devices, and uses a blockchain to distribute IoT data with guaranteed integrity. Furthermore, the middleware also offers that data is distributed in real-time via a second channel. We implement our solution using the Ethereum blockchain and the InterPlanetary File System (IPFS).

Keywords: Internet of Things · Blockchain · Data distribution · IPFS

1 Introduction

The Internet of Things (IoT) is a worldwide network of interconnected devices, which are able to process and store data, and in many cases provide sensor and actuator capabilities [3]. Blockchains are well-known as the underlying technology for cryptocurrencies like Bitcoin [16], but have also been named an enabling (and potentially disruptive) technology for application areas like supply chains [14], smart healthcare [12], or smart factories [8]. In a lot of these areas, it has been proposed to combine blockchains with IoT technology in order to store data from objects like sensor nodes in a tamper-proof, decentralized way, to process this data using smart contracts or off-chain, to distribute IoT data, and to provide services on top of this data [5,7,23].

Despite the manifold options to use blockchain technologies in the IoT, there are a number of challenges which complicate the wide-spread uptake of blockchains in this area. To start with, IoT devices are often hardware- or energy-constrained, and therefore do not provide the computational power necessary to participate in a blockchain network. Also, executing transactions and storing data in blockchains is expensive, which is not in line with the large number of interactions and the large amount of data to be distributed in typical IoT scenarios [30].

ⓒ IFIP International Federation for Information Processing 2020
Published by Springer Nature Switzerland AG 2020
A. Brogi et al. (Eds.): ESOCC 2020, LNCS 12054, pp. 177–191, 2020.
https://doi.org/10.1007/978-3-030-44769-4_14

Therefore, one particular question is how lightweight IoT devices can interact with blockchains in order to exchange data. Current research focuses on building specific blockchains for the IoT [6], with the explicit goal to provide more lightweight blockchain protocols. However, novel blockchain protocols do not only contribute to a significant fragmentation of the blockchain research and development field [24], but may also suffer from a smaller user base as well as a higher likelihood of bugs [17]. Therefore, it would be favorable if IoT devices could use existing, mature blockchains.

To achieve this, the work at hand presents a middleware for IoT applications, which facilitates the distribution of data via a blockchain, in case data integrity needs to be ensured. Because of the inherent overhead of using blockchain technologies for data distribution, the middleware explicitly facilitates data exchange also via a second channel. The second channel allows data distribution in (near) real-time, but does not provide the same integrity guarantees as the on-chain data exchange. We implement the middleware and test its performance in a fog setting, i.e., take into account that in many IoT scenarios, it is useful to host such a middleware at the edge of the network.

The remainder of this paper is organized as follows: In Sect. 2, we discuss the related work. In Sect. 3, we present the design and implementation of the middleware. Afterwards, we evaluate the middleware in Sect. 4. Finally, we conclude the paper in Sect. 5.

2   Related Work

The utilization of blockchains in the IoT has been proposed in many different papers. Typical IoT-related use cases are the utilization of blockchains to enable a tamper-proof log of IoT events, e.g., [21,27], the management of access control data, e.g., [18], or the purchase of assets, such as IoT sensor data, e.g., [30,31].

With regard to the storage and distribution of IoT data, Huh et al. [9] propose the utilization of Ethereum-based smart contracts in order to enforce policies for smart devices. Prybila et al. [21] present a solution to exchange data about distributed events in supply chains via the Bitcoin blockchain. Liu et al. [13] introduce a blockchain-based data integrity framework for IoT data, based on Ethereum smart contracts. Pešić et al. [19] present a high-level concept for applying blockchains in the IoT, following a blockchain-as-a-service model. Amongst other topics, the authors mention that this could be used for data sharing purposes. The concept has not been implemented so far. Shafagh et al. [25] propose a blockchain-based data management solution for the IoT, but also do not provide an implementation. However, such a proof-of-concept is presented by Sharma et al. [26] in their work on establishing a fog- and blockchain-based infrastructure for data exchange and computational tasks in the IoT.

Ali et al. [2] discuss the utilization of blockchains to enable data privacy in the IoT. Data items are stored in the IPFS, while the according data hashes are stored on the chain. The IPFS [4] is a Peer-to-Peer (P2P) distributed file system. It combines concepts of Distributed Hash Tables (DHTs), the Self-certifying File System (SFS), BitTorrent, and the version control system Git. The aim of the

IPFS project is to connect all computing devices with one common file system. An advantage of the distributed architecture of IPFS is that the nodes in the network do not have to trust each other and no user or node is privileged. This makes the IPFS an obvious choice to be used as a distributed file system together with a blockchain. Therefore, we also utilize IPFS in the work at hand.

Notably, Ali et al. [2] provide a decentralized data access model for the IoT, while in our work, the focus is on a middleware which helps to use blockchain capabilities in applications to distribute IoT-based data items. The data management part including the IPFS integration of data items presented by Ali et al. has not yet been implemented by the authors. Nevertheless, this concept comes closest to the work at hand.

To the best of our knowledge, none of the so-far discussed approaches to distribute IoT data via blockchains provides a proof-of-concept implementation for blockchain-based data distribution. However, this is done by Meroni et al. [15], who focus on artifact-driven process monitoring and apply both the Ethereum blockchain and IPFS for this.

A second important field of related work is the enhancement of current blockchain technologies to provide more lightweight solutions with regard to the computational power and energy consumption needed by a blockchain. One particular drawback of standard Proof-of-Work (PoW)-based blockchains is the extensive energy consumption [28]. This is especially an issue in the IoT, where devices may be battery-powered. Different specific-purpose blockchains for the IoT have been proposed to overcome this issue: Dorri et al. [6] present a hierarchical blockchain architecture consisting of multiple private immutable ledgers which IoT devices can connect to. A public overlay blockchain links the individual private ledgers. Zyskind et al. [32] present the Enigma platform, which uses a DHT to store data and to perform heavyweight, costly computational tasks off-chain. The IOTA Foundation [20] follows an entirely different approach for providing the benefits of distributed ledgers in the IoT. They deploy the so-called tangle, which does not organize transactions in blocks. Instead, individual transactions reference each other, forming a Directed Acyclic Graph (DAG).

As pointed out in Sect. 1, we believe that the utilization of already existing blockchain protocols is beneficial because of the more mature technology and the bigger user base, compared to novel protocols [17,24]. Nevertheless, the conceptualization and implementation of IoT-specific blockchain protocols is surely a promising research direction.

3   Solution Architecture

As pointed out in Sect. 1, blockchain technologies can provide different benefits in IoT settings, including, but not limited to (i) exchanging computational power through decentralized smart contracts, (ii) the tamper-proof record of transactions on the blockchain for auditing or accounting purposes or simply for data distribution, and (iii) increasing the trust in distributed data [7,11,23]. Within the work at hand, we focus on blockchain-based data distribution in the IoT.

Besides the opportunities the blockchain may provide to the IoT, there are also challenges which need to be addressed. As pointed out above, the energy and resource demands of state-of-the-art blockchain protocols may be problematic for constrained IoT devices.

Latency is another challenge: In many cases, IoT-based applications need to react to real-world events in a timely manner. However, contemporary block-chains possess long block times, which means that it may take a certain amount of time until a transaction is added to a block: A frequently named example is Bitcoin's median inter-block time of 10 min, but even Ethereum's inter-block time of 13 to 20 s[1] might be too long for time-sensitive IoT applications. Notably, even a short inter-block time does not guarantee that a transaction is added to a block in due time, since a number of different factors play a role by when a transaction is actually added to a blockchain, e.g., the current load of the miners, the number of transactions in the transaction pool, transient connectivity issues, and the transaction fee a participant might be willing to pay [29].

Taking into account the potential benefits as well as challenges when using blockchain technologies, it should be foreseen that the blockchain does *not* become the only means to provide a particular functionality, e.g., data distribution, in the IoT. In order to achieve this, we conceptualize and implement a middleware which is able to collect data from IoT-based data sources like sensor nodes, and to distribute the data via two different channels.

The middleware provides the means to handle the demands of time-sensitive IoT applications, and to distribute data on- and off-chain. For this, the following functional requirements need to be fulfilled:

– Allow data collection from arbitrary IoT-based data sources: Naturally, the middleware should allow interested stakeholders to collect data from different types of IoT data sources, most notably sensor nodes.
– Access data in a time-sensitive manner: Data from the data sources should be accessible within a given, guaranteed timeframe, if necessary.
– Access data with guaranteed integrity: The data which is collected should be provided to stakeholders with guaranteed integrity. Notably, this functional requirement may contradict the need for time-sensitive data access.

3.1 Architecture

Figure 1 gives an overview of the designed and implemented IoT-blockchain middleware. As it can be seen, the middleware provides the means to integrate arbitrary sensors via so-called sensor drivers. The middleware itself allows IoT clients to communicate with the sensors via two dedicated data distribution channels, i.e., the integrity channel and the real-time channel. The IoT client could be an arbitrary software interested in the IoT data and may get data via any of the two channels. Within the work at hand, we have implemented an IoT client which is able to measure different performance metrics and therefore provides the foundation for our evaluation (see Sect. 4).

---

[1] https://etherscan.io/chart/blocktime, as of January 2020.

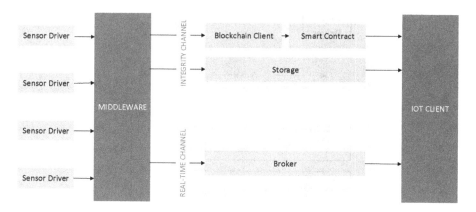

Fig. 1. Architecture overview

Notably, the middleware may run in the cloud or close to the IoT sensors, i.e., at the edge of the network. A cloud-based middleware provides the benefit that additional computational resources are available. The latter option can be used in order to decrease the communication delay between the sensors and the middleware, to benefit from a distributed architectural approach which mirrors the distribution of data sources in the IoT, and to allow the utilization of lightweight, IoT-specific communication protocols, e.g., the Constrained Application Protocol (CoAP) [1]. The basic approach to use computational devices in the vicinity of the IoT-based data sources is also known as fog computing [22].

In the following subsections, we discuss the core components of our architecture, i.e., the sensor drivers and the middleware including the data distribution channels, in more detail.

Sensor Driver. A sensor driver acts as the interface between an arbitrary IoT sensor and the middleware. Thus, it is responsible to collect the data from a specific sensor, with every sensor having its own driver. It may be the case that one sensor senses several phenomena, e.g., temperature *and* humidity. In such a case, one sensor driver collects the values for all supported phenomena.

The collected data is provided via an interface to the middleware. For this, the driver provides a phenomenon's data via IoT-suitable data distribution channels. In order to be able to differentiate the channels for different phenomena, each phenomenon gets its own channel. In the further course of this paper, a sensed phenomenon which is distributed via its own channel is referenced as *data source*.

Before the exchange between the driver and the middleware can be realized, the driver has to register at the middleware. The idea behind this process is that sensors can be added to the middleware dynamically, i.e., during system runtime. This avoids a hard coding of driver connections into the middleware and therefore adds flexibility. The registration workflow is made up from the steps depicted in Fig. 2:

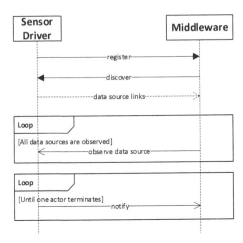

Fig. 2. Interactions between sensor drivers and middleware

1. When registering a new sensor, a driver sends a registry request to the middleware containing its own address.
2. The middleware answers with a discovery request.
3. The driver responds with a list of data source links it offers to the middleware, i.e., one link per phenomenon.
4. For every data source link, the middleware sends an observe request. That means in case the observation is accepted by the driver, the middleware is notified if a new value is received from the sensor.
   While we do so far not provide the means to negotiate Service Level Agreements (SLAs) between sensor drivers (i.e., data providers) and IoT clients (i.e., the data sinks) via the middleware, we foresee that SLAs could be integrated. Also, we facilitate the payment of penalties by a data provider if an SLA is violated. For instance, in case a data provider promises to deliver a data update every n time units, the provider needs to pay a penalty fee if such a data update is not provided by a sensor in time.
5. The notify message from the sensor driver to the middleware contains both the actual notification as well as the sensor reading, i.e., the new value. Thus, a push-based data distribution scheme is provided. As long as the middleware and the driver are running, sensor data is delivered to the middleware.

Middleware and Data Distribution Channels. The main functionality of the middleware is to receive data from the sensors (via the sensor drivers), and to distribute this IoT data via the two data distribution channels.

The integrity channel is used in order to distribute data items while guaranteeing their integrity. Since the blockchain is a tamper-proof distributed ledger, data integrity is ensured once data items are stored in it. However, storing complex data items in a blockchain may become expensive. To reduce the amount of data which is stored on-chain, our middleware only stores the hash of a data item on the blockchain, while the data itself is saved in a content-addressable storage.

The basic workflow of storing data via the integrity channel is depicted in Fig. 3. As it can be seen, the middleware is able to store data via the storage client (not depicted in Fig. 1), which is in turn responsible for the storage process. Once the storage client has successfully persisted a data item, the hash value of the persisted data item is returned to the middleware.

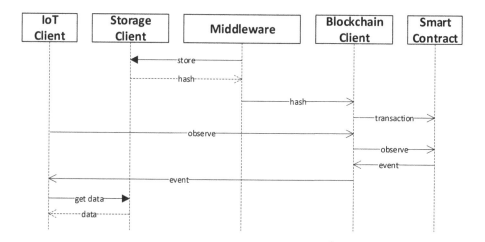

Fig. 3. Storage of data via the integrity channel

The middleware forwards the hash to the blockchain client in order to store the hash value in a blockchain. As the figure shows, the actual storing of the hash is done via a smart contract (discussed below) running on the blockchain, i.e., by sending a transaction containing the hash as a parameter to a function in the smart contract. Once the function is successfully executed, i.e., the hash is stored in the blockchain, the smart contract generates an event, which can be observed by the blockchain users, e.g., the IoT client. With this hash value, the IoT client is now able to get the data from the storage (via the storage client).

The blockchain client and the storage client are loosely-coupled to the middleware. In our proof-of-concept implementation, we use Ethereum for the blockchain and IPFS for the content-addressable storage, and use the according clients provided by these systems (see below). However, the middleware could also be used with other storage solutions and blockchain protocols. In this case, it is necessary to integrate according clients into the middleware.

For the real-time channel, we use a publish/subscribe mechanism. Via this channel, interested clients are able to subscribe to different data sources and to receive data items in (near) real-time. As Fig. 1 shows, the middleware sends the data to a publish/subscribe broker, which is responsible for the publication of the data and the subscriptions of interested stakeholders. Notably, data items can

Listing 1.1. Update-Function in Smart Contract "IntegrityService"

```
1   event MeasurementUpdate(
2     address indexed sender ,
3     uint8 function_code ,
4     uint8 digest_length ,
5     bytes32 digest
6   );
7
8   function update(uint8 function_code , uint8 digest_length , bytes32 digest ,
9   bytes32 id_hash) onlyBy(client) public {
10    require(registered == true && penaltyPaid == false);
11    if (lastUpdates[id_hash] > 0
12    && block.timestamp > lastUpdates[id_hash] + maxDelay) {
13      penalty += 1;
14    }
15    lastUpdates[id_hash] = block.timestamp;
16    emit MeasurementUpdate(msg.sender , function_code , digest_length , digest);
17  }
```

be distributed via the real-time channel, and at the same time via the integrity channel. While this is only possible with a certain delay, this allows to verify the integrity of data items distributed via the real-time channel.

Smart Contract. Listing 1.1 provides the core function of the implemented smart contract shown in Fig. 3. The excerpt checks the update rate of a data source, calculates penalties in case an SLA is violated, and emits an event to indicate the reception of new data. As programming language, Solidity is used. The function is called by the middleware (the *caller*) in order to provide the hashes of data items to an IoT client in a push-based manner. Notably, the smart contract is established between one particular data provider and one single IoT client (i.e., data consumer).

As it can be seen in Lines 2–5, the function gets a number of parameters, with *function_code*, *digest_length* and *digest* forming the hash used by IPFS to identify data items, and *sender* providing the address of the caller of the update function. Together, these variables constitute the event *MeasurementUpdate* (Lines 1–6). As the name implies, this event comprises a hash representing an update of a measurement from an IoT sensor.

The core functionality of the smart contract is provided by the function *update* (Lines 8–17). Apart from the already mentioned parameters, the function also is provided with the *id_hash*, which is the hash of the data source's ID. The identification of the data source is necessary to track the update rates of every single data source. The function modifier *onlyBy(client)* (Line 9) controls the access to the function.

In Line 10, we make use of Solidity's *require* construct to check conditions. In case the condition is not true, an exception is thrown and all changes on the state of the smart contract are undone. More concretely, we check if the caller of the function is registered, and if a penalty has already been paid out by the caller. As pointed out above, a penalty is due in case a data item (or rather hash) is not delivered in time, and despite this having been specified between a data provider and a data sink (via sensor nodes and middleware) in an SLA.

Notably, more than one SLA violation may occur during data distribution, leading to multiple penalties. However, the total penalty fee is only disbursed once, i.e., when an authorized person calls an according function (not shown in the listing) in the smart contract. If the total penalty has been paid, no further updates are accepted, and the function is aborted. The reason for a defined ending of the contract is the limited validity of an agreement between the middleware and an IoT client, i.e., that a client is not able to get data items from a source for an indefinite amount of time.

Lines 11–12 are used to check if a penalty needs to be paid: When *update* is called and the last update timestamp plus a maximum allowed delay (defined in the SLA) is less than the current timestamp, i.e., an update is delayed, a penalty is calculated in line 13. In the current implementation, we make use of a fixed penalty fee, i.e., one *Wei*, which is the smallest unit of currency in Ethereum. The penalty could also be calculated in a more sophisticated way, e.g., following a linear penalty function, but since the penalty function is not in the focus of the work at hand, we opted for a simplified approach.

Line 15 sets the timestamp for the last update from a particular data source to the timestamp of the block where the hash of this data item has been added to. Notably, the time a transaction is added to a block depends on the chosen blockchain and other factors not under the control of the sensor driver (see above). This can be problematic, since a penalty may become due even though a data item has been delivered in time, but its hash having been added to a block too late. This is a general problem if blockchains are used in potentially time-sensitive settings. Solutions for this are part of our future work. At the moment, the allowed delay has to be chosen so that blockchain-inherent delays do not become an issue.

By calling the *emit*-command (Line 16), the event *MeasurementUpdate* is broadcast. Events exploit the logging facilities of the Ethereum Virtual Machine. These logging facilities can be used to create callbacks in applications (here: an IoT client) which listen to the events. The events are stored in the transaction's log whereas the logs are associated with the smart contract which emitted the events. Parameters of the event can have the attribute *indexed*. Thus, these parameters are not stored themselves, but it is possible to search for the parameters and filter them.

When a listening IoT client receives the event, the client is able to build the hash of a data item and retrieve the data item from IPFS.

3.2   Implementation

Our approach to IoT-blockchain integration has been realized in a proof-of-concept implementation, using Python for the sensor drivers and Java for the middleware and IoT client.

The communication protocols applied by the integrity channel are determined by the used blockchain and storage technologies, i.e., Ethereum and IPFS. For the data exchange between the sensor drivers and the middleware and for the real-time channel, suitable communication protocols have been selected. Regarding the former, it is necessary to take into account typical communication issues in the IoT, e.g., potentially lossy links and the need for low-power communication [10]. Hence, we select CoAP as communication protocol [1].

Notably, CoAP offers the necessary request/response mechanism for the registration of new sensor drivers as well as the publish/subscribe mechanism used for value updates. Also, CoAP already provides mechanisms for device discovery and device registration, as needed by the middleware. However, CoAP's publish/subscribe mechanism is rather basic. Therefore, we select MQTT for the real-time channel [1].

We use Californium[2] as CoAP framework and Mosquitto[3] for the MQTT broker. For connecting the middleware as well as the IoT client to the Ethereum network, Web3j[4] and the Geth client[5] are used.

As pointed out above, the presented approach could be realized for other blockchain protocols and storage technologies, but for our proof-of-concept implementation, Ethereum and IPFS have been selected. To use different technologies, it is necessary to integrate according blockchain and storage clients into the middleware, and to implement a smart contract for the chosen blockchain.

The presented middleware is available as open source software at Github[6].

4   Evaluation

The goal of the evaluation is to test the performance of the implemented solution. We assume that the middleware runs on an edge device, i.e., we apply a fog-based system architecture. We use a single-board computer, i.e., a Raspberry Pi 3 Model B, as a typical IoT edge device.

To test the performance, we measure message delays using the real-time and integrity channels, i.e., the delay from the occurrence of a new data item in a sensor driver to the point of time it is received by a user (here: the IoT client).

4.1   Evaluation Setup

In order to execute performance tests, we have implemented a *virtual driver*, i.e., a sensor driver which has no connection to a physical sensor, and therefore represents a number of simulated *data sources* which regularly emit data items. Hence, the virtual driver generates artificial messages with hard-coded values. The amount of data sources and the amount of sent messages can be user-specified in the virtual driver, allowing us to use the virtual driver in order to execute reproducible performance tests. To be able to test varying loads, we use

---

[2]   https://www.eclipse.org/californium/.
[3]   https://mosquitto.org/.
[4]   https://docs.web3j.io/.
[5]   https://geth.ethereum.org/.
[6]   https://github.com/mcmon-dev/iot-middleware.

virtual drivers with 2, 7, 11, and 22 data sources in the evaluation setup. In addition, we use GrovePi+ in connection with the Raspberry Pi to also evaluate the setup with a real-world sensor which emits two different phenomena (i.e., represents two data sources).

For the Raspberry Pi, we use Raspbian 8.0 as operating system. The IoT client is a desktop application, running on a standard desktop PC. As blockchain, we make use of the Ethereum test network Ropsten[7]. In order to mitigate the influence of varying network loads, IPFS and the real-time channel are installed in a local network. The experiments are repeated three times to further mitigate varying loads in the local network and on the nodes.

During each experimental run, each (physical and virtual) data source emits a data item every 5 s. This is repeated 60 times, leading to an overall duration of 5 min per experimental run.

We use different statistical metrics, i.e., median, mean, quantiles, and standard deviations in order to assess the evaluation results. In addition, we make use of notched boxplots to compare the data.

Table 1. Delays in the real-time channel (in ms)

	Min	Q1	Median	Mean	Q3	Max	σ
Phy (2)	21.00	37.00	45.00	86.93	63.00	1785.00	169.234
2	21.00	39.00	50.00	96.26	73.00	3238.00	258.605
7	20.00	67.00	109.00	200.90	189.00	1856.00	268.4895
11	24.00	69.00	131.00	253.80	261.00	2407.00	350.524
22	26.00	129.00	321.00	2628.80	864.50	146121.00	15662.40

4.2 Results

Table 1 provides an overview of the delays for the real-time channel, i.e., the MQTT-based data distribution, which does not provide data integrity guarantees, for the 2 physical data sources (Phy (2)) and the 2, 7, 11, and 22 virtual data sources. The numbers provide the minimum, Q1, median, mean, Q3, and maximum for the abovementioned three evaluation runs. Figure 4a visualizes the delays of the real-time channel[8], but does not show a boxplot for the 22 data sources. The reason for this is the high increase of the median for 22 data sources, which would make the differences between the boxplots very difficult to identify.

As it can be seen in Fig. 4a, the median is increasing with the amount of data sources. Also, it can be seen that the boxes for the 2 physical data sources and the 2 virtual data sources provide similar results, indicating that the virtual driver resembles the performance of the physical data sources in a sufficient way. Another observation is that the upper whisker of the boxplot increases with the number of data sources, while the lower whisker is almost stable.

---

[7] https://ropsten.etherscan.io.
[8] With the boxplot notch indicating a 95% confidence interval.

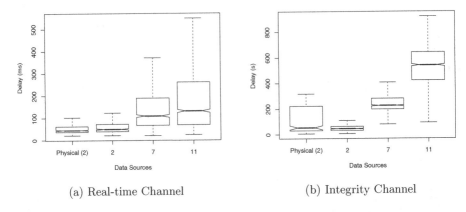

(a) Real-time Channel   (b) Integrity Channel

Fig. 4. Delays

The mean numbers shown in Table 1 confirm the results from the median and boxplot analysis. Interestingly, the maximum numbers for 2 virtual data sources are a significant outlier, but are compensated by other evaluation runs, i.e., do not influence the overall numbers significantly.

It should be noted that the usage of 22 data sources led to a quite high number of missing values for the real-time channel. In fact, roundabout 18% of the data updates were lost in the real-time channel when using 22 data sources. This indicates that this number of data sources might put a too high load on the Raspberry Pi, since for the other three test scenarios, no data items got lost. This shows that the implemented solution is suitable only for a limited number of data sources, which can be traced back to the limited computational resources of the used IoT device, i.e., the Raspberry Pi, and the high resource demand of some of the used APIs, especially the IPFS client.

Table 2 shows the numbers for the integrity channel, i.e., where the data hashes are stored in the blockchain, and the actual data items in IPFS. Not surprisingly, this leads to a large overhead, since it takes time until a transaction is added to the blockchain. Hence, the numbers in Table 2 (as well as Fig. 4b) are given in seconds, while the numbers for the real-time channel in Table 1 and Fig. 4a are given in milliseconds.

Table 2. Delays in the integrity channel (in s)

	Min	Q1	Median	Mean	Q3	Max	σ
Phy (2)	4.302	29.858	53.499	99.600	221.404	316.739	97.614
2	5.739	31.448	45.538	51.359	63.503	143.668	29.289
7	20.15	197.19	224.95	238.71	280.20	513.61	115.634
11	52.11	422.03	539.03	526.52	641.58	1180.60	217.532
22	47.45	723.11	992.98	1172.06	1503.20	3409.93	694.025

As it can be seen in Table 2 as well as Fig. 4b, similar to the real-time channel, the median increases with the number of data sources. However, for the integrity channel, the median increases stronger. This indicates that the integrity channel scales not as well as the real-time channel. This is also confirmed by the number of missing data items for the 22 virtualized sensor, which is about 33% and therefore significantly higher than for the real-time channel.

4.3   Discussion

In general, the real-time channel provides acceptable delays in case the number of data sources is not too high, i.e., with up to 11 data sources, the mean delay is roundabout 254 ms, which is acceptable for many IoT scenarios.

As originally assumed, the usage of blockchain technologies in the integrity channel leads to a very high overhead, with the mean delay being roundabout 527 s in the case of 11 data sources. Hence, the blockchain-based data distribution should not be used in scenarios where latency is critical. For scenarios where both data integrity and low delay times are needed, it is necessary to develop novel blockchain technologies (see Sect. 2).

However, it should be noted that the presented solution allows to distribute data in real-time, and to store hashes of these data items also in the blockchain, thus allowing to validate the data integrity afterwards.

Due to space constraints, we do not discuss the confirmation delays caused by the blockchain. However, we have made such measurements, which show that the blockchain delays do not differ significantly for the different evaluation scenarios. Therefore, the abovementioned delays for the integrity channel are influenced in a similar vein by the blockchain confirmation delays, and the increase in the overhead (compared to the real-time channel) can be traced back to the restricted amount of resources the hosting node (i.e., the Raspberry Pi) provides.

5   Conclusions

Blockchain technologies are frequently named as an enabler for data integrity in IoT scenarios, as well as facilitator of other functionalities in the IoT. Despite this, there is still a lack of proof-of-concepts which show how blockchain technologies can be used to distribute data between data sources and data sinks in the IoT. Therefore, within this paper, we have proposed a middleware which is able to collect data from IoT sensors and to distribute data via two different channels. The first data distribution channel utilizes IPFS as data storage, and stores data hashes within an Ethereum blockchain. The second channel is based on MQTT and therefore allows to distribute data in a timely manner. We have implemented the middleware and evaluated it with regard to its capability to be run at the edge of the network, i.e., on a single-board computer like a Raspberry Pi, and the overhead introduced by the usage of a blockchain for data distribution purposes.

In our future work, we want to extend the presented middleware in order to investigate further research questions in the blockchain/IoT realm. As has already been stated above, it would be interesting to discuss the integration of full-fledged SLAs including SLA negotiations, while also allowing more sophisticated penalty schemes. Especially, the applied penalty scheme should be extended by a mechanism to reflect the blockchain-inherent transaction delays, i.e., that a penalty does not become due because of such a delay.

Acknowledgements. The work presented in this paper has received funding from Pantos GmbH within the TAST research project.

References

1. Al-Fuqaha, A.I., Guizani, M., Mohammadi, M., Aledhari, M., Ayyash, M.: Internet of Things: a survey on enabling technologies, protocols, and applications. IEEE Commun. Surv. Tutorials **17**(4), 2347–2376 (2015)
2. Ali, M.S., Dolui, K., Antonelli, F.: IoT data privacy via blockchains and IPFS. In: Seventh International Conference on the Internet of Things, pp. 14:1–14:7. ACM (2017)
3. Atzori, L., Iera, A., Morabito, G.: The Internet of Things: a survey. Comput. Netw. **54**(15), 2787–2805 (2010)
4. Benet, J.: IPFS - Content Addressed, Versioned, P2P File System (DRAFT 3). CoRR abs/1407.3561 (2014)
5. Christidis, K., Devetikiotis, M.: Blockchains and smart contracts for the Internet of Things. IEEE Access **4**, 2292–2303 (2016)
6. Dorri, A., Kanhere, S.S., Jurdak, R., Gauravaram, P.: LSB: A Lightweight Scalable Blockchain for IoT security and anonymity. J. Parallel Distrib. Comput. **134**, 180–197 (2019)
7. Fernández-Caramés, T.M., Fraga-Lamas, P.: A review on the use of blockchain for the Internet of Things. IEEE Access **6**, 32979–33001 (2018)
8. Fernández-Caramés, T.M., Fraga-Lamas, P.: A review on the application of blockchain to the next generation of cybersecure Industry 4.0 smart factories. IEEE Access **7**, 45201–45218 (2019)
9. Huh, S., Cho, S., Kim, S.: Managing IoT devices using blockchain platform. In: 19th International Conference on Advanced Communication Technology, pp. 464–467. IEEE (2017)
10. Ko, J., Terzis, A., Dawson-Haggerty, S., Culler, D.E., Hui, J.W., Levis, P.: Connecting low-power and lossy networks to the internet. IEEE Commun. Mag. **49**(4), 96–101 (2011)
11. Kshetri, N.: Can blockchain strengthen the Internet of Things? IT Prof. **19**(4), 68–72 (2017)
12. Li, M., Xia, L., Seneviratne, O.: Leveraging standards based ontological concepts in distributed ledgers: a healthcare smart contract example. In: 2019 IEEE International Conference on Decentralized Applications and Infrastructures, pp. 152–157. IEEE (2019)
13. Liu, B., Yu, X.L., Chen, S., Xu, X., Zhu, L.: Blockchain based data integrity service framework for IoT data. In: 2017 IEEE International Conference on Web Services, pp. 468–475. IEEE (2017)

14. Lu, D., et al.: Reducing automotive counterfeiting using blockchain: benefits and challenges. In: 2019 IEEE International Conference on Decentralized Applications and Infrastructures, pp. 39–48. IEEE (2019)
15. Meroni, G., Plebani, P., Vona, F.: Trusted artifact-driven process monitoring of multi-party business processes with blockchain. In: Di Ciccio, C., et al. (eds.) BPM 2019. LNBIP, vol. 361, pp. 55–70. Springer, Cham (2019). https://doi.org/10.1007/978-3-030-30429-4_5
16. Nakamoto, S.: Bitcoin: A Peer-to-Peer Electronic Cash System, Whitepaper (2008)
17. Nofer, M., Gomber, P., Hinz, O., Schiereck, D.: Blockchain. Bus. Inf. Syst. Eng. **59**(3), 183–187 (2017)
18. Novo, O.: Blockchain meets IoT: an architecture for scalable access management in IoT. IEEE Internet of Things J. **5**, 1184–1195 (2018)
19. Pešić, S., Tošić, M., Iković, O., Radovanović, M., Ivanović, M., Bošković, D.: Conceptualizing a collaboration framework between blockchain technology and the Internet of Things. In: 20th International Conference on Computer Systems and Technologies, pp. 56–61. ACM (2019)
20. Popov, S.: The tangle, IOTA Whitepaper v1.3 (2017)
21. Prybila, C., Schulte, S., Hochreiner, C., Weber, I.: Runtime verification for business processes utilizing the bitcoin blockchain. Future Gener. Comput. Syst. (2020, in press). https://doi.org/10.1016/j.future.2017.08.024
22. Puliafito, C., Mingozzi, E., Longo, F., Puliafito, A., Rana, O.: Fog computing for the Internet of Things: a survey. ACM Trans. Internet Technol. **19**(2), 181–1841 (2019)
23. Reyna, A., Martín, C., Chen, J., Soler, E., Díaz, M.: On blockchain and its integration with IoT. Challenges and opportunities. Future Gener. Comput. Syst. **88**, 173–190 (2018)
24. Schulte, S., Sigwart, M., Frauenthaler, P., Borkowski, M.: Towards blockchain interoperability. In: Di Ciccio, C., et al. (eds.) BPM 2019. LNBIP, vol. 361, pp. 3–10. Springer, Cham (2019). https://doi.org/10.1007/978-3-030-30429-4_1
25. Shafagh, H., Burkhalter, L., Hithnawi, A., Duquennoy, S.: Towards blockchain-based auditable storage and sharing of IoT data. In: 2017 Cloud Computing Security Workshop, pp. 45–50. ACM (2017)
26. Sharma, P.K., Chen, M.Y., Park, J.H.: A software defined fog node based distributed blockchain cloud architecture for IoT. IEEE Access **6**, 115–124 (2017)
27. Sigwart, M., Borkowski, M., Peise, M., Schulte, S., Tai, S.: Blockchain-based data provenance for the Internet of Things. In: 9th International Conference on the Internet of Things, pp. 15:1–15:8. ACM (2019)
28. Tschorsch, F., Scheuermann, B.: Bitcoin and beyond: a technical survey on decentralized digital currencies. IEEE Commun. Surv. Tutorials **18**(3), 2084–2123 (2016)
29. Weber, I., et al.: On availability for blockchain-based systems. In: 36th IEEE Symposium on Reliable Distributed Systems, pp. 64–73. IEEE (2017)
30. Wörner, D., von Bomhard, T.: When your sensor earns money: exchanging data for cash with bitcoin. In: The 2014 ACM Conference on Ubiquitous Computing Adjunct, pp. 295–298. ACM (2014)
31. Zhang, Y., Wen, J.: The IoT electric business model: using blockchain technology for the Internet of Things. Peer-to-Peer Netw. Appl. **10**(4), 983–994 (2016). https://doi.org/10.1007/s12083-016-0456-1
32. Zyskind, G., Nathan, O., Pentland, A.: Enigma: Decentralized Computation Platform with Guaranteed Privacy. CoRR abs/1506.03471 (2015)

Author Index

Printed in the United States
By Bookmasters